Campus Crisis

ALSO OF INTEREST
AND FROM MCFARLAND

"Light of My Life": Love, Time and Memory in Nabokov's Lolita,
by James D. Hardy, Jr., and Ann Martin (2011)

*Baseball and the Mythic Moment:
How We Remember the National Game,*
by James D. Hardy, Jr. (2007)

*The New York Giants Base Ball Club:
The Growth of a Team and a Sport, 1870 to 1900,*
by James D. Hardy, Jr. (1996; softcover 2006; large print 2009)

Campus Crisis

*How Money, Technology and Policy
Are Changing the American University*

JAMES D. HARDY, JR., *and*
ANN MARTIN

McFarland & Company, Inc., Publishers
Jefferson, North Carolina

LIBRARY OF CONGRESS CATALOGUING-IN-PUBLICATION DATA

Names: Hardy, James D. (James Daniel), 1934– author.
Title: Campus crisis : how money, technology and policy are changing the American university / James D. Hardy, Jr. and Ann Martin.
Description: Jefferson, North Carolina : McFarland & Company, Inc., Publishers, 2017 | Includes bibliographical references and index.
Identifiers: LCCN 2017019934 | ISBN 9781476665207 (softcover : acid free paper) ∞
Subjects: LCSH: Education, Higher—Aims and objectives—United States. | Education, Higher—Economic aspects—United States. | Education, Higher—Effect of technological innovations on—United States. | Universities and colleges—United States.
Classification: LCC LA227.4 .H37 2017 | DDC 378.73—dc23
LC record available at https://lccn.loc.gov/2017019934

BRITISH LIBRARY CATALOGUING DATA ARE AVAILABLE

ISBN (print) 978-1-4766-6520-7
ISBN (ebook) 978-1-4766-2910-0

© 2017 James D. Hardy, Jr., and Ann Martin. All rights reserved

No part of this book may be reproduced or transmitted in any form or by any means, electronic or mechanical, including photocopying or recording, or by any information storage and retrieval system, without permission in writing from the publisher.

Front cover images © 2017 iStock

Printed in the United States of America

McFarland & Company, Inc., Publishers
 Box 611, Jefferson, North Carolina 28640
  www.mcfarlandpub.com

To our spouses and children,
who have put up with an awful lot

Acknowledgments

We acknowledge a debt of encouragement and support to Mrs. Dorothy McCaughey, rector of the residential college where both authors teach. She gave us time to work and believed in the project. Her support was a very present help through all the years of working on the manuscript. We acknowledge also a debt to Professor Billy Seay, retired dean of the Honors College at LSU.

Table of Contents

Acknowledgments — vi
Preface — 1

ONE • The Legacy of the Medieval University — 7
TWO • The Americanization of the University Experience — 23
THREE • Student Environments — 47
FOUR • Courses and Curriculum — 70
FIVE • MOOCs: Technology and Money — 90
SIX • SCOCs, Universities, Technology and Money — 111
SEVEN • For-Profit Universities: The American Dream Redefined — 134
EIGHT • The Limitations of Reform — 155

Bibliographical Essay — 175
Chapter Notes — 185
Index — 205

Preface

This book explores current academic issues, the most significant of which is funding, or the lack of it. American universities are chronically short of money, and since the crash of 2008, they are shorter yet. They lack the funds to enhance or sometimes even to maintain excellence. Public agencies, municipal, state, and federal, are not able to sustain support for higher education. Everything happening within the academy flows from that sad and simple fact. Moreover, lack of money is not a problem that universities can solve on their own. Tuition and fees do not cover costs and cannot be endlessly increased. Without substantial extramural funding, now mostly public, virtually all the 4,000 or so American colleges and universities would have to close their doors. Money, as Thomas Carlyle has noted, is miraculous, and that is never more so true than in university education.

This book also examines university structure and management, which have become contentious issues in a time of fiscal shortfall. Many voices have been calling for a fundamental restructuring of higher education. We cannot allow ourselves to be associated with that thesis. Actually, universities work well, and until the last classroom is closed, the last professor laid off, and the plant sold for scrap, universities will continue to function as they always have. Those who propose innovation, whether technological or administrative, have not shown a better way to educate millions of students at the university level.

Rules organizing the University of Paris in 1215 retain their effectiveness today. The basic university structure, which is hierarchical, anti-democratic, and non-egalitarian, sustains three fundamental university functions: collecting knowledge, teaching students, and educating the faculty. These three interrelated functions define a working university. There are, of course, in education as in everything, glitches, mistakes, and heartrending tales of woe. But generally, modern American universities are succeeding at their triple task. They do not stand in desperate, or even modest, need of internal reform. But they do stand in serious need of support.

We have examined American universities from both a narrative and an analytical perspective. Universities exist within the river of time, so we have considered them historically. In the twelfth and thirteenth centuries, universities were a product of creation; for us in the twenty-first century, they are a product of evolution. Leaving out their history, whether in Europe or America, gives the writer and leaves the reader with the impression that universities can be rearranged willy-nilly like a box of Legos. In our time, universities can be established but not created; they are now organic.

Universities are institutions, so we have analyzed them in terms of structure and function. We have found that neither politics nor technology can create a "new university." A political university is merely an ideological "re-education camp." Online technology can extend the reach of a university but cannot replace its campus or organizational structure; it can enhance only its function of collecting knowledge. And, if you start a university from scratch, you will build an institution with the structure and functions of the university we have now. The American university is the way it is and does the things it does because that is the way it works best.

Through all the history and analysis, we have asked a single basic question. Given the current (and inevitable) structure, given the current (and necessary) functions, given the current (and required) educational and research role in a democratic society, given all that, are American colleges and universities doing their job well? And the answer, it seems to us, is yes. American universities are doing their jobs quite well. They aren't perfect. Nothing is. For every ointment there is a fly. And the proposed innovations? Will they help? Because universities are doing a good job generally, the innovations will affect higher education only at the margins, sometimes for better but all too often for worse.

Our examination of the academy, and our experience within it (we are both lifers) has led us to several overlapping conclusions. Some are pleasing, to us, anyway; others discouraging, but that is always the way of the world. The first group involves the institutional university, a medieval survivor that, fortunately, works better now than it did then. American universities are run well, contrary to a lot of current chatter.[1]

True enough, universities are bureaucratic institutions; like all bureaucracies, they are run with a bias favoring routine over innovation and rules over people. This reality may be regarded as part of the human condition. But university administration is not really oppressive, though on occasion it is administratively intrusive. In spite of political correctness, academic freedom is generally respected, and administrators usually prefer achievement to incompetence.

Moreover, the basic university structure, inherited from medieval Paris, will remain intact. Professors will teach students as they always have. Students will be taught (and possibly learn) the standard academic subjects. Libraries will collect knowledge and university museums will preserve artifacts, all in the usual manner. The university will support research and publication by the faculty, just as before. These three basic university functions, teaching students, collecting knowledge, and supporting scholarship, seem permanent.

A second general conclusion involves "credential creep," the slow but inexorable rise in credentials a person needs to compete in the job market of a knowledge society. After World War II, the bachelor's degree was the social standard, but that standard continues to rise. In another working generation (40–45 years), a bachelor's degree won't be enough. Colleges and universities will benefit from this social trend, serving ever more customers, as some chancellors now call students, for ever-longer stints at the university. Students, of course, might see credential creep and its attendant costs a bit differently, but they will still need that next degree or certificate.

And what about those students? The time has come to abandon the pretty story that every student can learn "under the right conditions." If the teacher is great and the environment supportive, anyone can learn. That's the doctrine, but it is not true. And as higher education becomes ever higher because of credential creep, that comforting doctrine becomes ever less true. A quarter or so of a high school cohort won't be able to learn at the university level. That is what credential creep in a knowledge society means.

Further conclusions involve the current silver bullet for all ills in higher education: electronic distance learning. Far from being a course or two or five, students may well find that online "education" now includes entire virtual degrees or perhaps the entire freshman year. The American economy supports whole online universities. Hopes run high; universities can go largely online and, theoretically at least, reach everybody. The reality is that online courses will usually be a reluctant classroom supplement and not a good one. And what is the primary problem with online education? No matter what the academic discipline offered, no matter to whom, the course and the learning outcomes will be better if the course is taught and taken in person. It's a lot better to be there. That fact leads to a discouraging result. American higher education is moving in two simultaneous directions. On-campus students learn more, get better courses, and receive a first-class degree. Students online will get a second-class degree. Online "education" will be better than nothing but, all too often, not a whole lot better.

Online programs and universities are driven by the market, and so they turn education into a commodity. The academic credential has become an expensive commodity, bought with time and money. Neither the cost nor the value of the college degree seems likely to decrease in the foreseeable future. But colleges and universities will not benefit much from the growing market. The modest profits from online courses, after the always-larger-than-expected costs are paid, will not come close to bailing universities out of their current financial slough. Many colleges, perhaps most, will make no profits at all. But there will always be the costs.

A final category of conclusions deals with money, the most serious problem currently facing universities. Proposals to reform the academy bear little relationship to the primary problem of money. Public sector disinvestment in higher education will not cease; it is more likely to increase. Legacy and health care costs will place sufficient pressure on state budgets to make the academic squeeze permanent.

And what do money woes mean to college kids? A lot. Universities will not add faculty, tutors, and counselors to improve student learning, even though everyone knows that small learning communities on campus will improve student outcomes. The trend in academic personnel is leaner, not more ample. But neither will universities evolve away from mass education on campus to the elite system, where better students will do the work with less help. Current fiscal problems will lead to a continuation of current instructional practices, warts and all, along with the current mirage of fiscal salvation through the Internet. Current funding will ensure the continuation of current problems.

And a final note: America is becoming more, and more rapidly, a knowledge society, and universities are knowledge and idea factories. In modern America, knowledge is the biggest business of them all. Technology transfer and innovation generally are the most important things that a research university does. Universities will succeed to the extent that this general social need continues. Universities will also remain about the same as long as current funding levels continue. Reform, whether in institutional structure, college costs, curriculum, or research, will require a whole lot more money. Perhaps this is good news. Perhaps it is not. But it is reality.

• ONE •

The Legacy of the Medieval University

Is not our university a venerable institution? Surely, its annals are filled with illustrious graduates, interesting characters, significant discoveries, important events, and stirring achievements, all nurtured by beautiful architecture, remarkable natural vistas, and golden memories. Please send money.

At the same time, our university is bright and modern, on the cutting edge of contemporary culture. It pushes the envelope farther all the time. The new student union, glitzy as a casino, has a food court that serves international cuisine from twenty countries around the world. The student recreational center has climbing walls, a "lazy river," and exercise machines that allow you simultaneously to work out, watch television, monitor your heart rate, and tweet about it all. The dormitories resemble Buckingham Palace, and every student suite has a hot tub. The cafeterias appear regularly on food channels. The campus is connected to the entire world via Internet. Every classroom has a media center. Everything is up to date here. Please send your student to our university.

Strange to say, both these blasts of public relations blather are reasonably accurate. Universities strive relentlessly to have the most modern physical plant possible. But they really are venerable institutions, where academic and sentimental traditions persist. The traditions go back a long, long way. Modern American research universities are lineal descendants of the University of Paris, specifically from the university rules written in August 1215, by the papal legate Cardinal Robert de Courçon.[1] Research universities are equal in age to the Magna Carta and are no less important in the development of Western civilization.

To be sure, an immense extra-academic superstructure has been added to universities, but the medieval essentials abide. If one hacks through these administrative proliferations, through the residence life programs, the food service purveyors, student unions, IT departments, athletic programs, theaters, student publications, compliance officers of all sorts, the baronies of human resource management, through all that thicket, one finds that universities, like Gothic cathedrals, are survivors. Although the medieval university seems redolent of a mythic past, the modern American research university bears an uncanny resemblance to it. Like the University of Paris in the days of Thomas Aquinas, the modern university is a place set apart, where knowledge and understanding are pursued.[2] The future can be created here. One afternoon, Francis Crick and James Watson left their laboratory at Cambridge University, walked to a pub, and announced to all that they had discovered the secret of life. It was the simple truth. They had found the double helix of DNA. Universities are designed to make sure these things happen.

Universities nurture knowledge in three interlocking ways. They support the creation of knowledge, through research, thought, imagination, publication, collaboration, along with teaching, all of which serve to hone the faculty. Universities disseminate knowledge to students, and they also collect and preserve knowledge in libraries. The university has formed a community of knowledge for eight centuries. That's the ideal, sometimes honored in the breach but more often in the observance. Even when universities are less than the best, professors publish, students learn, libraries remember, and the ideal remains. Please send students and money. The need is, and has always been, urgent.

Origins

Universities emerged in the eleventh and twelfth centuries, amidst the mayhem of medieval cities. In the beginning, centers of learning were personal rather than institutional. A professor (master), in medicine, law, or logic, would announce that he was willing to teach a course of lectures. Students (scholars) would gather around him. If he were good and had something to say, the number of students would grow from a few into a crowd. These nameless students now attending, now dropping out, often came from great and dangerous distances to the few cities known for instruction. At some point, the students and teachers became so numerous and rowdy that some form of organization became essential. You couldn't have crowds of people jostling together in public squares and shouting to lecturers to repeat something. Masters and scholars in these proto-universities seemed given to fights, robbery, riot. And then it would rain, chasing masters and scholars into taverns, where they disturbed the regular patrons.

It could be even worse. Masters sometimes preached heresy. Occasionally they went further and did the unthinkable. They denounced the town council, usually for hostility to master and scholar and not infrequently for brutality. None of that was acceptable conduct, even for uncertain men like professors.

You couldn't accept those activities as a normal part of urban behavior. If you were a citizen, you would put pressure on city and church to reform the whole business of university education. The authorities in Paris and Bologna, two of the earliest university towns, intervened. One solution to the unruly crowd of masters and scholars was to run them out of town. A second solution was to profit from their presence. Profits won out, as they so often do. Authorities, both sacred and secular, moved to organize the masters and scholars, making the city marginally safer but significantly richer.

And the weather also helped out. After the year 1000, the European climate got a bit warmer, bringing general prosperity in its wake. Social order also improved. Outside invasions, whether the Magyars from the east, Arabs from the south, or Norsemen from Scandinavia, slowed down. Towns grew as trade expanded, making literacy and learning more important. Though universities were not yet established in any modern sense, they were moving in that direction. Extraordinary instructors, Peter Abelard in Paris and Irnerius in Bologna, drew students to town. Universities developed from occasional lectures to permanent institutions with stable curricula and degrees. As they settled into formal order, universities became a Western cultural necessity.

As universities developed, they responded to two powerful social forces: church and state. Kings encouraged universities and even founded a few (Holy Roman Emperor Charles IV in Prague). They thought universities should offer secular learning. And the universities responded. They offered arts colleges and degrees in law and medicine. The second social force was the Church. Everyone thought of universities as part of the Church's general magisterium. Most schools offered degrees and curricula in theology. Magnificos, whether secular or sacred, tended to be pleased at the learning offered in these growing medieval universities.

The scholars also mattered. In Paris, they were organized into nations (*natio*) based on language and in colleges (*collegia*) based on residence.[3] Almost everywhere, the scholars were usually in minor orders and had benefit of clergy.[4] Masters were often clerics, whether regular (St. Thomas Aquinas or St. Bonaventure) or secular.[5] Because of diverse pressures, neither king nor bishop ever gained complete control over the university and its masters and scholars.[6]

The scholars benefited from the combination of sacred and secular learning. A completed course of study could snag an important post in church or state for a well-placed application. Whether as portal to learning or the door to advantage, the university fulfilled the hopes of its early masters and scholars. Over time, costume, language, and university administration would change, but a Rip Van Winkle from thirteenth century Paris would find much of the rest of the university familiar.[7]

The desire for a university extended well beyond Paris and Bologna, for reasons ranging from knowledge to profit and prestige. But everything has costs. Masters quarreled bitterly, with each other and with their scholars. Scholars dealt in a cavalier manner with townspeople. Municipal authorities intervened more than once. At Bologna, alas, the student guilds took control of the institution.[8] In Paris, the masters would triumph, establishing the model for the modern Western research university.[9] In every city, the effort was always the same: combine study with municipal profit, social order, and royal/episcopal patronage.

In 1215, the papal legate Cardinal Robert de Courçon undertook a task that many had attempted before him, usually with quite modest success. Pope Innocent III asked him to look into the habitual contention at the University of Paris. Cardinal Robert was well placed to undertake what had always been a thankless task. The cardinal belonged to the Anglo-Norman aristocracy, with its traditions of opportunity and habits of command. Born in the 1160s at Kedleston, in Derbyshire, England, he studied at Oxford during the first generation of that college's existence. We know he then went abroad to study theology in Paris, and he even went to Italy, perhaps to Bologna to study law, perhaps to Rome where he would have met the great men of the Church. This is the only way that a career like his could have happened. Great preferment within the Church often came from personal acquaintance.[10] In 1211 he became chancellor of the University of Paris, a tribute, as well, to his learning, orthodoxy, and diplomacy, and perhaps to the power of the Angevin Empire. A year later, Innocent III made him a cardinal.[11] He preached against the Albigensian heretics and was a leading figure in helping to launch the ill-fated Fifth Crusade against Egypt. Cardinal Robert went on the crusade himself and died at the siege of Damietta in 1218 or 1219. He probably perished from disease, the usual scourge of military campaigns in those days.

Fortunately, before he left for the Levant, Cardinal Robert had undertaken a reworking of the rules of the University of Paris. These rules were designed to solve problems of authority. Who would run the university? Could the scholars be kept in order? Should the city restrain them? Could the masters learn to co-exist in peace? For most of the century before 1215, pope, king, and city had tried to create an effective university structure to manage its masters, scholars, Church (chancellor and bishop), and the city of Paris. A guild of masters had extorted recognition from town and university in 1170. In 1200, King Philip Augustus gave the university additional municipal privileges, partially in response to a riot. The year 1210 brought a new set of rules. Contention continued. Now, in 1215, Cardinal Robert was taking his turn at organizing an institution in which nothing seemed to work well but which all recognized as vital to the true faith, to a good society, to the advancement of learning, and to the prosperity of Paris. Everybody tried to make the university work because everybody believed in it.

Cardinal Robert did not attempt to invent something *ex nihilo*; he would fix what was already there. He established some firm boundaries in both form and function. The university could not be turned into a monastery: it must remain public and embrace both secular and sacred learning.[12] The masters already had their own guild, and they were not going to give that up. Their basic relationships within the university would remain the same. The cardinal respected established academic relationships.

Nonetheless, there was plenty of room for improvement. Start with the students. The young scholars simply milled around, going from to master to master.[13] Exams were irregular, ad hoc, and unsupervised. The masters were similarly undisciplined. New masters would randomly show up and start speaking. If they attracted scholars and collected fees, the guild of established masters would often boycott and denounce them. But bringing order out of chaos was a church specialty. In 1215, Cardinal Robert would knead the quasi-academic Paris masters and mob of scholars into a coherent institutional form.

The cardinal ordained a university controlled by the masters, who already dominated what passed for an academy. A savvy and charismatic leader, he confirmed essential academic authority and powers in them. That was the key decision. The masters would give the lectures, set the curriculum, run the "determinations" (examinations for a license), disputations, and public debates. The masters would decide who should receive a license (degree), and who should be sent away. These simple injunctions regulated the commanding heights of the academic world. That core decision by Cardinal Robert would never be reversed, and it would be replicated, first in Germany and then throughout the Western world, including the United States.[14] After a generation or so, pope, king, or city assumed that what was done in Paris was what ought to be done everywhere.

The cardinal restricted the masters' power as well as confirmed it. He ordained that those who proposed to educate others should themselves be educated. This was a genuine innovation and a good idea. Candidates to lecture in the arts, the undergraduate college, must have attended lectures for at least six years, and, before they lectured, the applicants would be examined by a committee including the bishop of Troyes, the bishop of Paris, and the chancellor of Paris. Should the candidate pass through this skeptical scrutiny, he could lecture on the standard curriculum, the *trivium* and the *quadrivium*, along with Aristotle's *Prior* and *Posterior Analytics* and *Topics*, as well as the grammar of Priscian and Donatus.[15] Who could doubt that everyone must know this stuff to be well educated? Cardinal Robert certainly knew it; consequently, all masters received the same examination before they could lecture, regardless of what they were teaching.

With that academic imperative, Cardinal Robert admonished the masters in the arts college to stick strictly to their curriculum. Masters had acquired a habit of engaging in long philosophical rants, the medieval equivalent of modern political digressions. The cardinal hoped to stop the rants, but he could not. Digression has become an academic habit.[16]

The cardinal also wanted something akin to a registrar's office. He ordained that each master was to have authority over his scholars, and no one "shall be a scholar at Paris who has no definite master."[17] There had been, and would be again, painful experience with young men about town on their own, pretending to be students. Kids need to be processed and supervised. The university began to keep lists of students, which meant, as it does now, a list of those who paid fees.

The decrees of 1215 for the arts college stood on their own, bereft of written elaboration. The cardinal never gave his reasons, nor did he give specific examples of what the masters' authority should be. The principles alone would have to suffice. And they have. Cardinal Robert set the general academic relationship of master and scholar from that day to this, though the details would be endlessly reworked.

The graduate program in theology also needed rules, and Cardinal Robert established some. No one might lecture in theology before the age of thirty-five, which was about ten years beyond the average lifespan at the time. The candidate must have attended lectures for eight years and attended theology lectures for five years more.[18] Those requirements might not be enough, more education might be desirable, but they were a start. Further, the candidate must be approved, both in "life and science." The age limit was the key. Since scholars often began to study at fifteen or sixteen, a master in theology would have to spend some twenty years or more at the university. In that time, he probably learned something.[19]

Here appeared the whole university system, sketched in rather than filled out, with some things mentioned and others implied. The lecture courses, the curricula, the qualifications to be a master, the examination of candidates for the faculty, licenses, university administration, dominance of the masters over the scholars—all the elements of a modern university are found here. Everyone who has been at a university, as student or faculty, will recognize the familiar outlines, some with a smile, others with a shudder.

The cardinal legate favored the chancellors and masters, to the cost of the scholars and townspeople. The chancellor had gained some vague authority over the whole university, which has relentlessly expanded over the centuries. The masters kept general control over the curriculum, the lectures, the examinations, and the degrees. When the faculty were united, which was not always the case, they could often dominate the chancellor as well. Probably for the best, the scholars remained subject to the masters in all academic matters. The interests of the town, primarily law and order, were ignored; the economic interests were protected. Cardinal Robert understood the importance of rent. Students were admonished not to occupy rooms and buildings without permission or payment.

The cardinal had established a hierarchy within the university, based on rank (then the bishop, now the administration) and on knowledge (the faculty). Municipal authorities were excluded from managing any part of the university. What the cardinal had done was combine the muscle and organization of the guilds, the ultimate supremacy of the Church, and the separation of town from gown. It's not yet the ivory tower, but it will be.

Looking back on it, the cardinal's effort seems almost miraculous. His rules of 1215 for the University of Paris were concise: only a couple of pages in Latin. The miracle lies not only in brevity, utterly unknown today, but also in reasonableness. The cardinal created a structure that could work, and that had a good chance of being accepted by everyone involved. Persuasion was probably the result of Cardinal Robert's charisma as well as his rank. He knew everybody personally, and that always counts. University masters were no more cooperative then than they are now, but the guild of masters did benefit from the cardinal's rules, and so they went along.

The bishop did also. Scholars and townspeople had little choice, but the mere existence of rules helped everybody. The cardinal had created both system and community, bringing university education out of the chaos of indeterminacy, where no degree, masters, or scholars had universal acceptance.

Cardinal Robert's organizational insight produced one of the great achievements of the Middle Ages. The leading modern historian of the medieval university commented that "[t]he great work of the universities was the consecration of learning; and it is not easy to exaggerate the importance of that work upon the moral, intellectual, and religious progress of the Middle Ages."[20] Churchmen knew in their hearts that learning led to the True Faith, away from heresy, while informing the simple piety of the *res publica Christiana*. The Church was the guardian of the whole community, and learning was the adornment of religion. Secular authorities had a slightly different view. Kings and town councils thought in terms of power, profit, and prestige. Universities began to appear everywhere. In the next couple of decades, there would be schools at Salamanca (1218, 1254, 1255), Padua (1222), and Toulouse (1230), and, in the next century, in central Europe as well.

Students had still a different view. Having been selected by local churchmen as a likely scholar and sent to the university, a student knew this was his great chance at social advancement. He passes his arts determination and studies law or theology. A degree puts him on the high road to success. He doesn't have to be a pardoner or a summoner; he can become a cathedral canon, or even more. Cardinal Pierre Thomas began life as a peasant and ended it as a prince. Most of the scholars were urban children of propertied and professional parents who knew what an education meant. Martin Luther's father sent him to university to become a lawyer and perhaps a minister to the prince. There was nothing unusual about that. Not everyone did so well, but all who succeeded at university succeeded in the wider world beyond. By the thirteenth century, the university was already the Golden Door to a better life. And for the *res publica Christiana*, it was the center of scientific and philosophical speculation.

In spite of initial success, the cardinal's rules required subsequent interpretation.[21] Like any organic law, they were sketchy rather than ample. They left much unexplained. The cardinal's rules worked better when he was present than after he left. A leadership vacuum meant that chancellors, masters, and scholars were unsure where the boundaries really lay or what the rules really commanded. After the cardinal's death (1219), power struggles led to violence. Between 1229 and 1231, the university nearly dissolved as instruction ceased. The people of Paris appealed to Pope Gregory IX, who added some details to the cardinal's basic rules.[22] Gregory's decrees covered the whole of university life, from intellectual matters to official conduct, to the inevitable misconduct committed by scholars and those pretending to be scholars.[23]

Pope Gregory expanded on the cardinal's solutions for familiar problems. He ruled that chancellors must swear that they will not accept "unworthy men" as masters. Chancellors must grant licenses (degrees, including the *ius ubique docendi*, the right to teach everywhere) only to worthy men and not be swayed with "respect to persons or nations." The pope then moved to administration. The university acquired the right to regulate "the manner and time of lectures and disputes"; those who violated these ordinances could suffer exclusion. The most important rules concerned scheduling. Enforcing them allowed the university chancellor to clamp down upon, and ultimately eliminate, freelance masters who set up shop on their own. The university effectively acquired its monopoly on higher education.[24]

Nearly as serious was the practice of monetizing the university. The chancellor was prohibited from demanding money or an oath of loyalty from a master whom he licensed. Nor could the chancellor sell licenses, a common practice. These abuses threatened the integrity of the university. The pope also addressed the defects of the masters, both intellectual and moral. Gregory admonished them to lecture on the approved books and avoid those not declared free of error.[25] Gregory also warned the masters of Paris to avoid wild philosophical speculations, which could veer into heresy. Finally, even when masters avoided heresy, they were not easy to live with. Many were arrogant and rambunctious, to say nothing of uncooperative, fractious, willful, and insufferable generally.[26] Not unlike today, the individual personality of the masters played a large role in academic success and peace.

Like all of high rank, the pope and cardinal favored the institution over the person and regularity over improvisation. No more cowboys allowed; the days of Abelard were over. The two prelates understood that human life is corporate and hierarchical. And a proper university should reflect that reality. The pope and cardinal cut back a bit on the academic anarchy. The masters would lecture at a particular time on a particular day, and students would be punished for absence. The chancellor imposed a semesterly calendar with specified holidays and requirements to attend Mass.[27] The university would function as medieval institutions should, a particular combination of obedience and privilege. It would resemble guilds and monasteries: all members obeyed countless rules and enjoyed the benefits of a privileged position.

Pope Gregory's reforms of the rules of 1215 set a pattern that has lasted for centuries. Reforms around the margins, and in the details of university structure, have become a permanent process. But the center has held. The numbers and complexity of university rules, regulations, injunctions, prohibitions, guidelines, lawsuits, and extramural interventions have multiplied endlessly. All seek to cure the university ills that cardinal and pope had denounced so long ago. Efforts at moral reform have always faced the stiff headwinds of original sin (now called human nature), which continues its doleful and gleeful progress through the hallowed halls.[28] So reforms will be proposed, and enacted, and mostly fail, forever.

Hierarchy

Medieval universities were anti-egalitarian institutions, with a distinct hierarchy based upon academic degrees, honors, rank, publications, and their absence. Nothing has changed. Most relationships within the university are fundamentally asymmetrical. Students occupy the bottom rung of the hierarchical university because of their relative lack of knowledge and utter absence of credentials. Near the top of the academic pyramid sits the faculty. Their eminence rests upon credentials, of course, but also upon custom and law, all arising from the rules of 1215. The faculty cannot be dislodged, if for no reason other than nothing can replace them. At the institutional apex, one finds the magnificos of the administration, the presidents and chancellors and provosts with their minions and bureaucrats. They run the institution because they run the budget, fill out the federal forms, keep the records, stuff the dorms, manage the students, and reassure the parents. They receive the incense and anthems that accompany high rank everywhere. But administrators do not run the academy. Professors, by virtue of learning and tenure, maintain an independent sphere of influence. Although students, faculty, and administrators can disagree on almost everything much of the time, the hierarchical structure itself has always survived the particular issues of the day.

Cardinal Robert based his academic gradations upon the disparity of knowledge between the masters, whom he favored, and the scholars, whom he did not. As a result, masters, especially doctors in law and theology, would come to attain a status equivalent to knighthood. Students lost authority within the university, but they did retain opportunity.[29] The scholars might not be much now; still, they had a chance to make it big later. The chasm in rank between the masters and the scholars was thought by everyone to be entirely proper. Some were closer to God than others. Rank is always regarded as grounded in reality, and all then thought it necessary for good order.

Modern universities continue the same distinctions in rank, persistent propaganda about "student ownership of programs" notwithstanding. Modern political ideals say one thing; academic history and psychological reality say another. And most people seem generally comfortable with rank in the university, which is normally earned and rarely inherited. Moreover, citizenship within the university is voluntary, and free social choices are modern icons as sacred as equality. Finally, in the nature of things, universities separate sheep from goats. For some to pass, others must fail. This applies to the faculty as well as the students. Universities accentuate inequality. Within the universities, equality is a publicly proclaimed ideal, while hierarchy is the reality of daily life.

The subordinate role of students does not mean that they have no rights. Universities publish student handbooks enumerating those rights in detail.[30] Nevertheless, the faculty retain authority over pedagogy. This arrangement, basically unchanged since the thirteenth century, has enormous institutional weight. After all, to this very day, no one has ever thought of any workable alternative. Of all the hierarchies in an egalitarian world, it is one of the most stable. The immense student protests in France in 1968 brought down the government but could not change the university. The student protests at Berkeley against the University of California in the 1960s left behind mountains of garbage, continuing bitterness and distrust within the university, student careers ruined, a few pregnancies, a number of drug busts, and the university intact. Recent protests at the University of Missouri over diversity, in which the administration surrendered to student demands, have resulted in the president and the chancellor leaving, freshmen enrollment down, donations to academics and athletics down, the student demands unmet, and the university remains as it has been. The uproar there has caused damage but not change. Academic protests are mostly therapy. The odd thing is that anyone would be surprised.

Generally speaking, now as well as then, professorial authority is not subject to any serious accountability. Within the classroom, and out of it as well, professors speak, teach, grade, reward, punish, assign work, give exams, and write recommendations as they see fit. The rules of the University of Paris basically equate the authority of a professor with that of the captain of a sailing ship. Still, professorial authority just drives some people up the wall. Politicians and reformers seek to ensure "fairness" and "accountability" to professors' academic decisions. The current fashion for grade appeal, with final resolution at a place and by persons far distant from the original decision, has led mainly to an inevitable emphasis on process over substance. In the end, academic decisions tend to stand as originally given. In any institution descended from Paris, authority is usually ratified. The dogs bark; the hierarchical medieval university moves on. Eight hundred years after Cardinal Robert, the faculty remain responsible for the university's intellectual life. We all take this for granted.

The research university supports faculty learning and research, faculty publication, and the most imaginative and productive professors.[31] On occasion, we have responded to colleagues who assume that the university is student centered. We offer the feeble response of evidence. If faculty learning and publication were not the paramount responsibility of the university, why are billions in grants from government, industry, and foundations annually awarded to university faculty members? Further, why are hundreds of billions in infrastructure, from electron microscopes to clean rooms, from libraries to labs, from cyclotrons to astronomical observatories, provided to university faculty? In this society, money is the measure of almost everything. "Follow the money," Deep Throat advised the Watergate reporters Carl Bernstein and Bob Woodward, and society generally does. University faculty work with libraries and equipment and grants and supplies that are worth far far more than the sum of all Wall Street and corporate bonuses. The annual allocation of billions to university faculty cannot be a fad or a whim. Money talks.

Because money does talk, the faculty of the two hundred or so premier American research universities and their professional schools are encouraged to attend conferences, give papers, write grant proposals, and publish articles, notes, comments, reviews, reports, and books. They are also urged to support the business of the university through technology transfer, legal and industrial consulting, and medical innovation. This expenditure of faculty time and expertise reflects the university's support of faculty learning. Nothing the university does is more important.[32]

Or reverse the point of view. Plenty of places have instructors, students, administrators, and counselors, but they lack the primary role of supporting the education of the faculty.[33] These places offer on-the-job training, short courses in industry, technical courses, and military education. They cannot be confused with research universities. Further, we suggest that the professor's very function denies the idea of a student-centered university. The professor is supposed to put pieces and patches together into patterns; to put things into context and into systems; and to investigate relationships between apparently disparate equations, things, and events. The modern philosopher Michael Oakeshott emphasizes professorial learning even more, arguing that many university scholars should not have to teach; they should "devote an unbroken leisure to learning, their fellows having the advantage of their knowledge from their conversation and the world benefiting, perhaps, from their writings. A place of learning without this kind of scholar could scarcely be called a university."[34] Oakeshott's idea can be found in sabbaticals, fellowships, and Fulbright grants for professors to think and perhaps to write.

Cardinal Robert believed that those with a formal education should teach those who wanted one, and he created around that idea a hierarchical system that *could* work. That system reflected the unequal relationship of apprentice and journeyman to the master in the crafts. Both apprentice and master craftsman would improve in skill and understanding over time. Why should not the same results appear with scholars and masters? What worked for the hand would work the mind. The cardinal bound faculty and students together in a community through their mutual efforts at learning and teaching. When things work as they should, both faculty and students resemble Chaucer's iconic wandering scholar: "gladly wold he lerne, and gladly teche."

Lectures

In modern American universities, the medieval methods of instruction continue in full force and flower. Lecture was then, and remains now, the basic teaching technique, primarily for three reasons. It makes more sense for the person who knows something to do the talking. Secondly, it is more efficient for a professor to lecture to a large number of students. Furthermore, in a democratic society, an enormous number of inadequately prepared students enter college. Lecture is the most effective way to bring them up to speed, insofar as that is possible. University critics are currently debating the value of lectures, trying to replace them with some mix of technology and learning activities.[35] Students do complain but mostly about lousy lectures. Yet we have rarely heard students complain about the lecture system, though we have heard a lot of grousing about lectures done badly.[36] A recent cultural phenomenon is the TED talk, where experts such as Bill Gates or Kelly McGonigal give a short online lecture from technology to personal development. College students voluntarily watch these, without either compulsion or credit. An even more popular version of the college lecture, the podcast, has become part of everyday Americans' digital consumption. The pedagogy of lecturing is not unreasonable. Those who know explain the material to those who do not.

Beyond the permanent value of lectures, in medieval Europe, lectures had an additional significant merit. Before printing, books were rare and costly, and many students began the course of lecture without one. The masters read from the text, Aristotle or Priscian, or the *Corpus Juris Civilis*. Hence, the practice was called lecture, literally, a reading. The master also read aloud commentaries by previous masters. In teaching the *Corpus Juris Civilis*, the master would read the text, then note what Irnerius had said, what Azus had said, what Accursius had said, what Baldus had said, what Bartolus of Sassoferrato had said, and what we now say. The student wrote it all down, word for word, ending several years in law school with the text, the best historical observations, and the most current gloss. In those days, students needed to attend class and stay awake. If the student persevered, as a reward for enduring the lectures, he had an immensely valuable book of his own.

Then, many professors lectured outside to gaggles of students who stood around them. In the absence of a lectern, an acolyte held the book that the professor was reading. The scholars, inkpots tied around their necks, pushed in as closely as they could: in the noise of the marketplace, ten feet away was a great distance. Everybody knew everybody else. The scholars and masters were not only under the same cathedral door; they often ate together and drank together. The relationship was personal (as with the wandering scholars in *The Name of the Rose*). Young men were often sent by their fathers to study under masters who were friends of the family. In Cardinal Robert's university, the institution had not yet obliterated the importance of personal relationships built around books and learning.

In medieval universities, students complained when the professors failed to lecture or cut the lectures short or did not read the text or spent class time on philosophical rants. In these cases, and they occurred all the time, students felt cheated, and they were. Students demanded professors pay fines for dereliction of lecture. Sometimes, they beat the offending non-teachers. Now and then, the students rioted. And well they might. They had a lot at stake. If they failed to get their own books, those years at university were set at discount. Complaints about bad lectures are nothing new. Only the definition of bad lectures has changed.

Today, students can buy their books, and some do. Most students are capable of reading the text, and again, some do. Every student can get online reviews and summaries of every text. The organic connection between book and lecture no longer exists. Now, the students do not complain about professors missing lectures; that draws applause. Complaints occur when professors *give* lectures, if they don't do it well. The lecturer is not entertaining, the students whine. He does not show enough pictures. She dispenses too much information. The material is too hard. The lecturer expects students to stay awake and take notes. Some lecturers even expect students to learn. This is all unfair, currently the students' favorite word. And anyway, you can watch a better lecture online. Defending themselves against the horrors of bad lectures, some students cut class, habitually. Others text. Some watch shows on their computers or smartphones. Most plug into social media. Inattention takes many forms.

Lecturers are responsible for most of the problems in the lecture but not all. Students today often put themselves more or less entirely through school and usually have a job, occasionally two or three, to pay for an appallingly expensive education. In lecture, they are usually waiting class out until they can return to their jobs off campus. Because they are stressed by life, they are less than receptive to learning. Meanwhile the lecturer lectures on. The medieval student lamented the lecturer's absence. The modern student laments the lecturer's presence.

The medieval lecture system continues unabated, despite complaints. And it should. From the institutional perspective, lectures are efficient, taking advantage of economies of scale. One professor, two hundred students or more, is an ordinary ratio at a state university. Four hundred students: better and better, as the bursar rubs his hands. A thousand students: it can be done. And it is done. If you build the lecture hall, they will stuff it. Even with a mere two hundred students, it's a hell of a bargain.

Modern critics of lectures pay only peripheral attention to the educational bargain and not much more to the students' effort to dodge the system and none at all to what the students might learn. The critics dislike lecture as a method of teaching, recommending various software programs developed from online learning platforms. They also tout student-centered learning, including group projects, collaborative work in class, "flipped classrooms," and experiential learning (learning by doing).[37] The emphasis falls on the community of student-learners. Team sports form the primary cadre of communal learning in most universities, followed by graduate students in the sciences. The learning is, so to say, bottom up rather than top down. It sounds more democratic. And it certainly appears more cooperative.

Lectures, by definition and by contrast, work top down, emphasizing the huge gap between those who know and those who need to know. Modern university critics prefer to disguise the teacher/student asymmetry in knowledge, which medieval universities emphasized.

From the foregoing, some critics might assume that American research universities are modern mainly in the material they teach and in the administrative apparatus they bear. Otherwise, they are anachronisms, quaint functioning antiques, having somehow survived from a long-distant time. Mostly true. Public relations puffery notwithstanding, universities are not modern democratic and egalitarian places. And they are not going to be.

A medieval tale of some charm and dubious veracity tells the adventure of a master traveling through the woods on Christmas Eve. He had with him a sturdy volume of Aristotle (known then as The Philosopher and Master of Those Who Know). He also had his sword, an accoutrement of his rank as a doctor. A wild boar attacked him. Prepared for anything, as a master always is, he thrust the Aristotle into the boar's mouth, rendering the beast helpless. The master drew his sword and cut off the boar's head, which he carried to a tavern to add to the Christmas feast. This myth has spawned a Christmas carol, the "Boar's Head," and illustrates the importance of learning, particularly Aristotle.

The myth touches upon the Western attitude that knowledge should be seriously pursued and widely disseminated as a general cultural good. By the thirteenth century, universities taught organized knowledge of every sort, secular even more than sacred. The wandering master was carrying Aristotle, who was an ethical philosopher, a logician, a rhetorician, and a scientist. The distance from the Boar's Head to the modern research university is not so far. The medieval university stands as a witness to William Faulkner's comment about things and times gone by: "The past is never dead. It's not even past."[38]

• TWO •

The Americanization of the University Experience

Europeans regarded their colonies abroad as small, distant replicas of the world at home. Colonists took their cultural attitudes into new lands, and both those who went and those who stayed thought that the old ways, though now newly planted, were the best ways. Making a home abroad meant bringing home with them. In Ireland, Ulster and the Ascendancy were designed to be as English as the shires, from government to church to manor houses and social structures. In Massachusetts Bay, colonists, fleeing the king's religion but not the country's culture, gave English names to their towns and counties. They thought of themselves as living in a New England, and a religiously better one.[1]

Planting the old world anew went beyond home and hearth to include church and state. All intersected at the university, which nurtured the attitudes that a godly people, believing in the true church, living in the king's dominions, must certainly possess. Trinity College, Dublin (1592) filled England's need for an educated Irish gentry and clergy. In Massachusetts, a college was founded only a half decade after the Puritans had settled (1636). When John Harvard, who had sold a tavern in South London to come to America, left the college his library, they named the school after him. Money gained from riotous tavern entertainment wound up buying books for a Puritan college, where enjoyment of any sort was discouraged, if not prohibited. The Lord works in ironic ways. Medieval Paris seems far from a college in seventeenth-century Massachusetts or sixteenth-century Dublin, but distance and time disguise similarity of function. Much of the old became new again.

But cultural institutions are not always replicated exactly. Over time, Americans have produced multiple adaptations of the university model inherited from Paris. On one side, American people, philanthropists, and politicians have built stupendous research universities, the best in the world, which fulfill, on a huge scale, the academic agenda that Paris had originated. On another, Americans have at times moved the three university functions (educating faculty, teaching students, and collecting knowledge) into separate institutions. While research universities do everything, community colleges teach but eliminate the creation and collection of knowledge. Public and private institutes and laboratories (Brookings, Hoover, Bell Labs) have excised teaching in favor of research. Americans believe in efficiency and bold experiment in everything but politics. We have the itch to tinker with the way things are. Everything happens in America.[2]

The Old Ways

Antebellum American colleges began as small schools in small places. Their limited educational missions included producing Protestant ministers and polishing the sons of the gentry. For ministers, colleges were vocational; for gentlemen, they were ornamental. Both missions served a serious social need. They still do.

Early colleges educated gentlemen and ministers but did not dominate the general culture. People in pre-industrial America, with its multiple religions, freedoms of the frontier, and widespread property ownership, still retained habits of obedience to church and deference to social authority. Colleges reinforced the prevailing social order, but most cultural values came from churches and politics. Not much has changed in that respect.

Nonetheless, if colleges in pre–Civil War America were not the sole center of intellectual life, they still prospered. Most major port cities (New York and Philadelphia) boasted a college, and some smaller places (Schenectady) did as well. Numbers of colleges and numbers of students grew after independence. Americans generally have approved of education, particularly when they do not have to endure too much of it themselves. People liked to say that they had been to college. Daniel Webster, arguing before the Supreme Court, stated that while Dartmouth was a small place, there were those who loved it.[3] And Americans did love colleges, giving money for scholarships, professorships, and books. The surest sign of general social approval came when people thought ladies also should have a college education. It would enhance their appreciation for the finer things in life; hence Mount Holyoke (1837) and Vassar (1861). Colleges were a good thing; soon no city or state wished to be without one.

Two • The Americanization of the University Experience

The early American system of higher education was not asked to do too much. Theological education was standard. Only the doctrine had changed since the days of Cardinal Robert. The rest of the curriculum was a Renaissance amalgam of the medieval arts curriculum combined with classical languages, literature, history, and philosophy. Such an education fit a gentleman's library, along with his need to write and speak in public life.[4] Yale College even offered a bit of Hebrew. This would, a Yale president noted, enable a Yale student to speak the language when he got to heaven. What could be more useful than that?

Because of their limited responsibilities, early American colleges were not yet the Golden Door to a better life. Horatio Alger did not advise the plucky urban waif to go to college. Work, discipline, thrift, and a keen eye for investment comprised the Alger formula. While colleges might suggest these virtues, life in nineteenth-century America taught them with a vengeance. Before World War II, colleges had not acquired a general responsibility for the social mobility of the many. Higher education was still an adornment for the few.

Except for the Protestant ministry, early American colleges were not vocational in their academic offerings. In place of educating for a job, colleges then educated for participation in polite society. Sociability was a large part of American college life. Friendship and the inevitable creation of social circles within colleges led, in the 1820s and 1830s, to the formation of the first college fraternities. These were begun in places like Union College in New York (1795) and Miami University in Ohio (1809). Founded by students themselves, usually a few close friends, fraternities survived the graduation of their founders, becoming institutions rather than clubs. They spread to other colleges. New fraternities emulated the old. The system was firmly in place by the Civil War. In joining fraternities, students both enhanced and restricted collegiality. One grew closer to "people like us" and more distant from those who were not quite "the right sort." Fraternities brought a bit of exclusivity, always delightful to those on the inside. They reinforced social hierarchy.[5] Little wonder that fraternities, and later sororities, have expanded, becoming a fundamental aspect of American college social life.

In many ways, the ideal of antebellum American colleges was the University of Virginia, founded in 1819. It was designed architecturally and intellectually by Thomas Jefferson. A large quadrangle with a center green and the library at the uphill side, it combined, in the English fashion, student lodging, classrooms, and faculty apartments. The "academical village" faced inward, where a colonnade gave onto the green, reminiscent, though on an American scale, of a medieval cloister.⁶ University life was firmly within the walls, with social grace as important as formal learning. The university as social community was an already established English way of learning, and Jefferson, who greatly admired the French, transported the English collegiate style to America.

The system of instruction found in Jeffersonian America is far distant from what prevails today. No modern student would submit to it. An unfortunate Jeffersonian student, sometimes chosen by lot, was forced to stand and translate passages from the classical texts. The next victim answered questions on the text and translation. Recitation was a public performance before a critical audience: however much classical literature it taught, it did hone speaking and performance skills. Discussion or questions were entirely inappropriate for the classroom and must be pursued after the formal instruction had ended. Jefferson, by including faculty and students in his cloistered academical village, hoped that postprandial discussions would occur around the fire in faculty parlors. Formal instruction would merge into social gatherings, a pedagogical practice not entirely without merit and occasionally supported even today.

Recitation was not the only horror of early American college education. A further medieval inheritance came in the form of a fixed curriculum.⁷ Colleges had no electives. Contemporary academic luminaries strongly supported the practice. They felt it reinforced a sense of solidarity within an academic cohort. Students taking the same courses at the same time would develop a strong sense of communal loyalty. This "efficient common life" mattered to Yale president Noah Porter as much as did any specific bit of learning. Part of being a Protestant minister, or a gentleman, was an acute sense of who belonged, and who, to their great cost, did not. In America, antebellum college education helped place young men in their appropriate social slot. Those young men, with their Latin and Greek, their social skills, their public confidence, justified American college education for a long time.

In antebellum America, most young men did not attend college, nor did they need to. They were not gentlemen, nor were they ministers. They received the bulk of their education from churches and newspapers. Protestant churches often taught basic literacy because the Good Book was considered the appropriate school of moral and social education. Newspapers were a common vehicle of American political discourse; they were fiercely partisan, just as churches were fiercely denominational. Churches and newspapers formed the popular school of lifelong learning for the whole population.

Two • The Americanization of the University Experience 27

In the America described by Alexis de Tocqueville, public schools were just beginning. They started in northern cities, Boston in particular, gathering in kids (almost all male, almost all white) who were not being tutored privately. They spread fairly rapidly in urban American, largely because teachers were public officials, of a sort, and were part of the dominant political machine.[8] The schools inculcated the civic values of literacy, piety, patriotism, and work. In the public schools, *McGuffey's Readers* were the general supplement to the Bible. Their stories, poems, essays, and parables all urged children to live a life of good works and hard work. Most Americans would be educated in the common schools as well as through churches, newspapers, and patriotic societies.

American colleges slowly adjusted to the robust life of mass education. As Jefferson was founding his cloistered academical village, Harvard began to evolve toward the Paris model. It founded a law school in 1817, when funds were given to establish the Royall professorship in law. Legal education in America had existed before Harvard undertook to teach it. It began as an effort to organize the common practice of "reading the law." The impetus was a desire for efficiency. In Litchfield, Connecticut, as early as 1784, a group of lawyers had organized tutorials in the common law, with classes held in a private home. Led by Tapping Reeve, later a Connecticut Supreme Court chief justice, ad hoc lessons became intellectually coherent courses. These courses in law did not evolve into institutions, with admissions, examinations, or degrees. They resembled the Salerno medical school of Gariopontus in the eleventh century. In Salerno, doctors accepted students who followed them on their rounds. The program was both organized and informal. The Salerno system lasted a couple of generations.[9] After medical education ended in Salerno, a medical college was founded at Montpellier. The nineteenth-century American experience in the development of universities recapitulated the medieval European history.

The Litchfield program ended in 1834. By then, Harvard had established a law school, with all the formal administrative accoutrements. The institutional coherence of Harvard attracted students and money. It carried the day. The new Harvard Law School was a distant early warning of what universities were going to become.

The Harvard Law School began as an academic outlier. But the pattern could be copied, and after the cataclysm of the Civil War, it was copied. The war altered America so profoundly that the Harvard historian George Ticknor wrote in 1869 that it had created a "great gulf between what happened before it in our century and what has happened since…. It does not seem to me as if I were living in the country in which I was born."[10] This was true of university education and a great many other things also.

America developed a new collegiate model. The years of war and reconstruction saw fundamental changes in American higher education. Land-grant colleges emerged from the Morrill Act of 1862, which provided federal aid for state universities at a time when most colleges were private and denominational. Then came elective courses. Between 1868 and 1871, Harvard president Charles William Eliot overrode opposition to offer electives, out of which arose different academic majors.[11] Then in 1876, The Johns Hopkins University was founded, utilizing the German model of graduate and professional education. Collectively, these innovations established the distinctive character of modern American higher education, which combines learning on both the mass and elite levels.

The drift toward graduate and specialized education, which began with the Harvard Law School, continued with Harvard College. Its postwar president Charles William Eliot was the most important university reformer in American history. He changed almost everything about Harvard. He abolished compulsory Protestant worship for the students. He supported graduate and professional education. Besides introducing elective courses, President Eliot expanded the humanities and introduced sciences. Harvard moved under his direction from moral and natural philosophy to the modern arts and sciences. Knowledge, and the need for knowledge, had grown beyond the old courses and recitation. Between 1840–1880, knowledge exploded in the old traditional disciplines, and several new ones appeared as well. Eliot's reaction to having more to learn was to establish courses to teach it. Eliot made research universities more modern and also more like medieval Paris.

Eliot's reforms, though simple in concept, added immensely to the complexity of the university. The social and educational unity of the prewar student class broke down. In everything but languages and mathematics, lecture replaced recitation. Professors became representatives of their disciplines. Colleges became less like grammar schools in spirit and practice and more like professional schools. It took a generation. Gilded Age America created two "Golden Doors," both involving immigration: one into the country, the other into economic prosperity. America began the long march toward an increasingly meritocratic and knowledge/credential society.

Eliot was not alone in remaking American higher education. The founders of The Johns Hopkins University project also opted for radical change. They decided to reproduce the German research university. They planned a modern curriculum, copying the German emphasis on science, medicine, and graduate work. German universities had established laboratories and demanded faculty publication. Hopkins wanted that also. No surprise that German industry, particularly in chemistry, looked to universities as a source of ideas and scientists. The intimate connection between the university and the larger society was reimagined in Bismarckian Germany. It was the Paris system, with science, not theology, at its core. The Johns Hopkins University was designed to bring this to America. If The Hopkins succeeded, which it did, other American universities would have to follow in the same direction, which they did.

Since the Gilded Age, American research universities have become ever more concerned with supporting their faculty, and more involved in creating culture, technology, and scientific insight. This Gilded Age trend has spread from the elite, touching even some of the community colleges. In an electronic age, any school can imitate the university of Thomas Aquinas.

Nearly New and Post-Modern

In the nineteenth century, Americans changed much about universities, making them more accessible, more diverse, and more professional. It may not have been quite as much fun, but it was certainly more comfortable to attend an American university in 1900 than a European university in 1300. Still, the basic university model remained unchanged. American institutions, like Paris before them, still educated the faculty, taught the students, and collected knowledge. But that, too, would change. In the twentieth century, Americans began to subdivide the university. The basic university functions could be performed in separate institutions. Community colleges would only teach students. Think tanks and research institutes would conduct academic research and foster publication. Endowed libraries, such as the Folger, would collect knowledge. Everything Paris did was still done, just not necessarily at the same place. Great research universities continue to do everything, but they are vastly outnumbered by more specialized institutions. American higher education has added components as well as subtracted them. Colleges add curricula, administrators, and athletes. They subtract one or more of the basic university functions.

Subtraction is politically popular. A stripped-down university is cheap and efficient. A community/junior college is in effect a stripped-down university, concentrating on undergraduate teaching. It doesn't bother with fancy libraries and labs; it doesn't support faculty research. Politicians support this model and always have. The community college boom began in the fifties, often as part of local efforts to improve local economies. It continues today on a national level with national support. President Obama himself has proposed free tuition at community colleges.[12] With presidential encouragement, it is unlikely that the growth of community colleges will diminish or that their character will change.

Community colleges are designed to serve the customers' needs, whatever those are. Students can take everything from algebra to welding. They can also get a good deal of personal attention, which helps insecure students succeed. Community colleges also help kids from poorer families who cannot afford to attend a university. Working adults can benefit too, picking up courses as time permits and need demands. Student dreams are invested in community colleges: for those with "luck and pluck," the dreams may well come true.

Community colleges can become enormous. In Orange County, Florida, (Orlando) Valencia Community College has grown to five campuses and any day may add more. The Miami Dade Community College System is the largest local college conglomerate in the state, maybe in the world, possibly in the galaxy. Even in Baton Rouge, Louisiana, the relatively recent Baton Rouge Community College (BRCC), born in 1995, has about 10,000 students and a continuously expanding campus. BRCC's growth has meant more buildings, more restaurants, a shopping center, bank branches, and a newly prosperous neighborhood.

Community colleges bring at least some smidgen of higher education to every area of every state. There are now 1,177 American community colleges, with over seven million students enrolled. And the growth continues, though more slowly since the Great of Recession of 2009.

One system in particular, Indiana's Ivy Tech Community College, has carried efficiency to an industrial conclusion. It has thirty campuses scattered across the state, and serves over 200,000 students. Like all community colleges, Ivy Tech offers a huge variety of pre-professional, academic, vocational, and apprenticeship programs. Ivy Tech's degree-granting centers are supplemented by classroom and testing facilities in more than 75 Indiana communities. Beyond that, Ivy Tech includes a "Corporate College" to deal with training and certification programs that businesses need. Ivy Tech provides every conceivable credential path for its students. Some go on to a four-year university; others take a single course or work on an accreditation program. Ivy Tech does it all. The system is fiscally friendly as well. Ivy Tech offers genuinely affordable education. Students in degree programs pay about $3,000 a year. That's far below the cost of a single university semester.

Ivy Tech has brought the factory model of management into the lower rungs of higher education. The modern factory system divides the work into discrete units, performed in specific order, at a certain tempo, by workers assigned to a single task, making an identifiable product to a particular standard of excellence. The factory system divides the workers from the managers by clearly separating their functions. Ivy Tech turns the faculty into semi–assembly line knowledge workers, only teaching students and having few tangential research duties. The whole thing is run by administrators who do not teach but who deploy teachers and graders who do not manage. By cutting costs, Ivy Tech attracts customers (students); by attracting customers, it cuts costs further. The economies of scale are not infinite, but neither are they negligible.[13] The dreamers who wanted inexpensive education, broadly scattered across the land, have not dreamt in vain.

Nevertheless, in this vale of tears, nothing is perfect. Junior colleges do not remain junior. Demand develops for something more. Students ask for advanced courses, particularly in subjects like English, mathematics, and the sciences, all providing credits that can be transferred to the university. Teachers want local access to advanced education courses for certification and graduate degree programs. Nurses need a program that will lead to the RN and BSN certificates. Are not these needs legitimate? And community colleges, with their close local ties, are happy to fulfill them. Bachelor's degrees slip in, along with a graduate degree or two. Junior colleges seek to add status as well as students.

After a while, community colleges, responding always to community demand, can turn into something resembling a four-year institution. Inflation involves titles as well as money. States often bow to local pressure, expanding the school's mission and changing its name to a college. The faculty also want community colleges to turn into something grander. It inflates their position as well as that of the school.

Junior colleges can become senior colleges for a variety of reasons. In 1959, the Louisiana Legislature, dominated by Governor Earl Long, approved the establishment of Louisiana State University (LSUA) in Alexandria, at the time as just a junior college. Earl Long wanted a college in a town that strongly supported him and the Long family. The college opened in 1961, but there wasn't much student demand for courses. The first degrees were granted in 1964, an Associate in Nursing certificate. LSUA was not accredited until 1974. Student enrollment remained low. Nonetheless, in the 1990s the college continued to add associate degrees every couple of years. Bachelor's degrees appeared in 2003. Student enrollment still remained disappointingly low. Never mind: LSUA has unwavering local political support.

Governor Long was not alone in getting a new college. State representative Allen Gremillion of Crowley helped establish a junior college at Eunice, Louisiana. The college at Eunice was an affiliate of LSU, as the state university headed off efforts by a rival college to set up a branch. Eunice is a small town with modest demand for local higher education. There was plenty of political demand, however. So the branch campus was placed in a sugarcane field, located at the edge of town, near the grass-runway airport used by crop dusters. LSUE has remained a junior college, offering no degrees above the associate level. But it prospered in several ways. The baseball team has made it to the junior college finals several times. Enrollment has held up; in the last couple of years, over 3,000 people a year have enrolled for a course, or two, or even more. LSUE has also acquired 94 administrators to manage 130-odd faculty. The whole enterprise must be regarded as successful, at least in local terms.[14]

Junior colleges are not alone in the subtraction business; indeed, they do not subtract the most from the university atmosphere. That distinction belongs to online distance learning, which, happily for their administrators, requires no campus, no buildings, no maintenance, no parking, no dorms, no food service, no football, no student union, no recreation center, and almost no faculty. This electronic model has been persuasive enough to intrigue the private sector. Substantial proprietary universities such as the University of Phoenix exist largely online. Register online. Take a course or two or more online. Electronically attend. Pass the exams in enough courses, and you complete a degree. And plenty of people have been doing it that way. Distance learning exists in the realm of electrons, which, fortunately, appear to be sufficiently numerous and cooperative to carry the traffic.

Corporations have subtracted teaching from the university model, ending up with research labs staffed by university graduates. Industrial labs began in Germany in the nineteenth century, particularly in chemistry.[15] After World War I, AT&T founded Bell Labs, and after World War II, private industries expanded their research departments, using Bell Labs as models. IBM was an early leader in computer research. More recently, companies like Apple, Google, and Microsoft have expanded electronic technology from mainframe to cell phone. They are not alone. Companies that manufacture foods also maintain research labs. Industrial labs, which are now universal, have been joined by "think tanks," some connected to universities, such as the Hoover Institution at Stanford, others independent, like The Heritage Foundation and others. Universities have also added non-teaching units, many based upon the Princeton example of the Institute for Advanced Study. Whether private, public, or some arrangement in between, the aim has always been to create an idea factory. This is not new nor is it American: Aristotle did the same thing with his Lyceum.

Bell Labs may be taken as an emblem of all of the others—mainly for its long life (1925–present) and its extraordinary achievements.[16] Privately owned, Bell Labs was evenly split between AT&T and Western Electric (now Alcatel and Lucent). It owed a great deal of its excellence to the quasi-official Ma Bell monopoly, which gave Bell Labs an opportunity for innovation and permitted primary research. In 1956, Bell Lab scientists John Bardeen, Walter Brattain, and William Shockley received the Nobel Prize for inventing transistors. In 2009, Bell Lab scientists Willard Boyle and George Smith shared the Nobel Prize in physics with Charles Kao for inventing charge-coupled semiconductor imaging sensors. Bell Labs also developed the laser and the UNIX operating system and made advances in information theory. In the area of pure research, Bell Labs sponsored the discovery of cosmic background radiation, for which Arno Penzias and Robert Wilson received the Nobel Prize in 1978. The telephone monopoly may have charged a lot for long-distance calls, but it also produced technological innovations and encouraged wide-ranging speculation in physics and mathematics. In both endeavors, Bell Labs operated like a university, just more focused and efficient. That, of course, was what the company had in mind in the first place.

Secrecy has always been a cardinal component of corporate technology research, which is not the norm in universities. AT&T and Western Electric patented new technology, of course, but permitted free publication of basic research. That was, and is, quite unusual. The Pentagon has followed the other path. The most spectacular, and also the most secret, of the non-teaching idea/innovation factories was, of course, the Manhattan Project. And, for the aficionados of conspiracy, secrecy reached its zenith in Area 51, at Groom Lake outside of Las Vegas. Area 51, which the government long denied existed, was rumored to be a center for research on aliens who had visited earth. Was this true? Well, there were rumors, some so startling that they were only whispered. Some strange-looking people were seen in Las Vegas. Could it be? Area 51 may be regarded as the opposite of universities, which are open both in access and information. But there is the similarity between universities and Area 51. You can see some mighty strange people at universities.

The public has not been unhappy with truncated university functions.

People like the idea of think tanks (which omit teaching) and community colleges (which omit creating and collecting knowledge). People also like additional university functions. In general, adding university functions has meant expanding the accoutrements and impedimenta of administration. Look at all the dormitories, food halls, student unions, compliance offices, classroom buildings, office buildings, libraries, broadcasting and computer studios, stadia, field houses, convention centers, tech centers, recreation centers, and health centers. All fall into the general category of university additions. So much money. So many employees. Empire building is a favorite university vocation.[17] It has also been a favorite political practice. New buildings always mean new jobs. Empire building is part of fundraising. A new building needs a name, as every donor knows.

New buildings proclaim empire, but empire is not restricted to concrete. The university also needs a new strength coach, along with two assistants, and a bungee-jump coach as well, and who could ignore the need for half a dozen assistant directors for compliance? How about a new department in something fashionable, such as digital rhetoric? To ask these questions is to answer them. The push for subtraction rests upon money. Administrators and professors push for additions, which feed their pride in having a really *full* full-service university.

Americans feel that no area of study or activity can be entirely legitimate without a university degree to corroborate its importance. Education is a good example. Teacher training entered the college curriculum as a result of the relentless expansion of public schools. In the 1830s and '40s, American educational reformers pushed hard for free public schools, which many could attend.[18] Democratic ideals prevailed; schools popped up everywhere. But schools need teachers. Teacher training began modestly enough, in "normal schools." Over time, the definitions of basic training expanded. These early schools stressed basic training for a year or two.[19] In a single generation, teacher education became a coherent university curriculum, with multiple majors and degrees at all levels. As for the normal schools, they followed the American path of academic mobility. First they became "teachers' colleges" then colleges with a more general educational mission. Finally, the most successful became state universities (Illinois State University at Normal, Illinois, for example).

Business courses followed education into the university catalog. After all, who could doubt the importance of business courses in a free market economy? As with education, business courses tended to clump together in separate colleges, the most famous of which is the Wharton School at the University of Pennsylvania. Over time, business colleges became, like education, a standard part of the institutional smorgasbord. Americans are interested in money—mostly making it, but also learning how it works. The workings of business and finance, like education, appeared sufficiently important and complex as to justify a university degree or two in those enterprises.

President Charles Eliot's introduction of elective courses did more than permit expanded offerings in the traditional disciplines. It also allowed new disciplines to emerge from the old. History remained a largely narrative discourse, but academic geography, geopolitics, political science, sociology, and economics grew out of the discipline of history. Psychology separated itself from philosophy. The emergent social sciences reflected both the rapid expansion of knowledge in the Gilded Age and novel ways of looking at the social world. They rapidly became standard academic disciplines, most by the time of the Great War and all by the 1950s.

Once upon a time, people learned to farm and to tinker by practice and by mishap. Craftsmen had always learned by practice and by mishap. There was little place for literacy and less for theory. Steam changed all that. In the nineteenth century, engineering and agriculture achieved enormous success within university walls. The professors supported it, particularly as both areas of study became increasingly mathematical and scientific. Even before the Civil War, America had schools of engineering, the most noted being West Point and Rensselaer Polytechnic Institute (RPI). After the war, as American education expanded, engineering and agricultural programs appeared everywhere. Cornell established an engineering college, and so did Yale (Sheffield), and the University of Pennsylvania (Morse). Under the leadership of Liberty Hyde Bailey (retired 1911) Cornell developed an agricultural school of international importance. Where the Ivy League led, the rest followed.

State universities, which taught everything but specialized in engineering and agriculture, sprouted up everywhere after the Morrill Act, and they have educated students in the millions. Private engineering colleges appeared, such as MIT, Caltech, and Georgia Tech. It became impossible to maintain that on-the-job training in field and factory was sufficient to master these technical disciplines. University education was the only answer. And research by the faculty was obviously of no less importance than the instruction of postulants. These new subjects fit seamlessly into the old system of creating, collecting, and disseminating knowledge.

Then came World War II, which did what modern wars do. It accelerated the existing academic trends of adding new courses, new disciplines, new labs, and new students. War also added immensely to government investment, regulation, and oversight of universities. Before the war, research universities had a distant relationship with the federal government, one that was basically confined to agricultural colleges. Technological warfare changed all that. As hot war merged into the Cold War, the federal government found that research universities were a prime source of scientists and engineers, to say nothing of the thousands of graduates in the STEM disciplines. The wartime symbiosis between Washington and universities became permanent.

Since then the connection between Leviathan and the research university has taken many forms. The government recruited faculty from campus, beginning with the Manhattan Project. Scientists and engineers were also gathered together on campus; the radar laboratory (RadLab) at MIT followed that model. Federal agencies (NSF, NIH, Department of Agriculture) have supported grants, contracts, and consulting gigs. The federal government gives student grants (Pell and National Defense Education Act) and underwrites student loans. The annual sums run well into the hundreds of billions of dollars.[20]

That kind of money always comes with strings attached. The federal Leviathan imposes, modifies, adds, multiplies and reviews regulations better than any political entity in the history of the world. Federal bureaucrats have created (and create still) proposal forms, prototypes, and protocols for investigation and experimentation, compliance and human resources report, and on and on. This pyroclastic flow of paperwork affects universities no less. It seems (and likely is) virtually endless, and it is a Sisyphean task to fill the forms out. The federal flow of forms and reports can suffocate a small private business, and universities devote entire buildings stuffed to the rafters and millions of dollars annually on compliance. If history is any guide, the flow from Leviathan will only get worse.[21]

The federal river of money has created a new academic relationship, one between gown, town, and government. Research university professors, especially in the STEM disciplines, are tied as closely to government and corporations as they are to their students. Indeed, the graduate students are usually funded by external grants. This system of "entangling alliances" has come to be called the military/industrial/academic complex. Because of it, research universities today are awash in obligations created by grants. The funds involved are so substantial that many schools could not open their doors without them. The fiscal dependence upon that complex has reinforced the university's traditional functions. These developments are permanent; indeed, they are expanding, not least because of the fiscal crisis of 2008.

Two • *The Americanization of the University Experience* 37

Within the modern research university, accountability and bureaucracy are welded together into an adamantine whole that can never be separated by gods or men, or even by women. Stuff this important cannot pass without notice. The philosopher Michael Oakeshott complained that modern universities do both too much and too little. He argued for a "theory of reflection," meaning that universities should address the interests of the society they inhabit. Oakeshott also argues that a university ought to be a "pause" for students, a time for reflection before entering the workforce and a lifetime career.[22] These two views of reflection are mutually exclusive. Society wishes students to finish as quickly as possible and to be educated as cheaply as possible.

Students in a modern American research university do not, therefore, "pause": rather, they pick up the pace markedly. As academic disciplines have become more technical, the student has more and more to learn. But the time to learn it has not expanded. Degrees are still to be earned in four or five years, more or less as they were in the thirteenth century. Far from pausing, the student crams.

A third Oakeshott ideal about reflection involves the faculty, and it is even less realistic. Oakeshott believed professors needed a leisured existence in order to reflect on society and their disciplines. American universities are not interested in that. But Michael Oakeshott was not really interested in vulgar reality. He had an ideal in mind, not the way universities had been but the way they should be now. He proposed that

> Of the scholars who compose a university, some may be expected to devote an unbroken leisure to learning, their fellows having the advantage of their knowledge from their conversation and the world benefitting, perhaps, from their writings. A place of learning without this kind of scholar could scarcely be called a university.[23]

Such a university, as the old song goes, would be "lovely to look at, delightful to know." But it ain't gonna happen.

There are, of course, those who regret the full-service university.[24] Supporters of liberal arts education find academic bloat in the multiple curricula. But there's no going back. Mass society requires mass universities. The critics weep in vain. Oakeshott to the contrary notwithstanding, the university of masters expands relentlessly in all directions. Open opportunity and institutional efficiency, as well as genuine expertise: that's the American Way of higher education.

Taking it as a whole, both additions and subtractions to the university model work fairly well. After a couple of centuries of evolution and reflection, American higher education now consists of universities and parts of universities, some virtual. Academic reformers have pared universities down and bulked them up. They try every conceivable combination of the basic functions of the University of Paris. At least in higher education, everything has happened in America. But even in America, people never quite reach the New Jerusalem.

Cardinal Newman

Six hundred years after Cardinal Robert de Courçon, another Roman Catholic cardinal from Oxford took on the task of defining a university education. In 1851, Pope Pius IX called upon Cardinal John Henry Newman to create a new Catholic University at Dublin.[25] Like Cardinal Robert, Cardinal Newman found much to reform in the university, and many problems in doing so. It was not enough to explain his educational philosophy in *The Idea of a University* (1852, 1877); he must also bring those ideas to reality.[26] For both cardinals, what was right must also work in an imperfect world.

Medieval origins aside, Cardinal Newman did not think that a Catholic education should be medieval in content. Science should not be neglected, for the modern university's mission is intellectual, not moral or theological. Professors would teach students how to think critically about modern subjects. Newman's ideas resonated within the North Atlantic cultural community, where *The Idea of a University* would become a standard by which professors and institutions could be judged.

On November 3, 1854, Cardinal Newman opened the new Catholic University. He addressed seventeen students, including the grandson of Daniel O'Connell, prophesying that they would be proud of the Catholic education they received. Newman was new to university administration, creating his university on the fly. He bought three houses for classrooms and student accommodation. He planned for a medical college and a law school. He employed an engineering professor to instruct in the practical and mechanical arts. He hired lay professors, an enormous departure from then-standard practice. He inaugurated evening lectures to include those who worked while they studied. All the while, he managed the daily business of an ongoing school, even cutting and serving the meat for the students' common meal. Newman did it all, and it wore him out. He left the Catholic University in 1858, with most of his work inaugurated but unfinished.

The university itself did not prosper for some decades. The basic problem was external to Newman's work. Lacking a royal charter, the private Catholic university could not offer degrees that were recognized by the crown.²⁷ But the institution did survive, a tribute to the breadth of Newman's ideas and the need for a Catholic university in Dublin.

Newman's attitudes toward university education reflected the changes in European intellectual life. By midcentury, industrialization and democratization had proceeded so far that nothing could stop them. The steam engine had taken over every aspect of commercial and manufacturing life. Trains and ships moved people at unheard of speeds, sometimes as high as thirty-five miles an hour. Physicians feared for the health of travelers whisked along at such a tempo. In 1852, the Crystal Palace Exhibition in Hyde Park featured large numbers of new machines as well as a smaller exhibition of the next big thing. That was industrial chemistry.²⁸ In matters political, the revolutions of 1848 were safely over, but the democratic impulses throbbed on. France had instituted universal manhood suffrage. The kingdom of Sardinia had issued the *Statuto*, a new democratic constitution. In America, the movement for women's suffrage had already begun. The 1850s seemed to be the preface to a new world, in which science would dominate industry and democracy would dominate society. A Catholic university, Newman thought, must interpret humanity's role in modern society.

Cardinal Newman began with a program to improve teaching, in technique and content. He wanted the faculty to form an intellectual community, somewhat of a cross between the monastic and Jeffersonian models. He wanted the students to learn things broadly cultural and scientific. Since Newman believed in the unity of nature, he wanted his university to emphasize the consequent unity of knowledge.²⁹ The Cardinal wanted the reality on the ground to move closer to the ideal of the good. This was a standard Catholic ideal.

Cardinal Newman also commented on public attitudes toward a university education. Six centuries of history had been inadequate to inform the general public about what universities do, and how hard it is to do it.³⁰ Popular opinion was wrong about a university education. The first and worst mistake was the notion that learning is easy. Anyone can do it. No great effort is demanded. Newman, who knew better, lamented "this most pernicious of delusions," that "[l]earning is to be without exertion, without attention, without toil ... the population is to be passively, almost unconsciously enlightened, by the mere multiplication and dissemination of volumes."³¹ The British public tended to believe that merely passing out a bunch of books would, in itself, allow any student to absorb complicated ideas. Much of the American public still believes that any student can absorb any discipline, at least under the right circumstances.

Newman might denounce popular misconceptions, but he could not hope to end them. Nobody wanted to hear the bad news that students might have to study. Even today, college brochures seem to convey the impression that learning is done with insouciance. Sit on the beach, sit in your bedroom, download everything worth knowing. It's easy and painless. Everybody should go to college. A college education can be attained without struggle. This attitude radiates hope and good cheer, and it is also utter rubbish.

People who believe that learning is easy fall into the pit of "popular delusions and the madness of crowds."[32] But some popular delusions are so comforting that they can never be erased. Delusion is the normative state of popular opinion concerning education. Newman recognized this and fell back on the hope that if more people were educated, the delusions would diminish. The university could enlighten the world. That was the hope, anyway.

For Cardinal Newman, teaching was the central function of a modern university. Since learning was hard, teaching must be superb. Excellence would require, as it always does, intense dedication within a supportive environment. Practical skills and information must be set in a framework of comprehensive patterns, both social and technical. Newman presented his critique of education in the introduction to *The Idea of a University*:

> The view taken of a University in these Discourses is the following.—That it is a place of teaching universal knowledge. This implies that its object is, on the one hand, intellectual, not moral; and, on the other, that it is the diffusion and extension of knowledge rather than the advancement. If its object were scientific and philosophical discovery, I do not see why a University should have students; if religious training, I do not see how it can be the seat of literature and science.[33]

A university education should be intellectual and social, not religious, and taught within a broad academic context. Effective pedagogy creates learning communities formed between student and professor, as well as between professors of complementary disciplines. Newman believed that everyone can be made happier through learning, arguing that knowledge is "most valuable for what its very presence in us does for us, after the manner of a habit, even though it be turned to no further account, nor subserve any direct end."[34]

Newman's understanding of learning informed his views of what a university ought to do. It should not be a vocational institution, though some of the learning on tap will inevitably have a utilitarian function. The university should teach how to understand rather than how to do. Newman also argued that, if "a practical end must be assigned to a university course," it would be that university graduates lifted up the whole society. The cardinal knew that the nineteenth century (like the present) demanded that a practical end be furnished, or at least announced. So Newman claimed that

> a University training is the great ordinary means to a great but ordinary end: it aims at raising the intellectual tone of society, at cultivating the public mind, at purifying the national taste, at supplying true principles to popular enthusiasm, and fixed aims to popular aspirations, at giving enlargement and sobriety to the ideas of the age, at facilitating the exercise of political power, at refining the intercourse of private life.[35]

The student became what he should be, rather than what he must do.

Newman proposed changes in academic detail rather than in institutional structure. The relationships between professors (masters) and students (scholars) would remain pretty much what they had always been. The university hierarchy would be unchanged. The university's three functions would continue as they always had. Newman did not object to the standard structures; he objected to the structures working badly. His reforms were designed to make the existing university work better in educating students, "those earnest but ill-used persons." Students should learn to turn pieces and patches into patterns. Professors would to teach them how to do it. Newman thought this sort of education happened rarely in his own time, if it happened at all.

Educational problems started with the faculty. They taught the wrong stuff, badly, a common complaint from the twelfth century to the present, and certainly beyond. Bad teaching is as common as the common cold and as ineradicable as sin. Newman's suggestions were remarkably Jeffersonian. The faculty should be brought together so that specialized knowledge could become broader through contact with those who taught different disciplines. Newman envisioned an academic village rather than a research laboratory. Learning was a group activity, as in the study of the Talmud, and only a few students "can dispense with the stimulus and support of instructors."[36] Equally, only a few instructors could combine the different functions of unfolding knowledge to the students and discovering new knowledge through research. Newman liked the new German scientific curriculum, but he did not support the German emphasis on individual student and faculty research. The university's primary reason for existence, Newman thought, was teaching students and thus enlarging society itself.

To be sure, some of Cardinal Newman's justifications for a university education seem fanciful. Do university graduates actually "cultivate the public mind"? Even less likely, can university graduates "purify the national taste"? How about "supplying true principles to popular enthusiasm"?

Newman hoped that a college education would improve and civilize a rude society in a time of surging democracy. His aristocratic hopes were rooted in virtue rather than experience. Still, as Western society becomes more technological, scientific, and industrialized, a good university education has become as important as Cardinal Newman envisioned.

Newman left Dublin with his university unfinished. But his book *The Idea of a University* quickly became an academic classic; oddly enough, it had an enormous influence in the North Atlantic Protestant world, from London to Vancouver and Los Angeles. Part of being educated in the Gilded Age English-speaking world was a familiarity with Cardinal Newman. His emphasis on teaching and on intellectual community provided a healthy counterpart to the growing emphasis on graduate and specialized education. Newman, in effect, urged the academy not to forget the students. He brought Jefferson up to date. Since Newman, universities have emphasized effective teaching and concern for student learning.

Newman lies at the core of university reform over the past few decades. Universities have become more focused on the things he recommended. And this is a good thing. Modern universities face two "hard and huge" tasks, teaching masses of students and teaching students who lack intellectual curiosity. Without Newman's concern for pedagogy, many, perhaps most, of these quasi-marginal students would not survive. In a democratic society, with a need for mass education, would the university itself survive? Or would the democratic societies survive? Newman may have overstated the social results of a university education, but he understood perfectly the social *directions* of a university education.

We are Newmanesque today, even if we haven't read his book. His ideas, usually unattributed, inform modern efforts to improve teaching, and his work has made the faculty's jobs easier, not harder. We ask today the questions Newman asked then. How can we teach better? How can we make it easier for the students to learn? How can we support learning and teaching as university functions? Cardinal Newman, like his contemporaries Charles Eliot and the progenitors of The Hopkins University, is an essential evolutionary step between Cardinal Robert's structurally flexible and hierarchical university and our own times of mass education.

Multiversity

Everyone remembers World War II. It was in all the papers. Newsreels covered it relentlessly. Movie stars went on war bond drives. Everybody was part of the war effort. The German minister Walther Rathenau, in World War I, had invented the concept of total mobilization. By the Second World War, everybody was mobilized. The home front was as intense as the war front.

The government also mobilized the universities. That took several forms. Scientists, engineers and technicians were recruited from the universities and exiled to Los Alamos to work on the Manhattan Project. General Leslie Groves found some of them to be difficult charges indeed, but he persevered, and so did they, and the result was The Bomb. Universities also housed V-12 programs, where students were pushed through degrees and basic military training to prepare them to become officers. Beyond that, universities housed military labs, the most important of which was the radar lab at MIT. By the time Colonel Tibbitts dropped Little Boy from Enola Gay, universities had found a comfortable accommodation between academic productivity and government needs.

As the Cold War replaced the Good War, the cult of usefulness persisted in universities. True enough, there had been an era when going to college was a leisure activity. The Newman/Jeffersonian idea of the university as a general civilizing force for society no longer dominated the times. A new apostle arose. Clark Kerr expressed the new reality in *The Uses of the University* (1963).[37]

Clark Kerr's book rested upon several basic assumptions, which he considered entirely true and therefore described without defending. The first of these assumptions located the university as an active citizen in the political and economic world. It was not an ivory tower, nor a cloister, nor a place of leisure but rather a constant actor. Secondly, the university would be funded, not by its students or its endowment but by external sources, primarily governments and industry. The modern university could not survive on self-generated income; it must be part of the military/industrial/academic complex. Further, the fundamental purpose of the multiversity was research, most of it sponsored, much of it secret, and all of it depending on the education and expertise of the faculty. Of the three pillars of the Robertian university, educating the faculty was by far the most important. The other two, curating knowledge and teaching students, were not in themselves contemptible, but they were collateral functions, sideshows to the main show. Further yet, the university's internal structure would be badly warped by the overwhelming emphasis on STEM research. But this imbalance, while something perhaps to be regretted, was still necessary. Of course, the multiversity radiates consequences and corollaries from these four basic principles, but it is the "Big Four" that describe how the multiversity will work generally.

Clark Kerr responded to current needs. In 1958, California had experienced a political earthquake. Republicans, who had held the state house since World War II, lost the election to Edmund G. "Pat" Brown, the Democratic attorney general. Pat Brown had a matter-of-fact, down-to-earth view of state government. He believed in water projects; California was a thirsty state, and the thirst was growing as the population expanded. He believed in roads and infrastructure. There were a lot of Californians in 1958, and immigration to the "Golden West" from the rest of the country was in full tilt. Everybody wanted to participate in "that California living." Pat Brown also supported education, from kindergarten to PhD and beyond. Universities were essential to the success of the millions in the Golden State. Concrete projects: that's what Pat Brown liked. There were no moonbeams in his makeup.

The California Board of Regents went along with the new governor, who seemed to have the right spirit and the right stuff. The Regents appointed someone after Pat Brown's own heart. In 1958, Clark Kerr became president of the whole California system. At the top stood the California state universities: Berkeley, Davis, UCLA, et al. Clark Kerr added to them campuses at San Diego, Santa Cruz, and Irvine. The middle tier included the Cal State colleges, and Kerr added to those as well. At the bottom came the community colleges. Kerr supported every community's effort to create and expand a community college. The universities specialized in sponsored research; in the colleges, professors both taught and published; in the community colleges, the instructors taught the masses whatever they could learn. The system cost billions, even in contemporary dollars. But it fit the times.

Those were prosperous years, from the late fifties into the late sixties, particularly for the Golden State. California was plugged into the space program. From Edwards Air Force Base to Cape Canaveral, University of California scientists were part of the manned space program. Grants in all scientific fields were easy to get and, because of the NDEA, more numerous and more generous. No university profited more than those in the California system. The multiversity that Clark Kerr described in 1963 was not imaginary. It existed on the ground. It worked well. It was of material assistance to the prosperity of the state. And it fit the California promise of a flourishing present and a glorious future.

In fashioning the California multiversity, Clark Kerr reproduced on a mass scale what Cardinal Robert had done, almost, as it were, in miniature. Both Cardinal Robert and Clark Kerr (often called Clark Kent in those heady days) built a university based on practical experience in the real world and in the academy. They held analogous positions. Cardinal Robert had been chancellor, and Clark Kerr was the CEO of the California multiversity. They built university structures from experience, on both sides of the campus walls. Cardinal Robert took two pages in Latin. Clark Kerr wrote several books. But the result was the same. Both built a university that worked.

Evolution

Modern American universities are medieval survivors, but they have not survived unchanged. They have evolved, adding elective courses, multiple majors, new disciplines, graduate and professional colleges, a huge administration, athletics, and millions of students. None of this existed when John Harvard made his bequest.

For modern research universities, sheer mass is the meat of the matter. That mass is found in three academic areas: students, administrators, and curriculum. Students are the most obvious, thronging campuses in their thousands, collectively millions. While the numbers have changed, the kids themselves have not. There have always been students without intellectual curiosity. There have always been students utterly resistant to learning. There have always been students whose primary interests were social and students who have run afoul of law, cops, and custom. There have always been students for whom the credential alone mattered. What has changed since Galileo and Fabricius of Acquapendente taught at Padua is simply the size of the show. The same kinds of students appear on campus now, but in overwhelming numbers.

Administrators may hide in their offices, but their numbers have increased in even greater proportion than have the students. No major state university has fewer than five to ten *buildings* filled with various administrators. Add another building for the athletic director and his supine minions. Maybe two buildings. Administrative bloat is often bewailed by faculty, though rarely by politicians. These wails are in vain. Bureaucrats are required by the federal government to monitor compliance and accountability. As federal programs grow, the number of administrators grows as well.

A final increase in mass has come in curriculum. At Louisiana State University (LSU), for example, you can graduate from one of 11 colleges; Rice University in Houston has over 50 undergraduate majors. The University of Southern California has seventeen graduate and professional programs. At the University of Michigan at Ann Arbor, each of its 43,000 students can choose from more than 200 undergraduate majors in 13 colleges. These are examples only and can be multiplied endlessly. In medieval Paris, you could study four things only.

Changes in mass have led, ironically, to continuity in structure. The university structure created by Cardinal Robert has been sufficiently flexible to incorporate any number of students, bureaucrats, and curricular additions. Functions of the Robertian university—educating faculty, teaching students, and curating knowledge—have become bigger and more expensive but remain unchanged in their essentials. The hierarchy of administrators, faculty, and students has proved to be entirely reasonable and has survived all efforts to change it, heartfelt as these efforts usually are. It still makes more sense for those who know to teach and for those who don't to attend lectures. Indeed, modern increase in mass has only reinforced the medieval form of the university. No workable alternative has suggested itself. We do not think one will. Cardinal Robert's university remains what it has always been, not because it is perfect but because nothing else works.

• THREE •

Student Environments

Joseph Stalin, the story goes, once remarked that quantity has a quality all its own. He was talking about artillery, explaining his preference for using huge numbers of mediocre field pieces instead of the German practice of using limited numbers of superb heavy weapons. Without realizing it, Stalin was also describing a basic aspect of American higher education: educate everyone to the limits of her ability to learn, however modest that might be. American universities and colleges admit millions of students and, like Stalin with artillery, always seek more. In the nature of things, some students will, by preparation, aptitude, interest, or inclination, be unready to learn the material. No matter. Many students from the huge horde might be sub-optimal, but they will still learn something and benefit from exposure to college. Education is never completely wasted. Even the poorest cannon does some damage.

Since World War II, American administrators have admitted an ever-larger percentage of the high school graduating class, now running close to 60 percent. The number of students has come to exceed 20 million.[1] The mass component of higher education characterizes America but not Europe, the birthplace of universities. European universities, damaged near to death by the twentieth-century war (1914–1989), had always been elite institutions, admitting two groups: the nobility and the brilliant. They are recovering but have yet to make an appropriate accommodation to current European social democratic notions of mass education. But America, with its variety of schools, from community colleges to research universities, has adjusted higher education to the needs of a democratic society.

Size is not the only defining characteristic of American higher education. University instruction also involves the student's relationship to society. President Jefferson and Cardinal Newman believed that an educated citizenry was necessary for a democratic society. Modern America has expanded on those attitudes, demanding that colleges prepare students for the world of work as well as make them good citizens. The quality of quantity in American higher education involves both democratic opportunity and socially useful instruction.

Large Numbers and Bell Curves

When you come on campus, you see a place swarming with students, some afoot, some on bicycle or skateboard, jaywalking and jayriding everywhere, melded into phone, Pad, or Pod, stoppered with headphones, immersed in youth culture, generally oblivious to the world around them. Their numbers can be so large that a green and park-like campus seems almost urban. On an ordinary class day, never mind a football weekend, a standard university campus might contain twenty to fifty thousand people. Multiply that by campuses in every state, and you get a number so large that it calls for formula rather than anecdote. Statistics help you understand what is going on in American universities.

You may want to refer, as so much of the social sciences do, to the Law of Large Numbers.[2] The Law holds that a large number of examples will produce results in which the mean, the median, and the average are the same number. The larger the number of trials, the closer the average will be to the mean and the median. It establishes stable, extended, and expected results from random actions. Flip a coin a large number of times, and you get about as many heads as tails. Increase the number of flips, and the parity between heads and tails comes even closer. Random events produce anticipated results.

How about a more complex example? A single die has six sides, showing numbers one through six. Each time you throw, it is a discrete event, as likely to come up one as any other number on the die. If you throw it again: same random chance. Five twos in a row? Sure. Six throws with six different numbers? That too. Each number is equal to all the others. But what about a million throws? That will produces an expected value, the average as well as the median and the simple mean. Add the integers up: one, two, three, and so on. The total is twenty-one. Divide by six (the number of integers), and the answer is 3.5. Over the very long haul, the die will land an equal number of times on the low half (one through three), and on the high half (four through six). The split between the two halves is 3.5, halfway between the highest low number and the lowest high number. The Law of Large Numbers brings order to lots and lots of random events.

The Law also works when the things measured are unequal, such as people. The distribution balance remains, though now it is in the form of a bell curve. In September 1994, Richard J. Herrnstein and Charles Murray published their sensational book, *The Bell Curve Intelligence and Class Structure in American Life*.[3] Most of the data came from the United States Department of Labor and the Armed Services. There was so sufficient an amount of it that the book ran to eight hundred pages and contained a good many statistically sophisticated conclusions. But the book raised a huge pother. A glance at the contents shows why. Herrnstein and Murray held that intelligence can be accurately measured, even across the spectrum of different languages and cultures. Statistically, some people were (are) smarter than others, and at least half fall on the dull side. The book further suggested that the amount of intelligence was due more to nature (genes) rather than nurture (social and school environment). The numbers favor nature in the 40 to 80 percent range, probably nearer the high end. Most people are born less than smart, and they stay that way. Society has developed elaborate programs that purport to repair social disadvantage, to release the individual's inherent but socially suppressed capacity. The authors argued that these programs do not and cannot work.[4] Beyond that, Herrnstein and Murray presented statistical evidence to show that intelligence test results comprise the most important predictor of social, economic, and general life success. Finally, the United States, if judged by its policy choices and public attitudes, ignores this reality utterly. Americans are uncomfortable thinking that some people are smart and others are not. And America is especially unwilling to accept conclusions that connect intelligence, or at least test scores that report facility with languages, to race and class.

The most hostile reviewers alleged that *The Bell Curve* justified racism by emphasizing the black-white differential on test scores. They argued that the book implied that the difference was caused by inferior black intelligence. More nuanced criticism dealt with the statistical analysis, or the assumptions concerning the nature of intelligence, education, or testing that were attributed to the authors.[5] While the level of discomfort among reviewers varied greatly, no one argued that the data was incorrect. The questions that reviewers raised centered around what the data meant.

What do tests actually test? For the most part, college entrance tests examine facility with two languages: one symbolic—mathematics—the other linguistic, which in the United States is English. If a student tests near the top of the bell curve in English and mathematics, that student will likely do well enough through the first couple of college years. There are no guarantees, of course. Character is destiny, not language.[6]

Still, *The Bell Curve* and the Law of Large Numbers provide some predictability concerning student outcomes. The tests show where additional teaching resources can help and which students should be directed to take advantage of them. They also introduce another variable in student life, which the university provides, and that is teaching.

The Art and Mystery of Teaching

Ever since the twelfth century, bad teaching has been a consistent academic problem. Once, it led to riots; recently, complaints have been less violent but not less widespread or heartfelt. In the past 30 years, as college costs have grown, parents, politicians, and students have become increasingly vocal about teaching. They blame professors for playing identity politics, for using the classroom as a political forum, for coming in unprepared, and for not covering the subject matter that the students need to know. In short, they feel that they are not getting their money's worth. Politicians denounce the waste of public dollars going to universities. Everyone is unhappy about some aspect of university instruction. Universities have more students than ever before, but they have rarely gotten less love. Their professors must do better.

We think of teaching as the professor being in the classroom, which for the most part it still is. There is a personal connection between the professor and the students, though as the class grows in size, it becomes quite tenuous. The professor knows the kids, at least by sight, and the kids know the professor, by sight and maybe by name. The professor's personality dominates the classroom. If it does not, that alone defines bad teaching. If it does, that is the beginning of good teaching. But mere personality is not enough. The professor must also care about the subject he's teaching, the kids he's teaching, and the way he is teaching them. Character is not only destiny; it is the core of good teaching.

Good teaching in some ways resembles pornography. You can't clearly define it, but you know it when you see it.[7] It is politically incorrect to say it, but good teaching is an art and a mystery, which no one can explain and which cannot be taught. If you can teach well the first day, you can teach well the last day, and all the days in between. This simple truth both saddens and angers many "educators." In reality, there is no teacher training for professors. A practicum in education might provide them some technical advice, such as test preparation, eye contact, whiteboard use, syllabus construction, rhetorical change of pace, and so on. But even if this training took place, it would not create good teachers. Good teaching is akin to star quality. Katharine Hepburn, once asked about star quality, was unable to define it but concluded with the jaunty remark that whatever it was, she had it. Good teaching has a bit of star quality along with occasional helpings of ham. Some people just have it.

Good teaching cannot be quantified. That unsettling reality burdens those who are required to evaluate teaching or administer universities. Good teaching involves performance, from a monologue to a conversation, to discussion, to acting. Moreover, good teaching is situationally based: techniques, style, activities, and props for one group of students would not be appropriate for another. Lectures, conferences, seminars, and medical rounds each demand something different from a good teacher.

Still more, since good teaching is subjective, evaluation must be also, and the style of the judge enters into the evaluation. Bureaucrats and bean counters tend to be censorious from necessity, as they must have something to count and report. Administrators are torn between the itch to correct and the need to support the troops. The best evaluation of good teaching recognizes the theatrical. The effective teacher can convey drama in anything, from automation to mitosis. The small is as important as the large. A good teacher can convey intimacy to a large group as if speaking one-on-one in conversation. In every case, it's a gift. Professors can only be judged, not measured.

The good teacher tends to be interested in the process of instruction and its effect upon the students. Perhaps the instruction has no impact. Then you need to change something. Add a question or two. Move around a bit. Make eye contact, starting at the back of the class and working forward. Put your lecture outline on the board, so both you and the students can follow it. Tell a story. Engage in a brief colloquy with a single student. Try a change of pace. Teaching, like baseball, is a matter of adjustment.[8] It is a process as well as a performance, a journey of improvement as well as a moment of communication. The better the teacher, the more interest there will be in doing it well.

You step on the stage and start the monologue. Everyone has seen it done well. Confident posture, charisma, an upbeat attitude, intense focus: the curtain is going up. Teaching is a form of drama. The audience will hear a story. It's going to be fun. And everyone has seen it done poorly. The performer seems insecure, finding it difficult to look at the audience. The "uh" count rises steadily to triple digits. Stage movements become jerky and uncoordinated. There's no eye contact. Story deteriorates into a ramble. The dramatic tension essential for rhetoric wavers, collapses, and the class falls apart. Private student reverie replaces attention to the presentation. There will be little learning here.

Everyone would like to avoid that scenario. Colleges need to help budding teachers develop good classroom personalities. You may not turn out a Neil deGrasse Tyson, but at least you can improve on Dolores Umbridge. The rookie season in the academic pulpit will set the tone for the remainder of a career. But one thing is essential: you must always try to be better today than you were the day before. This is how you express what is frequently called love. People rarely tell you this; they talk instead of lesson plans. But teaching is a calling even more than it is a profession. And everyone knows that.

And so we return to the bell curve. Whether from nature or nurture, excellent professors are rare outliers near the end of the curve. That fundamental reality means that no reform in academic structure will guarantee good teaching. Flip the classroom, add in-class activities, assign group reports, change exams into essays, add daily quizzes, use some peer grading, change the teaching system as you will, and the good professors will still teach well and the poor ones will not. The university is an institution, but teaching, however it is done, boils down to personal communication between people.

Good professors fare best if left to their own methods, and poor ones don't improve much from intense institutional intervention. In brief, with teaching, it is easier to muck it up than fix it up. Even if, by some miracle, teaching reforms and guidelines could actually enhance teaching, the most recent reform proposals being floated around universities completely ignore the core modern academic problem, which is a lack of money.

Actually, the universities rarely intervene to improve bad teaching. They assess it, they evaluate it, but they don't have a plan to change it. They hire professors and throw them in front of students, assuming, on the basis of little evidence, that the new guys will be satisfactory teachers. Review processes are usually quite formal, and no one should suppose they do much good. Universities do offer extensive sensitivity training, but it is designed to enforce political correctness and avoid lawsuits. University administrators appear to have little interest in fixing instructional deficiencies. And departments rarely terminate faculty merely because they can't teach well. When they let you go, and they do, it's scholarly deficiencies that matter. So nothing is done, and almost no one wants anything done, or even said, about formal training for professors.

Still and all, if help were to be had, what sort of help would actually help? Some technical assistance couldn't hurt, especially in putting together multimedia presentations. And how long could it take? The United States Army boils teacher training down to two weeks. It's not perfect, but it seems to work well enough. Some rudimentary teacher training won't solve all or even many deficiencies in instruction. It will help, at least a bit. And with more kids in college and college costing more and public complaint rising like a Greek chorus, it seems the better part of valor, at least, to appear to work on the problem.

The Shining Path

When Americans consider college in terms other than football, they usually think of what their money buys. Especially in today's depressed economy, parents push their students to take useful subjects, such as accounting or engineering. Politicians and employers demand "workplace readiness" from a university education. The kids should acquire skills needed for success in a job, along with the ability to fit into the professional world. Surely a university education should be more about what you can *do* rather than what you *know*. The university must prepare students for the technology now on tap and the society now in place.

But suppose you are a social radical on campus, one of many in this age of slow economic growth. You are discontented with the university because it supports our dysfunctional class system and values. You may complain that the university has always been that way, or you may complain that modern American universities have dramatically changed in the past few decades.

Either way, you may well be a critical university studies (CUS) theorist. You attempt consciousness-raising among your students, colleagues, and citizens. You may even cherish an educational program teaching massive change in society and university and in the social goals that each pursues. The university must be remade in structure to be more egalitarian and in curriculum to promote social change. You are not alone in your mission: Critical university studies theorists have been increasingly numerous and vocal since the 1990s. They publish attention-getting books.[9] They attack the corporatization of the university, high student debt, and administrators' willingness to exploit adjuncts and graduate students as a source of cheap labor. They support academic freedom and greater public support for higher education. Jeffrey Williams of the *Chronicle* suggests that, "In some ways, critical university studies has succeeded literary theory as a nexus of intellectual energy."[10] Johns Hopkins University Press is issuing a book series on the topic, and a couple of hugely popular CUS blogs (maintained by the shining lights of the field) keep their followers current with relevant developments at universities around the country. Some universities even offer university studies classes, in keeping with Gerald Graff's recommendation to universities to "teach the conflicts."[11]

Modern critical university studies theorists trace their line of descent from a Brazilian Christian socialist. Paulo Reglus Neves Freire (1921–1997) dedicated his life to improving the lives of the poor in Brazil and Chile, but it was his book, *Pedagogy of the Oppressed* (1970),[12] that caught the attention of American academics. During a time of cultural upheaval in the United States, Freire's message was fashionable: teaching and learning are political acts. He warned that professors shape students into helpless victims of an oppressive political system or to become oppressors themselves. Professors do this through an oppressive pedagogical system. American academics accepted Freire's theory wholesale, despite the fact that it had been derived from a very different educational and social situation. They agreed with Freire that The System and The Man are out to crush, or at least deform, the young students in their care. Even if professor and student have the proper political stance, the university's hierarchical structure will withstand their revolutionary efforts. Everything in the university—the people, the political attitudes, the institution itself—stands in the way of true societal change.

Since teaching is politics, the Freireans began with the notion that every educational transaction is unequal and adversarial. The teacher possesses a social advantage (entirely unfair) that the students lack. In this unequal dynamic, the professor is the oppressor, and the student is the oppressed. Inequality automatically makes every academic relationship, however casual, a contest for power played on an unlevel field by two parties, one always possessing an unfair advantage.

Freire called this continuing oppressive instruction the "banking" theory of education. The student functions as an empty bank account into which (whom) professors deposit socially acceptable ideas, making the unjust society more unequal yet. Slowly, over years and decades, the student's account fills up. At some point, the student receives a diploma and leaves the educational system for an assured social position in that unfair society. The former student becomes another oppressor.

The student has learned to become part of the system, to turn ambition toward socially useful paths. She has learned to accept, and fulfill, socially appropriate norms.[13] Having graduated, the young person slips into a social niche. Every parent wants this. Liberation has become almost impossible.

According to its critics, the banking theory of education harms student and society in three ways. In the first place, the student must always remain a passive learner. Stuff is stuffed into her head/bank account. She resembles a receptacle, not an actor. A banking education discourages students from experimenting to see if received social wisdom is actually wise. Consequently, the students' very humanity is gradually squeezed away.

As a second consequence, banking education reinforces the student/professor dyad, with the professor superior, intellectually, socially, and institutionally, as the "masters" have been since Cardinal Robert in 1215. Only a single role is left for the student, that of the unfree, the oppressed. Banking education prevents students from assuming an appropriate role as active partners in their own liberation. Freire was eager to demolish the asymmetrical student/professor relationship but found it difficult to suggest ways that it might be done.[14] Teachers really do know more than students, and a fair amount of passive learning, as opposed to active liberation, cannot be avoided.

The third effect of the banking method of education surpasses the others in social consequence. Current university education creates a culture of social silence, at least in the eyes of the critical university pedagogues. Dominant groups, already oppressive, rarely complain. Students banked into their education possess both a promising future and a lack of personal confidence to work for liberation. The general social culture is one of calm, rather than protest. Students must liberate themselves; nobody can do it for them. Silent students, who have not liberated themselves, demonstrate the success of banking education. Teaching enacts conservative politics.

Freire preached revolution, with a pessimism not inappropriate for a modern Marxist. He saw oppression as permanent. Freire's pessimism was accurate. There were, in fact, two significant revolutionary efforts arising from a rejection of banking education in favor of liberation. One was in Peru, where university students formed the core of a terrorist group *Sendero Luminoso*, the Shining Path. The path shone primarily with blood, and quite a bit of it.[15] The other was in Italy, emanating from the sociology department at the University of Trento. The liberated students became the Italian Red Guards, also a terrorist group. They specialized in bank robberies, airport shootings, and murders of politicians. These Freire-inspired uprisings showed that the culture of silence had limitations. The uprisings were violent, pointless, and suppressed. Liberation theology continues to float around in today's globalized world. Violent protests of liberation and frustration have become quite common.

Liberation theology is reappearing now on college campuses around the country, preached by a cadre of academic critics. Freire had become popular in America because he sympathized with the oppressed.[16] Today's university critics, many of them Marxists, are focused more on attacking the oppressor, anyway. They accuse the university of sins greater than bad teaching or inadequate student learning. The university is guilty of erasing people's narratives. Radical social critics don't bother with the details of university *delits*; they critique instead the fundamental university mission. It must be rebuilt in a revolutionary and egalitarian form.

University professors testify to Paulo Freire's unerring grasp of folk Marxism. Freire had adjusted nineteenth-century doctrine to fit the twentieth century. He believed that the university occupies one of the "commanding heights" of the public social structure. Professors following his lead suggest that universities stand in collusion with the banks, corporations, and government. Freire argued that liberating the university students could lead to liberating the oppressed masses. As Freire believed, the gown could change the town.

Well, the liberators have a long way to go. Student protests in the nineteen-sixties centered around privilege. These protests actually supported, rather than diminished, privilege. Students protested the war in Vietnam because they wanted to avoid the draft. Non-college men were being drafted all the time. Much of the protest movement was captured in a single moment. On the day that President Nixon replaced the draft with a lottery, a student at Georgetown was on his way to a protest meeting. He learned he had a high lottery number and turned around, going back to his room to study. Current privileges entirely intact, it was time to prepare for a privileged future. Students as a group hope their degrees will lead to a comfortable life, not death on the barricades.

In the end, Freire's educational theory created a vocabulary of discontent, which may be used to support any complaint by any member of the university community.[17] Critical university studies, with its Freirean sensibility, can seek liberation for professors as much as for students. In a university of masters, administrators hear the masters' complaints first. After all, professors live in the university. Students just come and go. Within every four, five, or six years an entirely new crop of students show up on campus, cut classes, pair off, take degrees, and, in their turn, disappear. Even the most discontented student sees liberation through graduation as more reasonable than liberation through protest. Poor Freire was a romantic, looking back with nostalgia to the good old days of 1830 and 1848.

Still, critical pedagogy has been a part of the academic culture, off and on, for nearly half a century. There must be something to it. That something cannot be intellectual rigor. Can one really suppose that learning quadratic equations will turn a student into an imperialist? Does teaching a student algebra using examples from the rain forest liberate her from social oppression and still improve her algebra? The questions answer themselves.

Critical university theorists claim to want to change the balance of power in the classroom itself. Knowledge must be "problematized." Everything academic must be negotiated, existing in a gray area where nothing may be entirely affirmed. Professors can no longer simply lecture and lead discussion. In such a negotiated classroom, grading is also a problem. Is it enough to give everyone who speaks up an A, regardless of what is said? The nagging question remains: in a classroom of "problematized knowledge," does anyone learn anything?

Outside Help

The historian Polybius began his *Histories* with a comment on learning: "There is, I trust, no one so sluggish and dull as not to be curious how the whole inhabited world, in less than fifty-three years, fell completely under the control of Rome."[18] Polybius assumed that everyone would be interested in the world they lived in. He was wildly optimistic. Cardinal Newman had a more realistic grasp of what people wanted to know. No matter the discipline being studied, most people did not wish to know it. And even for those who did, learning anything new is hard, tiring work, and frequently confusing. It is a long, slow slog. Since repetition is the heart of learning, the student must go over difficult material more than once. While knowing things may feel good, learning them does not.

And the news gets worse. From the beginning of everything, plenty of students have lacked intellectual curiosity; they are not really interested in *any* subject the university offers. Disinterested students quickly develop a system for coping with college. Learn a bit of something, pass the test, then forget it all at once. Repeat the process for the next test. In this way, you can make it through the semester learning nothing and retaining less. After all, you'll never use calculus in real life. Why do you need to know about Jane Austen? What good will French do you? A pervasive lack of intellectual curiosity can and does inform your entire academic career. And, of course, if you're good at the game, you'll graduate.

For the students, an absence of intellectual curiosity is an individual affliction; for professors, it is a pedagogical ecosystem. Every instructor has had classes where many or most students lack any interest in the material taught. They may be nervous and scared, as in calculus, or dull and passive, as in the humanities, but they all wish to pass and not to learn. As for the college instructors, who tend to love their disciplines and wish to teach, student indifference can, as one used to say, make them crazy. No one who has taught in college, looking out upon an inert mass of students—tweeting, texting, listening to music, watching Facebook or sitcom reruns on their laptops—has not sighed silently and thought, "There is nothing I can do. Whatever and however I teach, this group will not learn." Many will pass because they must, but few will learn.

Students who find learning difficult and uninteresting do have a way to cope. They look for outside assistance. The search for assistance is common, often appropriate, and on occasion, necessary. Some searches for outside help are traditional. In every culture, one may call upon divine assistance, though one always suspects that the gods help only those who help themselves. More mundane outside help is also acceptable. Students in classes consult regularly about take-home assignments. Students routinely tutor each other. Academic work is communal as often as it is solitary. From lab groups to dormitory study sessions, learning is usually a shared student experience. As it should be.

Students sometimes get desperate, though. Their searches for outside help can move beyond the legitimate and fall into the realm of cheating. One student copies something from another student's paper. This happens all the time, even though the chances are not good that the student next to you will be vastly more clever. Copying also runs afoul of a venerable academic axiom: a wrong answer on your neighbor's paper does not become a right answer when transferred onto your paper. Never mind. Students see the possibility of salvation. The need for help is great, the risks are usually low, and the reward can be quite high.

Mundane and often spontaneous cheating will be with the university always. In the electronic age, cheating has gone well beyond the do-it-yourself model. The furtive glance continues, but, like all aspects of American life, college cheating has become organized, monetized, electronic, and professional. "Paper mills" always existed, but now they boom. Just click. A professional paper writer will churn out an essay on any topic you choose. Your deadline is tomorrow? No problem. Paper mills have writers who can meet it. Having your term paper written by a professional is not inexpensive, but it can be a semester-saver for stressed students, particularly those who work and are overscheduled. The paper service also provides a lifeline to the large number of students who have trouble with English.

And, best of all, the mill-written paper is virtually untraceable, unless, by ill fortune, two people in the same class turn in the same paper. Just contact the mill from your own computer, and remember that "loose lips sink ships," in this case, your own academic career. With those simple precautions, a paper mill can save the student and has done so for years.[19] The lesson of the paper mill seems to be clear. A student doing his own work can scuffle along, but if you decide to cheat, go first class.

Teachers at all levels of education deplore the existence of cheating and lament its prevalence. Their condemnation centers on two things: personal loss and social disorder. The personal loss begins with what is learned. Cheating teaches how to cheat. The cheater misses the knowledge and skills on tap. All too often, these skills and knowledge are really needed later. At the social level, widespread cheating replicates the kleptocracies of Mexico, China, or Russia. Regimes riddled with mendacity do not work well, whether in Russia or South-Central-North-by-Northeast Northwest State College.

It can be difficult to draw a bright line between acceptable help and cheating. Tutoring in the dormitory is clearly on one side of the line, paper mills on the other. But a lot of work is collaborative. Group projects, whether in the laboratory or surveys or classwork, blur the contributions of each individual student to the final report. In many groups, actually in almost all groups, one or two kids carry the load for all of them. Groups tend to divide into workers and free riders. There is no penalty for those who slack; there is no extra benefit for those who work. In some disciplines, collaborative work is the norm, at least for juniors and seniors. This custom exacerbates the problem of the free rider. It's made even worse by professors who don't want to know who works and who skates by. Group work, after all, cuts the grading burden by somewhere between one-half and four-fifths. Outside help has many definitions.

However professors and colleges define cheating, students often have no scruples. They feel justified in cheating, in part because college is so hard. Everyone talks about grade inflation. Everyone gets an A. Nobody flunks out. It was much harder to graduate in my day. The reality is otherwise. Grade inflation and Mickey Mouse courses to the contrary notwithstanding, only slightly more than half of the entering freshmen graduate in six years. And a personal note: It has been our observation, both from gossip and experience, that college courses have gotten harder over the past generation, in part because there is so much more to learn (science and technology), and in part because, in a knowledge society, writing well is the most important and difficult skill to learn (humanities and social sciences).

Furthermore, as more kids go to college and need to go to graduate school, competition adds to the burden. It's not easier to get into med school, or law school, or business school: it's harder. Credentials are so important that sometimes you feel that you just have to cheat. You will do anything to get a leg up. There just doesn't seem to be any other way.

If that were all, tutoring would be the sovereign solution, but it's not all. Sometimes, perhaps much of the time, professors do not teach well. Partly it's rhetorical, but often problems are intellectual. Professors sometimes fail to organize the details of their discipline into a coherent "big picture." The professorial task is to organize knowledge even more than to inform. The professor takes bits and pieces of the discipline and molds them into an interpretation or a hypothesis. Mere scraps of information can come electronically, which is why God invented the Internet. Understanding the big picture comes from research, thought, imagination, study, and knowledge, and that is what the professor provides, at least some of the time. The academy is at its best when the most important outside help is provided by the professor.

College Learning Assessment

Learning assessments are nothing new. University students have been tested since before the thirteenth century. The results of those tests have usually determined the rest of their lives. It's been sink or swim. These days, testing has expanded; high-stakes exams, often called learning assessments, are applied to students at the top and the bottom of the university ladder. At the bottom, the No (Every?) Child Left Behind Act has ordained relentless testing within the schools in a desperate effort to attain a minimal level of achievement, including literacy, for all. By contrast, testing at the top works pretty well. Medical schools require their entering students to take, and do well on, the MCAT; law schools usually base admissions on a satisfactory LSAT score, and the GRE tests those who hope to remain within the academy. Once students complete graduate and postgraduate education, more assessment awaits in the form of professional exams. Teachers must take the PRAXIS exam.[20] Engineers who want to practice their profession are required to take the FE (Fundamentals of Engineering) and sometimes the PE (Principles and Practices of Engineering).[21] For attorneys-to-be, the bar examination is sufficiently difficult so that pricey post-law school clinics and courses have emerged to help them pass. Doctors take medical boards in their specialties. These exams are designed by real-world practitioners to test fitness to work; they form an effective effort at student accountability. Is the candidate skilled and knowledgeable enough to be loosed upon the trusting public as a lawyer, doctor, dentist, engineer, or teacher? Accountability is already standard professional practice.

Recently, the American public has been hearing calls for more accountability, this time with respect to what students are learning in college. The calls may have something to do with money, or the lack of it: in this weak economy, are we getting what we're paying for? Or they may have something to do with the eternal distrust between the old and the young: these callow whippersnappers are not what *we* used to be. Or they may have to do with the notorious "mushy" college courses that make the news, with titles like "On Being Bored" (Brown University), "Tree Climbing" (Oberlin College), "Demystifying the Hipster" (Tufts University), "Arguing with Judge Judy" (UC Berkeley), and "Tattoos, Piercings, and Body Adornment" (Pitzer College). Whatever the causes, it is interesting to note that Americans in the past decade have not been satisfied with simply complaining about money or whippersnappers or mushiness. They are demanding an objective report on the breeding ground of trouble. And they are eagerly reading some of the reports, objective or otherwise, that are being published. The news? College students are not learning much.[22]

One of the blockbuster reports was Richard Arum and Josipa Roska's *Academically Adrift* (2011).[23] The authors conducted broad and lengthy research on college students around the country and confirmed the popular suspicion that college students are more comfortable in a cyber world than a real world. They may know a great deal about sex, drugs, rock and roll, social media, and electronic games, but they are profoundly ignorant about their society and economy.[24] Further, they lack general cultural and academic knowledge.

Arum and Roska don't blame them as much as they blame the colleges for leaving their students "academically adrift," with few fixed educational priorities. Students are not being given a foundation in the culture, history, and economy of the world they live in. Even worse, Arum and Roska noted huge inequalities in college education. Some students are learning a whole lot and others next to nothing. Differences in college education quality often lead to differences in post-college life chances, whether in graduate/professional school or in the increasingly competitive workplace. Arum and Roska reminded readers that these inequalities do not lead toward the greater social good. They claim that colleges and universities are not the Golden Door they ought to be.

Academically Adrift did not simply make a depressing diagnosis. It also presented a remedy. Arum and Roska proposed a way for colleges to reduce student ignorance: administer a College Learning Assessment (CLA). The CLA is a standardized test produced by the Council for Aid to Education (CAE) that purports to test how much college students have improved during college. According to CAE press releases, it "provides objective and valid scientific evidence that students are mastering critical-thinking skills throughout their college experience, that they are independent thinkers, that they are capable of developing creative solutions to complex problems, and, most importantly, that they will be valuable and flexible assets to potential employers and organizations." It is already used at hundreds of colleges around the country.[25]

This CLA is a performance test, along with a couple of analytical writing samples. It presents students with a real-world problem and asks them to solve it feasibly yet imaginatively. Students also get a bunch of multiple-choice questions designed, as so many educational assessments claim to do lately, to test critical thinking skills.

The buzzword, of course, is "critical thinking," but the keyword in the CAE's press release is "employer." And the buzzword and the keyword are intimately linked. The CLA is not a test of knowledge, though that could certainly be added: it is a test of how knowledge is used. After all, that is what employers want. After all, it's always about the money.

Arum and Roska propose turning the entire university into a (relatively) high-level vo-tech educational experience. Up until quite recently, vocational education at the university level has been the province of schools of agriculture, business, education, engineering, technology, and architecture. Here, the object has been to teach students how to do something, such as design a factory, build a river-control structure, teach a lesson, or prepare a stock option. You went to college to learn how to do. A college degree meant you could do it, at least as an assistant to someone in the field. This is now being extended to the arts and humanities. Majors in history, literature, art, or philosophy also need to prove that they can do something. That something is analytic and synthetic logic married to oral and written communication. Business and government need people who can do it, and the liberal arts exist to provide them. They are becoming as much a trade school as any institution. The days of taking Latin, English, and history to become a gentleman belong to the era of Winston Churchill, not the era of Bill Gates.

The CLA, like Janus, faces both ways. It is often used by college administrators to examine their own schools' programs.[26] But it is also designed to assure parents, and society, that college students are soon going to be successfully functioning economic units. Perhaps we ought to see the CLA as written proof that students have developed what it takes—analytic, problem-solving, and communication skills—to succeed in the working world.

Arum and Roska's endorsement of the CLA is just the beginning. Institutions may use the CLA as a graduation test, with a passing grade demanded for a degree. The CLA might be employed as a supplement to an oral examination. Colleges could combine the CLA with an entrance exam to measure how much the students got out of their courses and how well the faculty taught and tested. Whatever the institutional decision on assessment, the CLA would certainly focus faculty and students upon real-world skills. Surely, that is a social good?

Apart from that philosophical question, there is the practical one asked by college faculty. Do CLAs work well enough to be worth the bother and the inevitable limitations? Students are not all going to learn what we teach them, no matter how much "critical thinking" pedagogy and testing we apply. In fact, the more testing is administered, the more "teaching to the test" will follow. Professors rightly fear that the CLA will set standardized and external learning goals; universities will be giving over their ownership of knowledge to corporate testing entities. A growing reliance on the CLA shifts accountability for learning from the student to the professor.

The nation's elementary and high schools illustrate the full horrors of accountability through learning assessments.[27] In Chicago, Houston, and Atlanta, teachers found their students couldn't answer questions on the test, even after relentlessly teaching only the test. So they simply erased the wrong answers and put in the right ones. That is the discouraging but predictable consequence of tying faculty accountability to student assessment. Another consequence is students' changed attitude to learning. They are now showing up at college expecting to be told what will be on university tests, too. And college students often expect their professors to tell them what the test will cover. Indeed, many students find that it does not happen nearly enough for their comfort or success. Student ignorance, lack of preparation, and attitudes hostile to learning exist in college as well as the schools. No learning assessment will fix that.

Even without CLA–based accountability, professors are told that, whatever the subject matter and whatever the test format, they must produce good test results.[28] The technique for achieving that good result is simplicity itself. It is repetition, which is the heart of evaluation. Information, like the dates of the Civil War, can be relentlessly drilled into the dullest young scholar. A writing sample or two? Students can practice writing until they learn basic grammar and syntax, until they can tell a gerund from a giraffe, can construct a semi-coherent paper, or until their hand falls off. Or until they can find someone to write the paper for them. It may take years. It will take years. But a college degree takes four or five years anyway, so it can be done.

The reason for a good teaching result is also simplicity itself. It is money. Colleges benefit fiscally from what is called student retention, and benefit even more if the young scholar hangs around long enough to graduate. Failing half the class in an introductory course supports neither retention nor graduation. So deans now check grade sheets (at least at LSU and presumably elsewhere also). The worldly wise look for too many "F" grades; the pure of heart look for too many "As," but the goal of encouraging retention is always met. As it should be. At small private liberal arts colleges, retention and graduation means survival for the school and the community.

So a CLA of the type endorsed by Arum and Roska fits into the retention/graduation nexus. The CLA attempts to identify skills that are taught in college, and its format is in use outside the academy. The State Department used to give (and may still) prospective foreign service officers a hypothetical situation, usually involving a deranged dictator in a third-world failed state who proposes to massacre a minority or nationalize an American asset: give a situation analysis and policy recommendation.[29] Modern corporate memos follow the same pattern. Students can learn the techniques for either a political or a commercial analysis; the CLA will certify them; employers will benefit from this handy sorting tool. The CLA movement is sufficiently broad that the inevitable has happened. Private corporations have been established to profit from the new educational fashion.

Some colleges and universities have created their own internal assessment. Accrediting bodies around the country are always looking for learning outcomes. Individual departments within the colleges are required to self-assess the faculty through student learning. Right now, these departments set learning objectives; in years to come, they will certainly be standardized. The local assessment programs have two great advantages. They cost nothing and they fit local conditions.

Whatever the form of learning assessment, several results of the assessment/accountability trend seem clear. Most universities will move toward some form of learning assessment. Some institutions will adopt a prepackaged commercial model, such as the CLA, the CAAP (Collegiate Assessment of Academic Proficiency), or the AP (Advanced Placement). Other universities will create their own combination of written and oral exams and a thesis. But almost every university will have something, or at least say they do. Secondly, the current political libido for assessment/accountability will slowly wane. Even the most entrancing trends have a shelf life. New trends, even more horrible to contemplate, will emerge. But, once established, the assessment/accountability tests will survive.

So "No Child Left Behind" has made it to college, as nearly two-thirds of the current student cohorts (its victims) do also. Beyond that, the learning assessments, by their very existence, will increasingly standardize college curricula. Further, a standard scale of student learning and professorial performance will gradually emerge. Both will deal with the scale as they always have, by adjusting to the task and cynicism about the results. But some version of the assessment/accountability/retention/graduation employment measurement is coming to a university near you.

Finally, a bit of a coda. The accountability movement arises from an optimistic temperament. Those who support CLAs certainly hope that they will improve student learning and professional instruction. They may find themselves agreeing with Donald Rumsfeld, who noted that only those things that are measured can improve. Those pushing assessment/accountability make the assumption that things measured *must* improve. Once measurement is in place, every student can learn the material if the instruction is good and the environment is supportive.

But, just for a moment, suppose that most of these things are not true. Suppose that the conclusions drawn by Augustine and *The Bell Curve* are valid. Nature and culture have imposed limitations on student learning. Not every student can learn the material, no matter how suave the instructor or how safe the learning environment. The material is too hard. Some students can learn a very little, and many don't learn much. A lack of intellectual curiosity always prevails over any instruction or assessment ever imagined. Measurement of any activity actually produces an organized mass of information. Yet, improvement is a possibility only, as anyone who has ever tried to improve retail service knows. Suppose that assessment/accountability exercises produce a lot of paperwork, an increase in the size of the bureaucracy, a midden of information, stress and angst, but change nothing substantive in student learning or professional instruction. We all know about sow's ears and silk purses. We also all remember an Addams cartoon, showing a lout driving sows into a silk purse factory.

The Golden Door

The raw numbers are depressingly familiar. Total student debt in 2016 has gone above a trillion dollars—and rising. This is a lot of money. The average student owes around $28,000, which is also a lot of money. Add these two numbers to a third, on which popular opinion and the census bureau agree: the economic advantage of a college degree in the job market is around $20,000 annually—$47,000 for college graduates to $27,000 for those with high school only.[30] And that is a lot of money.

These numbers form the framework of a public debate over college costs and benefits. Does college cost too much? You betcha, to quote the sheriff in the movie *Fargo*. Is student debt a burden and a scandal? Certainly. Is a college education really the benefit it's supposed to be? Financially, it certainly is. Going to college on the installment plan makes sense, which is probably why so many people do it.

The catch in this social equation is that it's not enough just to go to college; you must also graduate. Not everyone does. About one-third of those in bachelor's degree programs do not graduate within six years of first enrollment. The percentage is higher in community colleges, in for-profits, and in certificate programs. Failure to graduate means that the student has acquired a substantial debt but has gained nothing in the way of benefit. If you finance a car, you take on debt, but you also have the car. If you don't graduate, all you have is debt. Those who do not graduate are the real victims of the student debt system. For them, repayment is a genuine burden. But even for the graduates, parents and students frequently wonder if increased costs have cut too heavily into the ultimate payoff.

This debate appears on television news channels, in beauty salon magazines, around kitchen tables, and in legislatures. The Pew Research Center relates some statistics concerning the pervasive anxieties. Begin with parents. They have wildly sanguine expectations about their kids going to college. The Pew survey found that 94 percent of parents think their children will attend college. At the same time, three quarters of the same parents think that college is too expensive for most Americans to afford, presumably including themselves. The juxtaposition of these numbers suggests that Americans believe the children who cannot afford college will still go to college. A contradiction between hope and reality always increases public stress. Parents clearly think that the vector of their child's life depends on going to college. And it does. So my child will go. But how?

Parents' hopes and fears illustrate the American Dream. A college education has long been the Golden Door to social mobility in America.

An accounting degree or a mechanical engineering certificate enabled a student to enter the middle class. Families sacrificed to send a chosen child down the Yellow Brick Road to college, and out of current family circumstances. This story of focus and solidarity is part of an oft-told tale of family history in America. "Only in America" and "pioneering on the urban frontier" describe the possibility that an ambitious child could ascend the social ladder.[31] The story has been repeated enough to create a mythic truth about where opportunity really lay in the land of the free and the home of the brave.[32]

Not only did the people believe in education as the Golden Door; the president did as well. In 1944, as the Allies were winning the war, President Franklin D. Roosevelt pushed the G.I. Bill through Congress. It provided government support for the returning veterans to go to school. Millions did.[33] It transformed lives and remade the country. The G.I. Bill was so successful that it was extended to Korea and then to peacetime service, and it still exists. In the face of such evidence, who would not believe that a college education vastly improved life chances? Indeed, it is almost a surprise that only 94 percent of parents surveyed expected their children to go to college. In what country do the other 6 percent live?

A lot of parents endure a lot of stress as they confront the social dissonance. They become mighty anxious about the future of their kids, who must go to college but perhaps cannot. Some enter denial. College is not the Golden Door. The benefits are not worth the cost. Other parents and students adjust; in increasing numbers, students have entered community colleges, trying to get the first half of their education at reduced costs. They hope that this saving will put the rest almost within reach. Practically every student works part-time, and not a few work full-time. A college education now takes five or six years, but the student makes a bit of progress every semester. A great many students borrow money. What scholarships and grants (Pell and others) do not defray can be covered by a variety of expedients, from loans, to work, to more time to graduate. The days of "The Sweetheart of Sigma Chi" seem far away.

Students now often display a nervous seriousness not seen since the veterans came marching home. No one has to tell them that the job market is tight. Even the college graduates are scrambling for a good job. Every student knows that technological and communication skills are needed for jobs in a knowledge and service economy. College is a good place to get them.

This is particularly true for young women. Women still earn less than men. They know that the road to gender equality runs through a campus.

Increasingly, the favored child sent to college is a daughter. And why not? Women seem to excel in the college virtues of perseverance and social discipline. Women began to outnumber men on campus in the 1980s; in this millennium they exceed men by ten percentage points.[34] The gap grows.[35]

So here's where things stand: the need for a college degree has grown, while the costs of a college degree have grown even faster. If the parents and kids can't pay for college, then the public must. Federal loans pick up the slack. But the loans must be repaid upon graduation. And the federal piper is legally first in line for a cut of the graduate's income.[36] Graduates cannot dump the burden by bankruptcy. Federal law prohibits that.[37] College loans have reached five percent of all household sector debt. College attendance and debt together have become part of the politics of pain, akin to taxes.

Student debt has begun to alter the American family. Pew reports that nearly half, 48 percent, of households with students or graduate debtors find it harder to pay the bills. A smaller, but still significant, 25 percent say that student debt has made it harder to purchase a house, and a similar figure, 24 percent, say that student debt has affected career choices. Around 7 percent admit that student debt had caused college graduates to delay marriage and children.[38] Nonetheless, social reality has not changed since the G.I. Bill. HR departments, employment counselors, and business recruiters all say that a college degree is the essential ticket to a good job.

The Students' Verdict

"Boost, don't knock," the community civic clubs like Rotary used to say. A college education seems to have few boosters these days, but among them are most of the recent college graduates. They have been in college so recently that the rosy hue of nostalgia has not had time to distort their memories. What do these graduates, so often cast as victims, think of their college experience? Was it worth it?

Debt to the contrary, recent college graduates overwhelmingly say that their education has been "a good investment."[39] Some 86 percent think their college education and degree has been worth the cost in time and treasure. Only 6 percent of new graduates believe that college has been a waste of money for them. Similar results occurred when Pew polled those still in college in 2010 and 2011. Of this group, only 2 percent thought they were making a bad investment, while 84 percent thought that their college degree would pay off. These findings are quite dramatic, considering current public sentiment to the contrary. Whatever the problems with college, those just out and those still in seem satisfied enough with it.

The story goes that August and Frederick Duesenberg, when queried about advertising for their Duesenberg automobiles, replied, "Ask the man who owns one." This remark became the company slogan. Put the same test to those who own a college degree. What do they think their degree is worth? They tend to be glad they bought one.

• FOUR •

Courses and Curriculum

Every year, swarms of kids and parents visit college campuses. They all ask the same question: is this the place my student should go to school? The visitors, often accompanied by a student guide representing admissions, wander through the campus, admiring Victorian buildings and wincing at modern ones. They learn about scholarships. They are told about the variety of courses offered. They lunch at the campus food court. It's all quite serious, even a bit tense. The kids sort of know, and their parents really know, that a college degree is essential in the knowledge society.

Behind what the visitors see, hear, and surmise lie decisions to make and a general uncertainty about the future. Parent and child begin with a rough triage: some colleges are out of reach, for whatever reason, and others clearly won't do. This is the easy part. Some things are harder to see, even if one looks through the catalogues at degree programs and course titles.

Everybody suspects that colleges and universities come in various flavors. Indeed they do. They can be been plotted along an axis that runs from research universities to colleges that are hardly distinguishable from communes.[1] Urban community colleges are far distant in atmosphere from the small liberal arts universities. Confessional colleges seem utterly unlike the University of Texas at Austin or the University of California at Berkeley. Colleges exhibit a startling number of institutional variables.

These institutional variables guarantee that the student educational experience will vary greatly from one college to another. Research universities offer numerous specialized courses, usually taught in a formal manner. Smaller colleges teach the basic courses in standard disciplines, often with quite a remarkable degree of informality. Communes disguised as colleges offer relationships disguised as part of a course. The student experience depends as much on the institution attended as on the courses taken.

Research universities seek to offer as much as possible of everything possible. There, teaching merges into research. They offer a "multiplication of specializations through the proliferation of disciplines, programs, colleges, and institutes, with a strong component of graduate education."[2] Their pedagogy emphasizes the material. Research universities hold their faculty to a high standard of publication, grants, and innovation. Deans and professors alike tend to regard research as more important than teaching.[3] At research universities, the faculty form a privileged class within the academic hierarchy.[4] Professor Leonard Hochberg observes that they "are separated from the undergraduate student body by virtue of their role, seeing students only during class, and rarely during office hours."[5] Even when faculty and students do collide face to face, the interaction remains formal and centered on academic matters. Student and professor inhabit different worlds on the same campus.[6]

Smaller colleges, Hochberg notes, often have a "coherent curriculum with a strong core component of courses that are integrated (as with multidisciplinary or interdisciplinary foci)."[7] Their academic effort is directed toward student enlightenment, however the school defines that condition. In smaller institutions, school size permits many opportunities for students and faculty to get together on more equal terms.[8] The emphasis shifts from material taught to student learning.

Many smaller institutions try to ensure that a lot of teaching is conducted informally, in the Jeffersonian manner. These relationships can imitate Aristotle's lyceum, as exemplified today by schools like St. John's College in Annapolis. At some colleges (such as Union and Bucknell) professors go to fraternity houses to discuss the material and tutor the students. Students and faculty meet in cafeterias for ad hoc seminar sessions. Larger colleges attempt to imitate this sense of community: both at Rice and Yale, dorms have resident faculty members who are expected to teach in their offices as well as in the common rooms. Community, and the general optimistic outlook it supports, forms one of the great strengths of smaller institutions. Sadly, the weakness is also clear. Small colleges do what they do very well indeed, but what they do is often academically limited. They lack the intellectual power of large research universities.[9] Small colleges can't offer everything. Their strength lies in hope and possibility that you will learn all that they do offer. How the courses are taught is as important as what the courses teach. The university is, after all, an organism rather than a machine.[10]

Theme and Variations

In our society, which is a fascinating mixture of technology and therapy, of creativity and whine, an advocate can plausibly insist that almost any area of human endeavor should be taught in a university. Colleges are always adding new areas of study. Some may seem outré at first, but not for long. New courses soon become standard offerings. Established disciplines calve off new specialized sub-divisions endlessly. Biology becomes microbiology, genetics, biochemistry, biophysics, and more. Physics includes particle physics, part of which has become the new discipline of nanophotonics. And on it goes.[11] University curricula have shifted from permanently fixed to permanently fluid.

Fluid also involves courses: professors advance personal opinion as well as teach the material advertised. For example, American history professors have always enjoyed exceptional latitude for expressing political opinion in an academic course. Every college offers American history, though not the same history of America. There is a "standard model," and several standard variations upon the standard model. These courses differ so greatly that they may be seen as a paradigm of the institutional variables at work, with differences in content often accompanying differences in pedagogical style.

Professors usually teach some form of the standard model. This course marches steadily forward from discovery to colonization through colonial and revolutionary America, slavery, the Civil War, industrialization, the progressive era, immigration, racial problems, world wars, the Great Depression and New Deal, all the way through Cold War America, and, of course, the rise of baseball. It presents the American story as a chronicle of success—if not always attained, then at least approached. America has been a force for good in the world, standing for liberty, opening a golden door for immigrants, opposing tyranny abroad, and striving to provide prosperity and justice at home. America is exceptional, socially and economically. Many Americans still see their country as a "city on a hill." America is the land of the free and the home of the brave, just like they sing at baseball games.

The standard course leans in the direction of American nationalism. Professors emphasize the assimilation of immigrants into American ways. People come from all over, and here they learn English and seize opportunity. Their kids become part of the general American culture, and by the third or fourth generation they are marrying outside the group. It is called the "melting pot." Though now a politically incorrect term, it describes reality. Cultural and political assimilation is the path taken by the overwhelming majority of immigrant families, from the seventeenth century to the present. The melting pot continues to bubble.

This standard American history course has come to be seen as normative within the academy and appropriate outside. For the public, the professors who teach it just tell it like it is—and was. That's what happened, along with the *who*, the *how*, and a bit of the *why*. The standard model is a political statement of approval for America. In terms of current politics, it can be conservative as well as liberal; the commonality is found not in present issues but in past achievements.

Within the academy, however, some professors believe the standard model ought to be replaced. Not everyone thinks that American history is a chronicle of liberty, justice, and success for almost all. Those who are put off by the image of the melting pot also have a tale to tell. The story all depends on where you start. Instead of beginning with the Europeans and their standard stuff, how about beginning with the Native Americans (or First Nations, once called Indians)? In this version, the European invasion is a story of things being torn down, not built up. The arrival of the rascally Europeans marks the end of Native American history. The Caribs were wiped out, the Aztecs conquered and reduced to slavery, and eventually all the Native American cultures, from Tierra del Fuego to the Arctic shore, were brought under European control. The First Nations peoples were forced into new languages and European religions. They lost their lands, their freedoms, and their cultures, which were replaced by slavery, alcohol, and smallpox.

The deaths of millions of Native Americans, stretching from the sixteenth into the nineteenth century, did not unduly dismay the European conquerors. They simply imported slaves from Africa. Beginning in the sixteenth century, Europeans brought millions across the Middle Passage, mostly to Brazil and the Caribbean, but some (around 6 percent) to North America.[12] The slaves were finally freed in the nineteenth century, first by Great Britain and Mexico, then by the United States, and finally by Brazil. But Americans treated the newly freed and their descendants with discrimination, segregation, insult, contempt, and distaste. The Civil Rights movement made some dent in this sorry state of things. But social justice has remained elusive. American history, by and large, not entirely but mostly, is the story of enslavement, exploitation, and injustice. Using this narrative, there doesn't seem to be much grace shed anywhere.

The history course aforementioned may be regarded as the standard anti-standard. But it is not alone in dissenting from the majority model.

A third narrative of American history involves the natural environment. The First Nations peoples were excellent stewards of the environment, or at least lacked the technology to destroy it. The Europeans have increasingly polluted America and the world. The colonists and their descendants cut down the forests and eroded the soil. Vast areas of America have fallen victim to mining, industrial farming, and suburban sprawl. American history is the story of species extinction (passenger pigeons) and pollution (Cuyahoga River, which actually caught fire). America increased emissions so much in the twentieth century that it became the world's greatest polluter and uniquely responsible for climate change. The history of America is the story of degrading the planet.

The narrative may shift, from land back to people. America is unquestionably a nation of immigrants, first from northern Europe, primarily Great Britain and Germany. By the last decades of the nineteenth century, immigrants increasingly came from southern and eastern Europe. After the middle of the twentieth century, immigrants flowed more from Asia and Latin America. Those were the immigrants who wanted to come to America. Slaves from Africa, first brought to the English colonies in 1619, were not volunteers. Importation of slaves into the English colonies and then the United States continued right up until 1860.[13]

New immigrants have always received a suspicious scrutiny from those already here. Politicians form parties around nativist themes. Those recently off the boat were considered "greenhorns" and derided in their own communities as well as being disliked by others. Active discrimination followed the Irish, Jews, Italians, and eastern Europeans for generations, but it was much worse for the newly freed African Americans. Here, social segregation was given legal form.[14] After the Civil Rights movement, segregation and social discrimination diminished a bit but did not disappear.

Those born here have never ceased wondering if the newly arrived are quite the right people. American history, therefore, is a constant minuet of exclusion, group self-organization, discrimination, accommodation, education, generational change, assimilation, intermarriage, along with a struggle to retain the old cultural identity. The immigrant story has always been the juxtaposition of tradition and opportunity. The Jewish experience has been particularly well documented, from the stories of Abraham Cahan, the "worthy editor" of the *Jewish Daily Forward* in New York, to the Al Jolson movie, *The Jazz Singer*.[15] For the individual, the immigrant's journey was bittersweet, a life in the cultural middle as the parents' past slipped quietly away and the children loudly embraced what was culturally current.

Four • Courses and Curriculum

African Americans have had an immigrant experience somewhat different from the Europeans, Asians, and Hispanics. On Juneteenth, 1865, most of the freed slaves had been born in America, but as free people, they did not have a generally recognized place in American society. In much of the country, people opposed ending slavery because they could not imagine an appropriate place for free black people in America. Yet the role of education and economic opportunity was similar for all. So was the resistance to inclusion.

The historian teaching the course can decide which interpretation he wants, the standard model or some variant. The standard model focuses on general trends, while the variants emphasize specific social problems. There are always a lot of social problems, so the variants of American history courses go far beyond those outlined above. There is a feminist history of America, in which everything good, true, and beautiful appeared in Seneca Falls in 1848. Before that, darkness; after that, resistance to the light, and always "the horror, the horror." There are urban histories of America, labor histories of America, constitutional histories of America, and so on. Still, we ought to examine just one more American history variant.

A currently fashionable model of American history focuses on America's role in the world. The basic theme is usually the multiple iniquities of imperialism. The course can begin with Jefferson, include Lewis and Clark, proceed then to the Mexican War and the Spanish-American War, but must always emphasize the Cold War and beyond. It goes almost without saying that America started and sustained the Cold War. Instructors denounce America for opposing the dismantling of the great European colonial empires. America maintained a constant nuclear blackmail over the whole globe. It is entirely appropriate to blame America always. America is, after all, the greatest threat to world peace and has been so since Pearl Harbor. America pursued unlovely policies of aggression and racism in an effort to dominate and exploit the rest of the world. Anti-imperialist professors say that what goes on at home is equally bad, but local; they emphasize America as a blot on all the world.

In America, according to professors teaching the standard course, most things have worked out, most of the time, for most of the people, more or less. Those unhappy with America produce the alternate narratives. They argue that the sufferings of a single group define the America of everyone and every event. The single part is the whole, and the worst of the single part defines the whole.[16] Everyone can see the logical defects of this attitude, just as all can also recognize the fervor of belief.

Professors do tweak their courses on the basis of political opinion; other curricular change comes from their simple desire to make the course better. Courses *can* be improved. Add some new knowledge that has come from recent research, such as the material on exoplanets that has been included in astronomy courses. Some improvements involve the introduction of new techniques, such as computer drafting in architecture. Change the way the material is presented, moving from analytical to historical methods in introductory political science courses. Edward Fox at Cornell reworked the Western Civilization course in the years from 1947 into the early 1960s. Like others before him, such as S. J. H. Hayes at Columbia, Fox found that it took years to change a standard course in significant ways.

Professor Fox came to Cornell after a stint in the State Department as a policy analyst. He had lived through the dangers of appeasement as a student of William Langer at Harvard, and the experience sharpened his sense of the importance of geography and international politics in history. At Cornell, he saw that college students, even in the Ivy League, were ignorant of their cultural heritage and lacked the tools to understand the postwar world. Fox wanted a Western civilization course that would acquaint students with their cultural past and enable them to deal with an increasingly complex modern world. The cost of cultural and geographical ignorance was now (postwar world) too high.

The problem Fox addressed was not new then, and is with us still. The historian David McCullough laments the "historical illiteracy" of Americans. He means their general ignorance of American history, but the problem is obviously worse when applied to the whole sweep of Western culture. Cornell, like most universities, offers a two-semester course that runs from the Stone Age to the stoned students. That's a lot of years and a lot of stuff. In any reform of the Western civilization course, the professor must attack historical illiteracy by reorganizing the whole thing.

Fox began with geography. He included a historical atlas as one of the required texts and added map quizzes to the course syllabus. Fox believed that history made more sense when considered within a geographical context, a view that was going out of fashion in the postwar world. Fox continued his reform of the course by changing the text. But he did not do what had been so often done before. The normal response by a major scholar to inadequate texts is to write a new one, which is also imperfect but in a different way. Fox instead had scholars in the requisite fields write short books, around one hundred pages each, about the Roman Empire, feudalism, the Reformation, and so on. These books, about a dozen of them, were designed to be used with an assortment of primary texts and maps to provide a multi-level introduction to Western culture. Perhaps this combination would be less imperfect rather than differently imperfect.

Most innovative of all, Fox published a syllabus that was itself the length of a short book. It contained the material to be covered, as do all outlines everywhere. Fox added hints on how to write a paper, along with an example of excellent student writing. He included suggestions on how to study and how to approach history. He explained the importance of historical geography. Fox made the extended syllabus a continuing commentary on the material taught that week, making sure the material was always understood in context.

The strengths of Fox's course, indeed the course itself, has become lost to time. Edward Whiting Fox was a charismatic man, both as a professor and a mentor, and the course's success depended on his being there. Teaching is a performance art, and Fox's performance style was cheerful and encouraging. But in the academy, as elsewhere under the heavens, there is a season for all things. In post–Hiroshima America, Western civilization became progressively less fashionable. The academy migrated in the direction of world civilizations, where the texts emphasized non–Western cultures. The Fox course became increasingly isolated as an academic offering. Fox had worried that students did not know the foundations of their own culture; younger professors argued that the non–Western world was what mattered in a globalized economy. Excellence is no guarantee against the adverse judgment of newly emerging canons of orthodoxy.[17] When Western civilization courses waned in popularity, Professor Fox's reforms were lost in the wash.

Some university courses die, but most survive and evolve, a little at a time. Professors and deans fiddle with them, for reasons of ideological purity or to incorporate the latest research or to fit some administrative need or the desire to make things better for students. Sporadic but dramatic curricular revolutions do dazzle the public eye. People easily assume that no other alterations ever occur. Only a bomb-thrower can change the standard courses, often toward ideological rant. But the reality is otherwise. Like Paris, the great research university is a moveable feast.

Adjuncts

Courses change and so do those who teach them. Fifty years ago, tenured professors did most of the work; now it is adjuncts and part-time faculty. The dismal trend toward adjuncts has led to some shocking statistics. Now (2016), over half, somewhere between 50 percent and 75 percent of college faculty, are part-time teachers who are paid by the course and have a one-semester or one-year contract. These adjuncts have no benefits, no teaching assistants, no retirement, no assurance or often hope of a new contract.[18] Academic gypsies, often with PhD degrees, are paid a pittance, with the median salary now about $2,700 a course.[19] The annual income for an exceptionally diligent and lucky part-time college teacher is frequently in the $20,000–$30,000 range. Adjuncts' annual income often falls below the poverty line for a family of four, and many receive some form of federal aid, such as Medicaid or food stamps.

Many adjuncts can teach only one or two courses at a university, and they have to teach in more than one school. Teach two freshman courses at a state university, another at a community college, another at a state college, and round that busy schedule out with a course at a suburban junior college. The adjunct's office is in the car, there is no time to advise students, tests must be made easy to grade, and the final exam must be short. These multi-school adjuncts—"freeway flyers"—are increasingly common in metropolitan areas. They are the *sottoposti* of the academic world, lower than serfs, who were at least tied to the land. For these lower-than-serfs, college teaching can be the very definition of a hard-knock life.[20]

When describing the faculty, university public relations people like to boast that all of the full-time faculty have a doctorate. The same puffs rarely say much about the less-than-serfs who teach so many of the university students. The academic gulag, while not exactly a secret, is not at all a matter of pride. It is, rather, a matter of necessity. Universities increasingly lack the money to do all the things they need to do. Corners must be cut. Universities defer maintenance on the physical plant. They also cut the budget allocated to teaching. Since every class must be met, deans and provosts have increasingly resorted to adjuncts and part-time faculty. The adjunct gulag is often blamed on deans and chancellors, but the real blame rests at the state capital and falls upon state legislators and their budgets. No internal university reform ever spoken or imagined can change that standard, permanent reality.

The adjunct gulag archipelago has an obvious impact on the lives of the less-than-serfs who inhabit it; it also affects the courses they teach. The pedagogy may well be, and often is, entirely satisfactory, though the adjuncts must of necessity skimp on student help and tutoring. Problems lie instead with the courses. Adjuncts have neither the time nor the authority to change and improve the basic courses they are assigned. The slow but constant improvement of the courses and curricula, part of the teaching task of the permanent faculty, cannot be undertaken by adjuncts. When the adjunct *sottoposti* teach most of the students, the courses remain static, and the university, even when the teaching is excellent, does less than its best. No one can be satisfied with that.

Honors College

Honors education is an issue of growing importance in the academy. Colleges and universities have begun to advertise their programs, in part to draw high SAT/ACT students, in part to draw more students of all types, in part to increase their rankings in the *U.S. News and World Report* annual ladder of esteem. In addition to puff, universities are investing money in honors programs to make them better, whatever that is deemed to mean, and more visible, which may be more important. Trawling for funds has come to the point where sizable donations have been received, enabling donors to name the college after their families. The newly christened Ogden Honors College at LSU is one example among many.[21] Where money is involved, actual importance may be assumed.

Honors colleges mean different things to different constituencies. For politicians who are constantly cutting college appropriations, honors college means more education for less money. Even though honors colleges may be spending more money, they are enhancing the prospects of the politicians' constituents' kids, and they are doing so more cheaply than it would cost to sustain a first-class university across the board. For parents, helicopter and otherwise, honors colleges provide their children with an edge, a leg up the ladder to the next level of education. Parents understand credential creep and know that their children will need graduate education of some sort: an honors degree will help them get it. Universities find honors colleges enormously valuable advertisements. A prominent honors college allows a university to appear to be academically stronger than it really is. This is the blowfish technique. What works in nature will certainly work in culture.

And then there are the students. In theory, of course, honors courses and honors colleges offer opportunities for intellectual engagement. In reality, students overwhelmingly view honors colleges as the way to fly first class. Begin with the perks: honors students live in honors dorms, away from the hoi polloi and with better accommodations all around. Beyond that, honors students get first crack at summer programs, internships, and conferences. These opportunities are few, but the ones there are go to honors students. Honors students also get priority in scheduling. They get the classes they want when they want them, and in an era when universities are cutting costs by cutting classes, honors students alone do not feel the pinch. Finally, honors students agree with their parents on one thing, at least: they have a better chance of getting into a graduate or professional school and a much better chance of getting a scholarship. One author spent twenty years teaching honors at LSU. In that time, only a single honors student failed to get into graduate school somewhere. Since it costs the same to fly first class as it does to fly coach, or baggage hold, why not go honors?

The modern boom in honors education, particularly at large state universities, has come from unwise and excessive dedication to equality. Everyone must be represented at a public institution. The only way to do that is to let almost everyone in. Only then can the proper amount of inclusion be demonstrated to voter and judge alike. But this policy runs afoul of a simple human truth, enunciated by Gilbert and Sullivan: "If everybody's somebody, then nobody's anybody." Beyond inclusion, there is the growing problem of money. Tightening state budgets mean less money for universities, which cannot afford to improve or even support every area of study. Too many kids, not enough professors; in some schools, not enough classrooms. The combination of public disinvestment in universities and the need to stand out from the crowd has made honors colleges a perfect refuge for those who need to excel (and appear to excel) in order to move on to graduate and professional education.

For Cardinal Robert, honors colleges were irrelevant. The entire University of Paris was an honors college. President Jefferson and Cardinal Newman created universities in the Robertian model; they were intimate learning communities and there was no need for an honors program. America, however, is a land of social giantism. Universities in the twentieth century grew well beyond what the cardinals had in mind. As universities expanded, particularly state institutions, they became more impersonal, and the education offered became merely basic. Take the kids in; push the kids on; get them through the routine stuff; get them out. Make room for the next cohort. Honors colleges have emerged as the antidote to that.

Honors programs come in two flavors. One is honors courses in departments. History departments offer honors American history. Biology departments offer honors biology. Mathematics departments offer honors calculus. These courses are sometimes quite different from the regular offerings, and sometimes they are the same, only more so. Calculus, is, after all, calculus, and the Civil War ends the same way in honors courses as it does in large lecture sections. The other alternative is honors programs or colleges. They offer a variety of honors courses not found in the departments. Some courses are interdisciplinary, such as an examination of the history, politics, economics, and aesthetics of the international art market. Here the honors program draws faculty from several departments. Interdisciplinary honors programs have no traditional canon of accepted courses, like Shakespeare in English or calculus in mathematics. Courses in the interdisciplinary honors programs can cover anything, and somewhere they do. Imagine, for example, a course where Shakespeare is considered in the context of public obligations, sacred and secular. Students would examine the nature of public authority, from the *Oresteia* and Aristotle through Aquinas and Shakespeare to Benjamin Nathan Cardozo, Karl Popper, and George Orwell.[22]

Honors colleges also offer boutique courses, which, increasingly, have come to dominate honors offerings. These courses are not interdisciplinary, nor are they team-taught. They frequently consist of topics that the department has rejected. In both interdisciplinary and boutique courses, honors colleges offer something denied to the vast bulk of university students. In return for limiting enrollment, honors colleges offer a good deal of personal interaction between professor and student and substantial emphasis on communication skills.

In general, two things emerge from this mélange of honors courses. Exclusivity is a constantly present but never acknowledged value. Beyond that, honors programs have no traditional canon of courses that must be offered—every math department must offer calculus—and there is no history of what is an appropriate honors course. It's all ad hoc in the honors world, especially with the boutique courses. You make it up as you go on. The emphasis is always on imagination and innovation on the part of the faculty and intellectual agility and communication skills on the part of the students. No surprise that everyone wants in.

Critics may well be skeptical about formal honors courses, but there is one place where honors delivers everything promised and more besides. The sociologist Ray Oldenburg coined the term "third place" to describe locations and environments different from home and work. Home and work are highly structured; the third place is entirely free form. The emphasis there is on spontaneity and sparkle, not duty and diligence. They are not class, they are not dorm, they are not beer pong, they are not the part-time job. Honors colleges form an extended third place.[23] For some people, the third place is a beer after work, but for honors college students it is a way of life. Honors colleges form a wonderful club for smart people, the only one on campus. It's hardly surprising that honors students cherish the experience.

Back before World War II, deans didn't worry much about honors programs because there weren't any. Colleges and universities creamed off less than 10 percent of a high school cohort. The students were relatively similar in background education; they came from propertied families, and had finished high school with fairly good grades. Honors courses weren't needed because there was no huge gap between the Gentleman's C and the "On-to-Graduate-School A." The regular courses fit every student well enough.

Indeed, during the Depression (and before), kids normally went to work at age 15 or 16 or so. They dropped out of school, after the tenth grade or perhaps even the eighth. For most African Americans, high schools weren't even available; eighth grade was about as far as you could go, unless you went to live with a relative in a large city or a state capital. Colleges drawing from a relatively homogeneous economic stratum found little need for honors courses.

Then came the war. Almost 16 million young and not-so-young Americans participated, and the G.I. Bill was designed as part of the general social payment owed them for their time in service. The G.I. Bill was available to all, whether you were starting in fifth grade or graduate school. The vets who flooded onto campus were different from the kids. They were serious students with well-defined career goals; many were married, and most felt a nagging urgency to finish up, get a job, go to law school, go to med school, set up households. They created a new social and intellectual environment on campus. Professors began to discuss honors courses as a way of dealing with the suddenly extensive gap between the well prepared and the marginal students.

Further, by the 1950s, a college degree had become the social and employment standard. It became important to graduate; but a few students needed to learn something in the process. They were going on to graduate school. This kind of outstanding student attended every single college. The story goes that Cleanth Brooks, after he left LSU for Yale, was asked about the LSU students he had taught. The best at LSU were as good as any at Yale, Brooks replied.[24] Well, in that case, shouldn't the best students at LSU get a Yale course or two? There were plenty of courses for those who needed a bit more help; how about something for those who needed a bit more course?

Beginning in the fifties, and increasing in the next decades, honors courses and programs sprang up almost everywhere. College enrollment did not drop after the initial surge of veterans; it continued to rise. Gaps in preparation and attitude between the best students and the run of the mill did not diminish either. If honors courses made sense in 1950, they made the same sense to the same degree in 1960 and 1970 and beyond. Honors programs became an academic adornment that most colleges had and a few, like Arizona State, boasted about continuously. Honors colleges, like the universities themselves, differed widely from place to place. Because of these variations, we will use one university as an illuminating anecdote.

Louisiana State University and Agricultural and Mechanical College received its modern imprint from Governor Huey P. Long.[25] Long was an autocrat in state government and a populist in social policy. He wanted LSU to be open to every high school graduate in the state, even those who could not read.[26] Open enrollment became a tradition at LSU. The gap between students who were prepared and those who were not grew in the decades after the Depression, to become, to say the least, genuinely stupendous.

Huey Long also made education at LSU virtually free. If you lived at home, a hundred bucks would cover most of an academic year. Long tied the university to the people of Louisiana, to such an extent that Huey's brother, Earl K. Long, remarked that a wise politician did not interfere with LSU, or with the main state prison at Angola. For poor people in a poor state, LSU was the high road to opportunity and prosperity.

Open enrollment, designed to give everyone a chance at a university education, inevitably meant that a large number of unqualified students, along with a small number of gifted students, arrived on campus.[27] As LSU's enrollment continued to rise in the 1960s, some administrators suggested the university needed a program for the best and brightest. Couldn't just leave them in the lurch! In 1967–1968, with support from one of Baton Rouge's leading families, the Sternbergs, LSU established an honors program.[28]

The honors program was based on the Rhodes College version of the Columbia University program, Contemporary Civilization (CC) and Humanities. The Columbia sequence grew out of a course established in 1917, War Aims. Peace came before War Aims was fully established. Still, President Nicholas Murray Butler, who had set it up in the first place, wanted to keep it. Columbia resisted the temptation to rename the course Peace Aims, none of which were ever achieved, and moved it instead toward a course in political philosophy. CC and humanities were interdisciplinary courses, defying the trend toward disciplinary specialization that had begun after the Civil War. Over time, CC and humanities became a two-semester sequence. The Columbia program seemed just the thing for the two-year honors survey at LSU. At LSU and at Columbia as well, the purpose of the sequence was to give the undergraduates a grasp of the Western culture in which they lived.

LSU Honors was designed as an interdisciplinary program apart from departmental honors. The faculty remained housed in their departments, and the honors director had to cajole the chair and faculty in order to get his staff. When the director was an effective negotiator, the honors program flourished, but "if not, not."[29] By the late nineteen-seventies, "not" dominated. The director then lacked the charisma to charm the chairs. He had a hard time getting faculty. The number of courses declined. Even the second half of the freshman survey was in danger of collapse.

And then the cavalry arrived, just as in the movies. In the 1981–1982 academic year, a new arts dean decided to boost the honors program.[30] He looked for a new honors director. The usual sprinkling of earnest humanists applied. The dean's choice, though, was Professor Bill Seay, a somewhat skeptical psychology professor with exceptional administrative skills. Even so, nobody expected much to change.

The new director kept what he had inherited, in pedagogy and intellectual content. The freshman survey remained a team-taught, six-credit-hour course that combined lecture and seminar sections. The emphasis remained on the humanities, especially literature, art, philosophy, and history. The first semester covered Greece and Rome, the second medieval Europe. Professor Seay also added courses. He expanded the freshman survey to four semesters: twenty credit hours over two years. The sophomore year covered the Renaissance to the modern world. Taken together, LSU Honors sequence provided a coherent introduction to the modern Western world.

After a couple of years on the job, Professor Seay became convinced that honors needed to be an independent college rather than a satrapy within the arts college. Without independence, honors could not expand into the sciences. Professor Seay managed to persuade the provost to create a separate honors college. It would have its own building and dormitories and a faculty on permanent loan from the departments. It all came together over a single summer. It's always easier to build a new niche than reform another one.[31]

Dean Seay's greatest asset in running LSU Honors was his relationship with the faculty. He knew when to leave people alone. The honors faculty were all volunteers. He tried to place them in teaching situations where they could prosper. Most did prosper, both as teachers and as scholars. And most honors faculty stayed on in the college as long as they could. The honors college exemplified Cardinal Newman's ideals of faculty collegiality. And it was fun teaching there.

In university reform, and perhaps elsewhere as well, ontogeny really does recapitulate phylogeny. Dean Seay at LSU did just about what Cardinal Robert had done at Paris. Both kept what was already in place and built upon that. Both paid primary attention to courses and faculty and tried to bring order to a program that was still coming together. Even the scale was similar: a dozen or more faculty (masters) and a couple of hundred students (scholars).

At the turn of the millennium, Dean Seay retired, and the honors college began to slip. A great many faculty left with Dean Seay. The interdisciplinary freshman/sophomore sequence continued to be taught, but the sections were smaller, and the new administration emphasized boutique courses taught by individual faculty members. By 2015, the interdisciplinary sequence was gone, and about a dozen boutique courses were about all that remained. Ironically, as the LSU honors college became intellectually less vibrant and diverse, it became financially more secure. It is now the Ogden Honors College. Honors has no set curriculum, no courses that must be taught (such as Shakespeare in English). So huge curricular changes are not unexpected.

LSU, with its scores of students, differs dramatically from the nation's premier program, Barrett College at Arizona State University. Founded in 1988, Barrett has grown like bamboo in the monsoon, reaching 5,400 students by 2015. That's the size of a state university. Barrett offers honors housing, honors courses, priority registration, access to internships, and an honors degree, pretty much what every honors college offers. The basic course at Barrett, an un–Newmanlike interdisciplinary sequence, is called The Human Event, with an emphasis on diversity, primarily geographical and gender. Every Barrett freshman takes a section of The Human Event, which lasts a year. Beyond that are scores of boutique courses, which, in the nature of things, range from something solid to fashionable fluff. Today, most honors programs resemble Barrett's. The emphasis is on cultural diversity, designer courses, and student preferment. The old Columbia sequence, built around Newman's interdisciplinary plan, seems hopelessly quaint. But there's no going back in academic fashion. Barrett is the model for the immediate future.

Barrett's success shows that honors is a growing academic phenomenon. As universities get bigger, honors gets bigger. As the job market gets tighter, honors-based student preferment becomes more important. It may be facetious to call a college the size of Barrett a "small college within a great university," but it is clear that for students who can manage it, honors is the only way to fly. An honors degree is too valuable a credential.

Identity Curricula

In our time, the "glass of fashion and the mould of form" in public affairs is identity politics, where loyalty depends on who you are rather than what you think. You are your race. You are your ethnicity. You are your religion, your nationality, your gender, your sexual orientation. Outside the university, identity politics has produced electoral blocs and group spokespeople. Within the university, it has produced identity curricula.

Identity politics works in part as a holdover from the immigrant experience, and in part as the culmination of several civil rights movements. It is based on the notion that political power and social justice can only prevail if everybody in the group sticks together, votes together, and marries within the tribe. That can produce general acceptance by all. But what happens when the kids go to college, as they must, regardless of race, creed, or ethnicity? Do they, ought they, leave their identity behind when they enter the ivory tower? Never: identity must be reinforced there. The university is the seedbed for the next generation of leaders, who cannot lead the group unless they identify with the group.

Currently prominent among identity courses are Black, Gender, LGBT, Asian, Hispanic, Native American/First Nations Studies. Not every research university has all, but all have some. The list will grow. New groups will make their claims, and established groups will appear on new campuses. The faculty rarely doubt, at least out loud, the academic legitimacy of identity courses and programs.

These identity studies departments, institutes, and programs have a good deal in common. They are all interdisciplinary. Professors include those in literature, history, and contemporary politics, along with art, music, cuisine, and religion, in a bouillabaisse designed to convey the nature of a particular culture: our people are a great people, unjustly put upon, but now coming into our own. Professors in the social sciences brandish battalions of studies documenting group progress and continuing disadvantage. In identity courses, professors emphasize, enhance, and distinguish the group from all of the others.

The chair and the faculty determine the exact mixture of these academic disciplines within the identity group program. They do so with one ear cocked to hear politicians' pronouncements. Identity courses within the university are frequently influenced by identity politics without, where the action really lies. The emphasis is not upon a homogenized America but upon preserving cultural differences.

Everyone acknowledges that group injustices underlie identity politics programs. A therapeutic society is always sensitive to things that are unfair, and it eventually responds sympathetically to assertions of injustice. The academic programs are simultaneously a public recognition of the legitimacy of grievances and a standing effort to make things better. Most Americans take group distinctiveness for granted. Identity programs focus on those things that define the group and on the group's position in society. It is the institutional version of the talking cure.

Group studies, once established in the university, inevitably move in one of two general directions. They can reinforce the emotional heat that led to their establishment in the first place. In this case, the program remains quite close to the appropriate political groups outside the university. The group studies program finds its role in consciousness raising. The program becomes a sounding board for grievances. Or it may go the other way, becoming more academic. The emphasis shifts from plaint to pedagogy, from being impassioned to being informed. The curriculum may be grounded in ethnology, demography, history, literature, sociology, or constitutional law.[32] A serious course of study can emerge from each academic emphasis. Ethnic studies, gender studies, black studies, et al., can take a place beside other established area studies. It has happened at Harvard.

Whatever road they take, identity group programs can never stray far from the theme of past exclusion. In modern America, past exclusion demands present remedy, usually social, always legal. The current political climate gives legitimacy to lawsuits against discrimination.[33] For every lawsuit, there are a hundred public and a thousand private accusations that race, gender, orientation, or ethnicity swayed a corporate or academic decision. So group identity programs will continue in universities for at least the next couple of generations.[34] The research university pays close attention to the prevailing social culture.[35]

The Appearance of Bias

The university often resembles a drum. Political racket from within the university is heard all over the place.[36] Universities are extremely good at expressing political polarization. Decibels increase the farther from the ivory tower the sounds travel.

The university itself generally ignores the racket, even in cases of egregious display.[37] Professors have to believe in something, after all, whether secular or transcendental, and the First Amendment protects their uttering it. The university believes in the First Amendment, though the general public does not. Academic freedom is a genuine university value; it is one of the major differences between the university and the larger world outside.

All of the above is well known and is illustrated periodically on television and in court reports. Less acknowledged is the somewhat chastening reality that students do not always pay much attention to professors. Exceptions do occur, of course. Students attend raptly when professors discuss the test, or grading, or when they present technical information that everyone in class needs to know. Generally though, during class, students are on their laptops, playing games, browsing Facebook, doing homework for other classes, and in fundamental ways not being in class at all.[38] Students now are not much interested in being in a single place, doing a single thing, and doing it seriously. They wish to be everywhere simultaneously, and technology allows them to have the electronic illusion that they are.

Moreover, simple prudence prohibits rattling the professor's cage, though students are young and do commit unprofessional and provocative behavior. It's not that they actively dislike the faculty. They just try to coexist. Students are rarely interested in faculty political opinion. Most students are apolitical; others are so deeply committed politically (usually to a single issue) that a professor expressing a contrary opinion does not move them. In general, the students practice a live-and-let-live policy vis-à-vis the faculty. With that attitude, the ships can pass peacefully in the night.

But there is an exception. If group grievances are mentioned, the professor is challenging the very core of the students' identity. Students become resentful and offended. But identity resentment, especially at a rolling boil, is not the same as learning, and the business of the university is learning. American research universities often face student demands for the institution to take a radical stand on current issues. But the campus cannot become an ongoing protest or a revolutionary training camp; those conditions were precisely what Cardinal Robert was trying to reform. As long as bombs do not replace books, the research university can remain what it was founded to be, a place of inquiry, creativity, knowledge, and freedom.

Outside the university, the drum has sounded so long and so loudly that liberal academic bias has become a social cliché. Over time, whether they were delighted or outraged, people have come to believe in the existence of academic liberal bias. Those public attitudes get reinforced from time to time. In this digital age, some student takes a phone video of an especially dreadful professorial rant and posts it on social media. It goes viral and is replayed on news channels. This produces the standard charges of left-wing bias, along with comments on student indoctrination. In due course, the particular news story about academic bias becomes stale. Months later, a new video appears and the news cycle repeats itself. Things rarely get to the Ward Churchill level, but, at the same time, the sense of a pervasive liberal academic attitude is continually renewed. People tend to see academic bias as part of the cultural landscape. It's no longer news in the sense of being something new; it's news in the sense of the same old song being sung again.

Experience

Justice Oliver Wendell Holmes, Jr., wrote that the "life of the law has not been logic: it has been experience."[39] The clear implication of Holmes's observation is that universities constantly change as knowledge and experience demand. Part of the change involves the things taught. Western civilization courses are now seen as politically incorrect, and in many schools the subject is no longer offered. Latin and Greek do not have the audience that once they had. STEM has replaced the classics in public esteem, and computers have become essential to every discipline. Academic curricula, like the law, moves toward intellectual coherence and supports important social values.[40] In a startling reversal of Gresham's Law, the intellectually solid outlasts the merely gaudy. But the intellectually serious can vanish as well. Classics courses, along with all the beauty of Greek and Roman language, literature, and philosophy, are making a slow but steady retreat. Now the classics are taught to a few; in decades to come they will be taught to almost no one. There is a time, saith the preacher, for wisdom, and there is also a time for wisdom to be lost.

• FIVE •

MOOCs
Technology and Money

The business show *MONEY* used to begin with the confident assertion, "Even when they say it's not, it's always about money."[1] And, of course, it always is. The program headline fits universities well, though they frequently pretend to be above mere money, unlike those worldly ventures that must satisfy customers and make ends meet. The *MONEY* headline seems especially poignant now, with student costs growing and external support flagging. Money dominates the management of all universities. Continual endowment drives, appeals to legislators, scholarly grants, and stiff tuition hikes never bring in enough to cover present costs and future plans. It has been that way since the thirteenth century. Colleges do go broke, but more often, they trudge along, with needs unmet and opportunities unrecognized.[2]

Money is not alone in being miraculous; technology also promises to change everything. The current craze in technology is the Internet. If social media can reach billions of people, surely online education can reach millions of students. The economies of scale promise to solve most university problems. Could (cheap) electronic communication repair, even remake, the entire academy, from the Ivies to the smallest branch of the most obscure community college?

Although universities all over America struggle with money problems, the problems are too varied for us to illustrate with a single representative institution. Nor can we point to a single educational-technology fix that has solved the fiscal crunch in any college budget office. So even if one size does not fit anything, we fall back on two specific examples, a state university that shows the depth of public disinvestment in higher education, and a recent candidate for fiscal savior: the Massive Open Online Course, or MOOC. Taken together, they may illuminate some of universities' fiscal problems and the chances, however remote, of a solution.

Aristotle warned against generalizing from the particular. It is commonplace among economists that the plural of anecdote is not data.[3] Keeping Aristotle and Brimmer in mind, we illustrate rather than prove. Cognizant of the variety of academic institutions, we offer one observation and report three reformist ideas. Start with the ideas. Many critics outside the university think that changing the law will change the university. Pass legislation, and you can change anything. Further, many believe that online education is the wave of the academic future. Electronic efficiencies will solve the fiscal crisis. Finally, the electrons democratize universities by increasing outreach to those previously excluded. These ideas exhibit a characteristic American optimism: universities really *can* be fixed—and paid for. It's just a question of how. And the observation? Money, particularly its lack, affects universities in several ways: the rising costs of education and research, the rising student costs in debt and time, and increasing public disinvestment in higher education. Consequently, proposed academic reforms, whether electronic or administrative, deal more with money than with excellence in teaching and research. And so we begin three chapters on technology with a look at money.

Debt and Disinvestment

We remember the time before. Then, the state university was the pride of the people, and the Golden Door to social mobility. Johnny and Jane came marching home to opportunity provided by the G.I. Bill. The university seemed closer to the citizens. Those were the days.[4]

They began to slip away in the nineteen-seventies, perhaps in public response to student protests. By the nineties, with student protests a fading nightmare, the distance between school and citizen did not diminish. It increased, as the costs of education grew beyond the range of private budgets. So students borrowed money and worked to put themselves through larger, more impersonal schools. By the twenty-first century, university costs had grown larger than the states could afford, even with federal help. State universities, once icons of public pride, now have become icons of public burden.

An old Supreme Court case from 1899, *Cumming v. Richmond County Board of Education*, illustrates the dilemmas arising from the eternal equation of more public functions than public funds.[5] The school board of

Richmond County, Georgia, decided to reallocate the funds available. They had the same amount of money as the year before, but that had not been enough to educate everyone then and would not be so again. Georgia, of course, then maintained segregated schools, which were surely separate but far from equal. The school board decided to close the "colored" high school and use the funds saved to open enough elementary schools to educate, to some extent, anyway, every black child. The white high school remained open. Some African American parents sued, claiming discrimination under the Fourteenth Amendment. The school board replied that it had made a reasonable educational decision. It did not have enough money to educate everyone through high school. Better to provide some education for all than more education for some. The Supreme Court held that the school board's decision was constitutional. Public officials can spend the money as they think best.

Things have not changed much since Mr. Cumming sued Richmond County. Politicians trying to finance public education face several interrelated problems. There's not enough money, of course. The cost of a university education has risen faster than inflation for decades.[6] Student debt has grown beyond what the kids and their folks can pay. The global amount has climbed to more than $1.3 trillion, and average individual debt has reached $28,000. None of these trends seem to be going away or even really slowing down.

As the state lowers its support for higher education, public universities have increased their fees and tuition to match the loss. The equation seems simple enough. The state transfers its deficit, a few millions at a time, from its budget to the collective budgets of parents and students. In Louisiana, one example among many, the fiscal 2013–2014 budget cut about $28–29 million from the LSU appropriations, more or less the amount LSU received from tuition and fee increases. Much, if not most, student debt originates in state fiscal policy. These problems make every policy decision on funding universities seem undesirable, indefensible, and necessary.

The Louisiana numbers are scary but not unusual.[7] Begin with the LSU total budget for 2013, which was about $445 million. This total does not include athletics, which has its own budget and turns a profit. It does include undergraduate and graduate/professional education. Although half a billion is a large number, it is comparatively modest for the amount of education it buys. Half a billion counts heavily in a strained state budget, or it would if the state were actually paying it. But Louisiana is not paying the full half a billion, or even half of the half billion. The state pays around 138 million, slightly more than half of half the total half-billion-dollar university budget. This number has plunged from where it was in 2008, when Louisiana paid 230 million to support the LSU campus at Baton Rouge. Of course, in 2008, the state budget was healthier and education cost a little less.

To be sure, $138 million cannot be called peanuts and would be a serious strain on the state budget if the state had actually paid it out without getting anything back. But the state did get a refund in the monies paid by LSU for pension contributions, workman's compensation, and the like. That refund came to about $128 million, making the net state contribution to LSU's administrative budget around $10 million. In future years, the numbers will be a bit different, and some fine year, maybe, the state will make a profit on LSU. That's the way to manage a budget.

So, what is the impact of current university financing trends on the students? The dimensions of the problem ought to sober every soul. Public university tuition nationally has risen over 125 percent since Bill Clinton's day. At Louisiana State University, the student tuition bill rose from $172 million in 2008 to $289 million in 2013. Those numbers, both local and national, catch the eye. That's real money, as Everett Dirksen used to say.[8] Quietly moving revenue obligations was once derisively called The Old Army Game. The state cannot forever transfer its fiscal obligations to kids and parents.[9]

Nonetheless, fiscal pressure on student, state, and school will only grow. States will not cease disinvesting in public universities. Increasing health care costs (Medicaid) means that states must ration the educational dollar. The goal of equal opportunity in a knowledge society becomes more distant. *Cumming v. Richmond County Board of Education* may be forgotten, but it is not gone.

The core of the fiscal problem is simple. In an industrialized economy, unlike traditional societies, people are expensive and goods are cheap. Education adds to the expense, making universities and hospitals the costliest institutions around. University education is inherently labor intensive, requiring expensive specialized "knowledge workers," frequently called faculty. Nothing can be done about that. Manufacturers increase productivity by churning out more things with fewer people. Universities, so far, at least, have only been able to automate at the margins, with language and mathematics labs. And even those labs require IT specialists and tutors for the students, who need a lot of help. The results from the labs have been mixed, to be as upbeat as possible. Colleges remain high-cost operations, and the better the college, the higher the cost.

Already labor intensive, universities seem likely to suffer ever-greater fiscal problems. Tighter state budgets mean a good deal of competition for the public dollar. Senator Lamar Alexander of Tennessee has said, publicly and often, that the crisis in state university budgets has a single cause, and that is Medicaid. This opinion is so politically inflammatory that other politicians will not even acknowledge having heard it. And no wonder. Senator Alexander predicts that Americans will face the choice between treating the current uninsured or preparing the next generation to compete in the globalized knowledge economy. The costs of each may limit the services of the other. But neither public health nor public education can be abandoned.[10]

Unfortunately, there is no cheap form of higher education, and there never has been. Higher education is not like generic grocery-store labels or off-brand gasoline. Nobody can get it for you wholesale. There is only one possible bargain. The main public university in every state is the best academic bargain. These cost a bit more than the compass colleges, but they are a lot better, and their degrees have a national resonance. You can go from a state university to a major law, medical, or graduate school. Nonetheless, even if it's the best educational bang for the buck, state universities cost a lot of bucks.

In his fiscal analysis, Senator Alexander may have been too modest. Legacy costs, often called entitlements, both in health care and pensions, will grow faster than state income. The most pessimistic have already begun to wonder if a state can go bankrupt. Almost everyone assumes that public disinvestment in universities is permanent. Perhaps cost shifting from state to student is also permanent. The new normal is discouraging.

Distance Learning

Distance learning is not new. Universities have long had courses conducted by correspondence. It's a cumbersome process. Professors send course outlines and assignments on paper to students, who reply on paper, in the form of completed quizzes, essays, examinations, and reports. Every student question requires a letter or email, and the answer requires another. Neither the student nor the professor feels really good about the results. Most students have never taken a correspondence course, and those who do usually take only a couple or so. Part of the reason is supply. Universities have a limited repertoire of basic courses, which are the only ones that the university accountants say are financially feasible to offer via correspondence.

Still, correspondence courses can fit special circumstances. We remember a correspondence student who had left college to get married. But after a couple of years she was ready to go back; she took a correspondence course in history to raise her GPA and re-enter college. It worked as planned. She graduated and then earned two masters' degrees. In all of that time, more than a decade, she took only the one correspondence course. Neither of us has known a single student who preferred correspondence, whether snail or email, to attendance. The system has its uses, but no one loves it.

Technology has wonderfully transformed distance learning, first with audio and videodiscs and now with the Internet. The discs made distance learning more entertaining and improved the variety of material being offered. The Internet has added real-time connectivity. Students can ask questions and get answers, sometimes finding the personal touch of a classroom in a distant location. The student can see, hear, and talk to the professor, now and then, anyway, which makes online learning simultaneously immediate and distant.

The Internet can also bring distance learning up to scale. Change occurs in the size of the operation, while the things being created/manufactured or sold, whether lectures or widgets, remain the same. The economies of scale cut production and marketing costs, making it cheaper to do what you're doing the more you do it. Online education promises to do the same thing. A course is more efficient if more students take it.

Administrators at brick-and-mortar colleges have already found that expedient. Just increase the size of the lecture hall. Add a few more kids. Go from fifty to a hundred, a hundred to four hundred, four hundred to a thousand. But as class size increases, so does the student's feeling of alienation and anonymity. She has become only a seat number. Ironically, social media, which can be genuinely anonymous, softens that impression of distance. Skype and chat rooms can seem intimate. Since the online student is not immersed in the classroom crowd, she may feel freer to ask questions and offer comments. The student can imagine that she is part of a small virtual community with the instructor.[11] The illusion of intimacy, nurtured by social media, can carry over to online education.[12] That sense of intimacy is not an insignificant pedagogical virtue.

Alas, online courses have a lot of defects. Distance learning, even in correspondence courses, has always raised questions of student preparation, student performance, and student identity and student cheating.[13] Whose work appears in the professor's mailbox, physical or electronic?[14] After all, every student wants help, needs the credit, and has friends or money.

Universities have tended to overlook these problems because the correspondence clientele was small. But problems grow when clientele grows. Online course scale raises all the usual problems of distance learning a couple of orders of magnitude.

Other problems with online courses include the roles of faculty and the university. Who owns the intellectual property invested in an online course? Both the university and the professor have legitimate claims. There is more. Professors must ensure course quality, and their teaching skills can be stretched to the limit. Electronic courses reach so many that assessment becomes a matter of profit and public relations. There is more, and that is academic credit for online courses. Universities usually offer academic credit only to students already enrolled. More yet: How can a university offer to broadcast a *free* online course, undercutting its own campus offering? Finally, there is the problem of failure. Most on-campus students pass most of their courses most of the time. Students in some online classes fail much more often than they pass and drop out even more often than they fail. Student wastage on this scale concerns both the institution and the public. And it should. Having the kids on campus can't solve all academic problems, but having them at a distance makes things worse. Still, the advantages in scale, outreach, and finance are enticing enough that administrators have developed protocols to regulate online courses and degree programs. Every college catalog already includes courses and programs that are all or mostly online.

Online education also reinforces two long-standing university myths. The first concerns those who *should* be students yet are not. Out there, who knows where, but out there somewhere, languish thousands and thousands and thousands of people longing to come to the university.[15] But they can't. The high cost of education, job and domestic responsibilities, arbitrary admission standards, subtle quotas, elitist prejudices, all keep these deserving students out.[16]

The second myth is like the first, though it deals with the single genius rather than the merely ignored. Out there somewhere is the brightest kid in the world, someone so creative that she will change the entire culture. The next Steve Jobs. The next Albert Einstein. The next Florence Nightingale. The next Al Capone, whose extraordinary managerial skills should be taught in business courses. And that young person is not in college. Silly rules stand in the way, or perhaps it's money, or maybe ethnic background, but something keeps her from being a student. So compelling is this belief that it has been made into movies, such as *Good Will Hunting*. Hollywood doesn't lie, does it? Everyone has a story about someone they knew or might have known or could have known who is kept out. In modern America, anything that should be true is true. The plural of *anecdote* may not be *data*, but it is frequently *belief*. A couple of examples, true or not, wield a charm that is denied to rational analysis.

These two myths have enchanted professors and the public for the last century or so.[17] After all, the myths are inclusive, democratic, decent, and hopeful. Surely colleges should act upon them. And they do.[18] One result of these attitudes is college entrance exams, which were originally supposed to widen the pool of applicants. Another result is the open university movement, which flourished in the decades after World War II.[19] The open university offers admission to anyone. It teaches courses anywhere and in anything, more or less by anybody. An open university deemphasizes exams, curricula, prerequisites, and credentials. It is free, or mostly so, and its egalitarian views have gone on to animate Wikipedia. If society could only open up, knowledge and enlightenment would spread to people not traditionally thought able to absorb it, or not traditionally allowed to try. The G.I. Bill (1944) embodied the ideals of extensive admission. It transformed America in the hoped-for direction of equality and inclusion. These two myths created an environment that allowed both professor and institution to support educational outreach. Those kids are out there. It's our duty to open the university doors to them. It's the right thing to do.

The Development of MOOCs

For several decades, universities have had a love affair with computer-based learning. As far back as 1960, the University of Illinois at Champaign set up PLATO (Programmed Logic for Automated Teaching Systems), which could manage up to a thousand students, each learning lessons independently. PLATO thrived, evolved, and remains; it is the longest-running university-based computer learning system in the world. Other universities also ventured into the brave new world of electrons. In 1969, Michigan, Michigan State, and Wayne State universities interconnected their mainframes in order to share instructional use of computers. Besides these rather niche educational forays, many universities began studying how to evolve their regular courses into online formats. The rapidly developing market for personal computers helped. Indeed, online courses were developed at approximately the speed as the personal computer movement. By 1985, Nova Southeastern University in Florida was awarding its first accredited online doctoral degree in computer and information sciences. The University of Phoenix Online was born in 1989; suddenly students everywhere were able to earn bachelor's and master's degrees through their computers.

The electron snowball really picked up speed through higher education then. Universities, businessmen, public servants: they all saw the future, and it was calling them to invest in courses offered over the Internet. Online higher education would help American universities achieve their highest pedagogical and social goals. Professors could improve their courses to educate students better. And they could reach many, many more students: those millions yearning to be free of their blue collars. Those presently left out could be brought into the life of the mind. It goes without saying that some cannier, economic-minded individuals expected online education to help universities achieve financial goals as well. Since the general public was no longer entirely convinced that a college education was good value for the money, education could be made less expensive. What if we could teach thousands of students in a single course? That would be a real bonus.

It did not take long for some enterprising professors to propose such gigantic courses. One day in 1993, Professor James O'Donnell, a philosopher at the University of Pennsylvania, was standing in his shower, wondering how to spice up his course on St. Augustine.[20] He had a genuine inspiration: why not present the course, via the Internet, to anybody in the world who wanted to take it? No one had done that before. It would be a real innovation. Here was born a Massive Open Online Course (MOOC),[21] which probably surprised the deans at Penn with its enthusiastic reception. Professor O'Donnell enrolled five hundred students from all around the globe, including places outside of Philadelphia.[22] It's a wonder that the University of Pennsylvania didn't exhort more of its professors to go big or go home. The Augustine MOOC remained one-of-a-kind there at the turn of the millennium.

Others in higher education thought Big Learning was an idea worth pursuing, though. Gigantic online courses, and gigantic collections of regular online courses, were beginning to become popular with the open source movement. In the nineties, academics pushed the idea of sharing resources freely. According to David Wiley, who was at the Utah State University Center for Open and Sustainable Learning, the goal was "technology-enabled, open provision of educational resources for consultation, use and adaptation by a community of users for non-commercial purposes."[23] Creative Commons was founded as a non-profit to publish and distribute academic content. Much of its sharing took place over the Internet. MIT began offering its OpenCourseWare, aiming "to publish nearly every university course for free public access for noncommercial use." Massive Open Online Courses offered real possibilities for more free academic outreach.

The next step was to go even bigger, to a group of universities putting out multiple large-enrollment online courses. In 2000, Columbia University started Fathom, a consortium including Chicago and Michigan. The online courses that it offered lost money, and the whole venture ended in 2003. But the Fathom idea would survive. At the same time, Yale, Princeton, and Stanford created AllLearn, an electronic consortium that was formally nonprofit. Just as well to admit that up front. The whole thing also lost money, no surprise there, folding in 2006.

These early efforts at bulk online education ended when course and cost problems exceeded expectations. But the true dreamers in the world of MOOCs continued to tinker. Present failures could not diminish the promise of future success. What professor or administrator could resist electronic educational outreach, with its potentially mass audience? Particularly when it could be highly profitable?

The next iteration in MOOCs came from Stanford University. In 2011, Professor Sebastian Thrun really sized up the Massive Open Online Course. He thought he might teach an artificial intelligence (AI) class with no limits and no costs. He offered this course free to anyone, anywhere. The response was genuinely fabulous. Enrollment took off, eventually reaching about 150,000 people, or at least 150,000 names. The AI course included lectures, demonstrations, explanations of formulae, homework assignments, quizzes, and tests. It was essentially an electronic version of the classroom course. Thrun apparently assumed that the electronic delivery system would change his AI course in scale, but all else would remain the same.

All else did not remain the same. Some of the problems were internal to the course, involving various elements of pedagogy. Pace was a big problem. Thrun moved too slowly for some, too rapidly for most. Moreover, not everyone was at the computer at the same time. Formulae and explanations had to be left up for days. The whole presentation would have benefitted from a studio setting, an editor, and a director. Perhaps a cognitive therapist could have helped as well. And certainly the AI course, like all university education, needed increased repetition of the material offered.[24]

Other instructional problems, though serious, seemed insignificant when compared to issues of scale itself. Professor Thrun's MOOC attracted unprecedented numbers of students, not every one of whom was suitably prepared for the course. Not every student prospered. About a 130,000 dropped out. Many of the 12,000 or so who saw it through to the bitter end failed the course. Only about 1,000 did well, though they did very well, getting perfect or near-perfect grades. About one half of 1 percent really benefitted from the AI course.

The academic wastage was as fabulous as the enrollment. Even the Chinese civil service examinations during the Mandarin period passed a larger percentage than that. Beyond student failure, another serious question emerged: who were these "students"? They had no verifiable identity. And while we're asking questions that must be answered before MOOCs can be taken for credit: who did the students' work? There was no way to tell. Forget those who dropped out: no one did their work. For the thousand-odd who did well, who submitted work under their names or pseudonyms? Professor Thrun's AI course had no student integrity at all; as originally established, it had no possibility of ever having any.[25]

Institutional problems in MOOC-world are equally serious. Just to start somewhere: what kind of credit or certification is earned by those who do well in a MOOC? Stanford University offered a "Statement of Accomplishment" to those who passed the AI course, but no certificate of any sort. It added a specific disclaimer that the MOOC carried no Stanford academic credit, no grade, and did not count toward a Stanford degree. If you wanted credit, you had to enroll in Stanford University (if you could), and take the AI course in person. It is offered on campus, and, to one observer, that campus version seemed uninspiring at best.

Professor Thrun was one of the first to offer a solution to administrative questions about fees and academic credit. He built an institutional framework for his MOOCs. Having declared his AI course a success, in spite of indications to the contrary, Thrun recognized that it needed improved graphics, a better script, and more thoughtful pedagogy. Further, he realized that all MOOCs need a director to turn professors into polished performers. Courses on the Internet require a lot of planning. So he founded Udacity, taken from the words "university" and "audacity." He hoped it would become a new online university.

Udacity offered eight-week courses, basically two in a standard semester. It began with courses in computer science then moved into mathematics and technical courses. By spring 2012, Udacity had six courses and two hundred thousand students enrolled. Things seemed to be going pretty well.

But the difficulties were more numerous and more serious than Thrun had supposed. An institutional framework did not solve them. Begin with the students, who did not necessarily understand how to work with online instruction. Add the absence of human help. A spectacular instance of these problems occurred at San Jose State University (SJSU) in the spring of 2013. Udacity, in conjunction with SJSU, offered three basic mathematics and statistics courses. Students floundered so quickly that the courses had to be suspended. True enough, many of the San Jose State students would be classified as "at risk," but the main impediment was the absence of personal help with the math. The online program alone could not teach the material. The kids needed human instructors also. The problems inherent in a lack of tutoring are built into the MOOCs. Electronic education appears to magnify the risk for at-risk students.

And always there is the problem of money. Professor Thrun hoped that Udacity's courses would remain free and he could retain open enrollment. Thrun was able to keep open enrollment, but he had to monetize the course. Udacity now charges fees, both for courses and exams. Services offered by institutionally based MOOCs have increased in number and expense. The fees have also expanded. What began as a fee for a proctored exam has morphed into a fee for the whole MOOC. Thrun discovered, as others have before him, that education costs money.[26]

In the past few years, Udacity has been moving in the direction of certification courses.[27] The IT course takes less than a year to complete, at a cost of about $200 a month. Certification is offered to students who pass an $89 proctored final. Udacity has also formed a partnership with AT&T, the "Nanodegree" plan, teaching programming skills to students who want to qualify for an entry-level IT job at AT&T. Udacity increasingly resembles the model of Ivy Tech in Indiana. Udacity has not become the free, open online university that Sebastian Thrun once envisioned.

But back then in the golden dawn of MOOCs, Udacity was not alone in churning out MOOCs by the armload.[28] Indeed, it was superseded by bigger fish in the MOOC pool. On May 12, 2012, Harvard and MIT announced edX, a non-profit consortium that would supply a number of MOOCs.[29] Each university pledged $30 million to fund edX. It began with several courses in the fall semester of 2012. The initial offerings were standard engineering courses, based on the current classroom curricula. After beginning with the familiar, edX expanded its menu into the humanities. Here, instructional and evaluation techniques are wildly more complex than is the case on campus. Here, students must be coached and judged more than simply measured. This pedagogy takes time, people, and money.[30] College education always does.

EdX does not offer course or degree credit for its MOOCs. It gives a "grade" for those who finish the course: a minority, if past continues to be prologue. Finishers also receive a certificate of mastery, if they pass. EdX also presents a variety of ways to take its courses. One may audit a course, which is entirely free, with no certificate. One may elect to work for an edX certificate, for a fee, but the Harvard/MIT consortium offers no credit of any sort. Further, edX offers an "XSeries Certificate," again for a fee. The student has to complete a group of "verified courses." Yet again, no college credit. Only when an institution or business voluntarily decides that edX offers a valuable service will college credit be an option. For example, Arizona State University (ASU) has recently partnered with edX to educate students in its "Global Freshman Academy." If a student pays for the $49-a-course "Verified Track Option" of the MOOC, ASU will treat the edX course as a regular academic offering. EdX courses are also officially recognized by the many businesses around the world that use it for a cheap form of employee training. By March 2016, edX was offering more than 700 courses to more than seven *million* students.

EdX has learned some lessons from Udacity's pedagogical challenges. The courses are divided into "weekly learning sequences." These are supplemented by quizzes to evaluate student progress, online tutorials, and even online labs. The edX pedagogical model of small learning modules and instant student assessment is becoming the online standard.

EdX was not designed to make money. That is fortunate because it has not. Harvard and MIT have retained open enrollment, regarding edX as an element of educational outreach.[31] The goal is to reach as many people as possible, including those who are using it for job training. Harvard and MIT do not now plan on offering an electronic profit center. But not every institution can take that attitude.

EdX shows that Harvard and MIT understand the wonderful world of MOOCs. The two universities have neatly avoided the contentious issues of student identity, student integrity, and academic course credit. Harvard and MIT recognized that MOOCs, like all other forms of university instruction, cost money. Having planned for a loss, administrators were not discouraged when losses occurred. In terms of content, the two universities offer a lot of standard courses, reformatted for online presentation, containing the standard intellectual content. They have also created courses designed specifically as MOOCs. Harvard and MIT regard edX as a public service. As a public service, it will probably continue to flourish.

At the time Harvard and MIT were announcing their partnership in 2012, a third leviathan was plunging into the MOOC pool. Coursera, a commercial company with $16 million in initial venture capital, was founded in 2011 by two Stanford University computer scientists, Daphne

Koller and Andrew Ng. They brought together Stanford, Princeton, Michigan, and the University of Pennsylvania. In the spring semester of 2012, Coursera offered 43 courses to 680,000 students.

Coursera had a big opening season. It has grown mightily ever since. In July 2012 it added a dozen new partners, three from abroad — Edinburgh, Toronto, and EPF, a technical university in Lausanne. In America, Coursera added Duke, Virginia, Johns Hopkins, California Institute of Technology, Georgia Tech, Rice, the University of California at San Francisco, Illinois, and Washington. In the fall semester of 2012, Coursera offered more than a hundred MOOCs, which its website described in a catalog that ran to scores of pages. By spring 2016, Coursera was offering 1,580 courses, in ten different languages, to 13.5 *million* students (Coursera calls them "users") from 145 institutions.[32] Coursera has reached takeoff.

If courses alone are the essence of a university, Coursera is an instant university. But it is a university unlike all others. It offers no academic credit or degrees. Its credentials, such as a "competency," may have a commercial application, perhaps recognized by some businesses as a substitute for a college degree. To earn academic credit, its millions of users must be enrolled in some college or other. There are not many new things under the sun, but Coursera comes pretty close to being one. But what sort of new thing? Will Coursera be a public service? Or will Coursera be the most successful for-profit educational business plan of them all?

As early as January 2014, Coursera added a further commercial enticement: it inaugurated "Specializations," an educational concentration not unlike a major. A Specialization consists of a group of content-related courses intended to help students deepen their understanding in a subject area such as history or physics. In a year or so, Coursera has managed to offer 25 Specializations. Students in these Specializations may earn a "verified certificate" if they pass the courses and take an exam. To no one's surprise, Coursera has monetized the Specializations. Each verified certificate in a course costs $49, and a Specialization may have as many as seven, eight or nine courses, with a "capstone course" as an additional requirement. The number of users gaining the certificates is still comparatively small. By January 2015, in the Johns Hopkins Data Science Specialization, 266 students completed the program. But the numbers are growing. And, even if $49 seems like a modest sum, adding it up in all of the Specializations in all of the Coursera courses at all of the Coursera universities, the total sum for 2014 reached over $1 million. Coursera may well make money, not just a paltry million here or there but real money.[33] Coursera is also moving into corporate partnerships. Negotiating with private corporations, it is tailoring Specializations to fit corporate needs. Corporate connection seems to be a general trend in entrepreneurial online education. Coursera benefits; the corporation benefits.

Things were moving so fast in MOOC world that, even before fall 2012's million-student semester, a major analysis of MOOCs had appeared. On May 1, 2012, Lawrence S. Bacow, former president of Tufts, and William G. Bowen, former president of Princeton, published *Barriers to Adoption of Online Learning Systems in U.S. Higher Education.* They announced that online systems "have the potential to improve faculty productivity and lower institutional costs without sacrificing educational quality."[34]

While their assertion was upbeat, the authors did not ignore the changes that must occur at the institutional level. Bacow and Bowen observed that online courses have two primary characteristics that set them apart from the traditional classes on campus. MOOCs are "interactive," meaning, for them, that any student anywhere has access to learning modules at any time. Connectivity need not be confined to classroom, tutoring, or question time; it can have nearly continuous real-time feedback. A second characteristic, adaptability, means that the professor can customize instruction to fit any student's specific needs by using learning outcomes from millions of his other students. MOOCs are infinitely adaptive to student strengths and deficits.[35] Bacow and Bowen argued that MOOC–ish characteristics of connectivity, interactivity, and adaptability can help a college to cut instructional costs. At least that was the fond hope in 2012.

Bacow and Bowen supported the MOOCs' capacity to help the university footprint grow while teaching each student separately. The university outreach can become immense, and the "inreach," so to speak, can be intimate. Bacow and Bowen suggested that keyboard-to-monitor can work better than the professor-to-student in the classroom. Large-scale instruction usually costs less than small classes. This squares the academic circle. It sounds remarkable. All that remains is for it to work in reality.

Within the maze of hopes, fears, and predictions, few things seem clear. How will professors assess online students' progress, especially in the humanities? Still, online technology is sufficiently interactive, connective, and adaptive to provide education where rote learning is a core activity. Languages, both symbolic and linguistic, come to mind. Students can get genuine benefit from MOOCs in some disciplines. Bacow and Bowen succinctly described advantages of online education. But they omitted any mention of what intellectual virtues might be developed by using the new technology. "Highly interactive machine-guided online learning requires fewer facilities, fewer faculty, fewer teaching assistants, and may be easily scaled to accommodate large numbers of students."[36] The bottom line is the bottom line.

So university administrators start with what matters most, which is money. They hope to save enough on faculty to cover the considerable startup and support costs for home-grown MOOCs. Probably not, though. The promised savings will be too small in amount and too distant in time to justify counting on MOOCs for profit. If it costs millions to produce a television show, it will cost at least something to produce a MOOC.

The prospects for profit grow still bleaker when comptrollers shift their attention from IT to faculty. Online education will hasten the already noted drop in the numbers of tenured faculty, though the Internet has had almost nothing to do with starting that trend. Reduce the tenured faculty to whatever level you will: the students' needs remain as great as ever, whether the kids are online or in class. The job mix changes, but the costs of instruction remains high, and the number of teaching assistants grows like Topsy.[37] Most universities and colleges will not experience substantial savings in instructional costs through electronic distance learning; indeed, they will incur costs by creating MOOCs. Harvard and MIT have been right all along. Coursera may figure a way to draw a profit, but most universities will not.

Let's turn from tech and teachers to the MOOCs themselves. Can they offer the same "learning experience" as a classroom? The same "learning outcomes"? In theory, they can. Optimists (administrators and reformers) consider the massive online course as just a bigger version of a regular classroom: same professor, same material, same credit, a few more quizzes, but still requiring exams, papers, and reports. But in practice, MOOCs offer a skimpier version of the IRL (in real life) courses. Daniel Bonevac, professor of philosophy at the University of Texas at Austin, has taught over 50,000 students in his edX MOOC, Ideas of the Twentieth Century. He admits, "How effective are MOOCs for those who finish them? A typical college course has about thirty-five hours devoted to instruction. A typical MOOC includes videos totaling less than half that time. Reducing a fifty-minute class to one or two five-to-fifteen-minute videos is difficult. Even if done successfully, it leaves out a lot."[38] Professor Bonevac has stated the hideous secret of online education. MOOCs are inherently inferior educational instruments. No matter how brilliant the professor, no matter how imaginative the course, no matter the strength of the sponsoring institution, the resulting MOOC is inferior to the education on campus. The online degrees are second-line credentials. The implications are surely clear to all. As MOOCs become a standard part of higher education, university credentials and education divide into a superior program on campus and a second-rate program available online. This excellence gap does not bode well for MOOCs, nor, do we think, does it lead to the general social good.

And who *are* the students who finish MOOCs? Not everyone is enrolled in college. Many MOOCers have already graduated, often with advanced degrees.[39] Some are retired, taking a MOOC or two or more for general interest and enlightenment. Academic credit for these "users" is moot. But the largest percentage of MOOC-completers report that they're in it for career benefits.[40] Other MOOCers imagine that they are both interested in the topic and able to do the work. AI is not really that hard. How much math could you need? Do you really need to know about circuits? For these students, academic credit is impossible. The point is simple enough. MOOCs large enough to fit all students are too large to fit any.

And back to money. If students get credit for MOOCs, those MOOCs will be monetized. As the MOOCs are monetized, they become part of the academic standard practice. To the extent that the university goes online, teaching assistants, tutors, and adjuncts collectively become the faculty. And with college education increasingly organized around electronic distance learning, universities may limit classroom instruction by banning online students from campus. Universities will offer a first-class education on campus, and, over time, a second-class education online. A first-tier college education will become more expensive and limited than it is now. Pull on that single string—the necessity of human contact for an effective student learning community—and the whole promise of MOOCs diminishes drastically.

As MOOCs stand now, and we do not anticipate serious change in this, they are best categorized in terms of money and institutional provenance.[41] This approach rests upon the view of MOOCs as an industry, selling hope and credentials. Begin, consequently, with for-profit MOOCs, such as those offered for retail sale by Udacity and Coursera. In this setting, college credit and student identity are irrelevant; only the fees for service matter. The second group of MOOCs are the major non-profits, such as Khan Academy, edX, and the foundations, from the National Science Foundation, the MacArthur Foundation, the Bill and Melinda Gates Foundation, and so on. The large non-profits also do not concern themselves with student credit, and, generally speaking, do not monetize their products. A third category, university-based-and-originated MOOCs, are vitally interested in both student credit and monetizing their products. They are out to make a profit for the non-profits and offer course credits and degrees as the way to do that. So far, disappointment has exceeded success. A final category of MOOC progenitors involves private capital invested in (possible) educational profit. Venture capitalists have put money into Coursera, and the companies interested in higher education include Andreessen Horowitz and Kleiner Perkins Caufield & Byers. A second group of outside investors involves companies whose core business lies elsewhere, such as Alphabet (Google) and Pearson publishing. The details of which institutions might be involved in which category of MOOC development will certainly change, but the categories themselves seem quite stable. It's best to look at MOOCs in terms of where they come from rather than what they try to do.

But there is always an outlier, and MOOCs are no exception. PBS produced a brilliant MOOC, Carl Sagan's proto–MOOC, *Cosmos*. Sagan was a distinguished professor of astronomy at Cornell who possessed exceptional communication skills.[42] He prepared for *Cosmos* with regular appearances on the *Tonight Show*, where he combined wit with information and good humor. That's a potent combination. *Cosmos* itself displayed a wide variety of studio shots and on-location scenes; it had intellectual coherence, and dealt with an entertaining topic. Everybody watched it. *Cosmos* was, of course, neither interactive nor adaptive. And it was too basic to be a university course, but that could be fixed.[43] A professor could add new material while expanding the program/course to include assessments and chat rooms. But excellence is an expensive virtue. The university simply cannot afford to do its MOOCs as well as Carl Sagan did *Cosmos*.

The cost and the excellence of *Cosmos* brings us full circle, back through the IT and studio needs and swarms of teaching assistants to the fiscal gains inherent in using MOOCs. We are left with a couple of questions. If MOOCs may cost about as much as campus instruction, how do they benefit a college? It appears to be in every college's interest to use some other college's MOOCs. And even if MOOCs save a bundle, do they add to the excellence of a university education? Deans are beginning to answer these questions in various ways, and, over time, their answers will determine the future both of MOOCs and universities.

The Future of MOOCs

"The future is now," said George Allen, the Washington Redskins coach, as he traded draft choices for established players. The foreshortened time horizon also applies to MOOCs. Technology will improve, but MOOCs, for good or for ill, will depend on ratings and demographics, which means the numbers of students and how well they do. Broadcasting, no matter the content, has its own imperatives. None of this has changed from the heady days of 2012, which everyone proclaimed the Year of the MOOC. MOOCs are broadcasting, just as a classroom is narrowcasting.

Scale remains the primary virtue of a MOOC. In theory, and probably in reality as well, a MOOC can reach something akin to social infinity. A billion students is not impossible; indeed, it is easy. Big is the only way a MOOC can work. But, with large numbers of users, MOOCs run into the most politically incorrect reality ever given public voice, the Bell Curve. Size and excellence are always at odds. So let's move quickly on to a second consequence of academic scale: MOOCs are, and will remain, impersonal and anonymous. No one administering the course will know anyone taking the course, and those taking the course will not know each other. Social media's illusion of community among strangers will inform the personal interactions within a MOOC. Yet whatever wisp of imagined community exists, the students remain isolated. Connectivity is never quite the same as propinquity. Scale takes away as well as gives.

Despite the drawbacks inherent in all massive online courses, universities have begun including them as part of their degree programs. Arizona State University has built MOOCS into its Global Freshman Academy, which is an electronic freshman year. Students can take courses in any or all of three ways: traditional, online, or MOOC. Their transcripts will not indicate what version of the course was taken. By fall 2016, students will be able to take their whole freshmen year online. Some kids may have done it while still enrolled in high school. Others may be international students waiting to transfer to America after they finish a part of their degree at home.[44] The MOOC version of freshman year is dramatically cheaper than the online version that is built around specific ASU courses. ASU students taking the MOOCs will pay no more than $200 per credit hour, while their fellow students enrolled in ASU online courses will pay $480 to $543 per credit hour.

ASU expects a flood of students in the MOOCs that edX is shaping for it. Perhaps 25,000 students will enroll in some of the ASU MOOCs. Nonetheless, Phil Regier, university dean for educational initiatives at ASU, admits that "there's a lot of uncertainty" about how many of those students will actually verify their identity as they enroll in the MOOC or pay for the certification process. He also admits that there is a good bit of uncertainty about how the hoped-for flood of students will be managed pedagogically: in other words, the typical problems of MOOC courses. But he and the ASU administrators/bookkeepers have no uncertainty about the rightness of this revolutionary step. MOOCs are going to be an integral part of higher education at ASU.

A few graduate schools have begun to use MOOCs as well. In March 2015, the University of Pennsylvania's Wharton School announced a new series of online graduate courses, one each in accounting, finance, marketing, and operations management, along with a "capstone project," where theory would meet reality. The Wharton School offers this program through Coursera, as Pennsylvania is part of the Coursera consortium. The student's cost for the entire program is a modest $595. No student receives university credit for these courses but can obtain a "Coursera verification certificate." Wharton also adds a bit of incentive. The university will waive application fees to a graduate business program for the top 50 students in a year. Even more, Wharton offers up to five $20,000 scholarships to already admitted MBA students who "excelled in completion" in the online series. The program itself is an example of electronic marketing, not dissimilar to television sales channels, with their combinations of enticements and discounts.

Nonetheless, Wharton justifies the business education specialization series as educational outreach. A Wharton spokesman announced that "A key component for us as an institution is the possibility to identify talent from a pool of participants who might not have considered business education before."[45] Wharton advertises its Business Foundation specialization series as a public service. And such a position, while a bit self-serving, is not entirely untrue. It fits the academic myth of the millions of worthy students once excluded who can now be reached. Sometimes the medium is the message.

The future of MOOCs resembles nothing so much as a gigantic, electronic, decentralized, and academically diverse community college, with graduate programs appended. Both MOOCs and community colleges concentrate entirely on teaching, ignoring the two other university functions that have come down from Cardinal Robert. MOOCs do on an international scale what Ivy Tech does for Indiana. Both community colleges and MOOCs have been embraced in part because they were seen as a solution to the high cost of a research university education. Community colleges have been a less-expensive alternative for students than four years on a university campus. It has been the dream that MOOCs will succeed in their turn. And almost everyone embraces the outreach and diversity that community colleges have brought to higher education. Again, MOOCs might have the same effect. Finally, MOOCs and community colleges have sufficient scale to alter the structures of American higher education generally.

MOOCs arouse both anticipation and apprehension. Will MOOCs really change Cardinal Robert's community of masters? Or will MOOCs change little in universities but add a new element to the college scene? Fitting in seems more likely than change. MOOCs will serve as ancillaries to the main scene of instruction, which remains on campus. The future of the MOOC really is now, unless, of course, it was yesterday.

• SIX •

SCOCs, Universities, Technology and Money

Remember *Sunrise Semester*? It was an early morning class offered over network television. *Sunrise Semester* began in 1959 and was supported by the University of Chicago. Most people thought (correctly) that it was an effort to fill dead air, to give networks the appearance of public service, and to lead into the morning shows. But *Sunrise Semester* was also an open electronic course, the first using new technology, a proto–MOOC, as it were. Of course, as the networks began early morning programming, *Sunrise Semester* disappeared. It had been a broadcasting stepchild. After all, everyone knew that educational television was an oxymoron and that anyone who thought otherwise was also a moron.[1]

Victor Hugo noted that nothing is so powerful as an idea whose time has come. The same is true for technology. The broadcast technology on tap for *Sunrise Semester* was not adaptive, nor interactive, nor connective. With television, all you did was receive; with the Internet, you can now be an active part of your "classroom." The Internet offers a sense of community across distance. Human nature being what it is, people like to feel connected. People feel more connected when the particular communication both instructs and delights.[2] That's the promise of online education.

Academic credit turns online connection into serious business. Course content, student enrollment, even scale, all depend on college credit. With it, online courses are brought within the college catalog. In addition, with credit comes testing, checking student identity, and monetizing the course. College does these things for (and to) students on campus; it does the same for students online. Academic credit: that's the key to it all.

Students are always desperate for credit, so they will take courses anywhere, even online. Online, they will also face the usual academic hoops and costs. They will pay fees, since they will have to be enrolled in some college, somewhere. Only then will they be eligible for credit in online courses. They will have to pass proctored examinations. They will have their identities checked, maybe by submitting documents, maybe through biometrics, maybe through keystroke analysis, probably through all of these methods.[3] And only a student with at least a fighting chance of passing will be allowed to register for credit in online college courses. No university can accept the 50 to 90 percent dropout rate, which is not uncommon for MOOCs. Universities are not in the business of sponsoring student failure.

Generally, college administrators have drawn courses from the standard curriculum, creating an online section of an on-campus class. Charging for the online courses, and giving credit for a passing grade, means that the university is making the cyber offering part of a degree program. And, lest one overlook the obvious, other universities are hawking their own electronic courses. Can any university afford to offer nothing but fluff and junk? No, its comptrollers reply, it cannot. So every university rushes to offer online courses and degrees from the standard curriculum.

Universities are seriously concerned about the scale of their online courses. They want these courses as big as possible, increasing revenue along with efficiency. A university can offer a single on-campus section of freshman biology or psychology or history and put the rest of the sections online. Freshmen have no choice. Or the university can go even bigger, opening online freshman biology et al. to students enrolled elsewhere, either at other universities or in high schools through dual enrollment programs. General education courses are low-hanging fruit, ripe for exploitation by deans and accountants. Administrators would be derelict in their duties if, in these straitened times, they ignored the Internet's combination of temptation and opportunity. Look at how well Arizona State University's Global Freshman Academy outsources its need for general education.

University online courses are broadcast like MOOCs, but they differ from MOOCs in all other substantive ways. New things require new names, as Aristotle reminds us. So we call proprietary online courses offered to students for credit Small Closed Online Courses—SCOCs. Universities can present SCOCs with the same regularity as they do courses on campus. The SCOC model might not fit every course in the catalog, but it is certainly compatible with a lot of them. University administrators anticipate a bonanza. Just put our stuff online as SCOCs, and all will be well, or at least cheap.

Perhaps that fond hope might be a bit optimistic. There are few game-changers in this vale of tears that is higher education since 2008. Online education is probably not one of them. A university president wishing to wave this magic wand must tackle politics, student costs, and general academic culture as well as technology. True enough, universities can force students to take a basic course, such as mathematics, online, because it's offered nowhere else on campus. But the scale is limited, the cost savings modest. The bigger problem is excellence. The teaching relationship and the learning community have been diminished. The Internet does not make university education better, and that alone justifies skepticism.

Steve Blank: The Entrepreneurial University

Everyone is in sales—the old saying goes. This even applies to professors who prefer to think that they contemplate the good, the true, the beautiful, and the ways of nature. Reality tells another tale. Professors routinely sell themselves to committees that hire and promote. They sell their political positions in the unlovely venue of faculty meetings. They sell their ideas to peer review for publication and grants. They sell their knowledge in consulting contracts. They sell their university to parents. They sell their academic discipline to students, some of whom are pretty skeptical. They sell their personality, if any, in public lectures. Most of the time, the customer base is small. The sales techniques are familiar. By regarding themselves as above and beyond sales, many professors seem greatly given to pretense. The television show, *The Big Bang Theory*, which like all comedy is serious, shows many true things about the professing profession.

To be sure, universities can be insular places, though less so now than before. Still, professors can work in an environment as isolated as that enveloping bureaucrats, cops, and clowns. Nonetheless, however ivory the tower, the outside world pushes at the gate. Cardinal Robert founded the university by outside decree; it did not organize itself as do bird flocks and beehives. But Cardinal Robert did turn the university inward, away from the disputes of the city and the royal court and toward teaching and ideas. The university quickly acquired its own customs, standard curriculum at every level of learning, and a hierarchy of rank and degrees. An inward orientation of work and attitude has persisted, giving the university its sense of standing slightly apart from the world.

These days, with a fiscal crisis threatening its massive external funding, the inward-facing university no longer makes as much sense as it once did. Universities are tied to the real world, both by funding and function. Given that symbiosis, professors might do well to sell their ideas, knowledge, understanding, and communication skills in the real world. Some have done so, but many professors are not so inclined. Nonetheless, professors and their universities need to develop a new attitude, looking outward from the campus to the world beyond.

Anecdotes, as Roger Brimmer has noted, may not add up to data, but they can lead to understanding. So we offer an anecdote in the person of Professor Steve Blank, a college dropout who now teaches at the Stanford Business School, the Haas School of Business at Berkeley, Columbia, and Caltech. Steve Blank is, in one way, entirely atypical. He is a "technologist," for want of a better term, who came to the university after retiring, more or less, from business. Blank has been a serial entrepreneur, with at least eight Silicon Valley startups and IPOs under his belt right now. Blank developed his ideas about business from doing business, separating what worked from what did not. In another way, Steve Blank fits the academic mode perfectly. He has thought about startups as a whole, and written about what he has come to understand from creating them. One of his books, *The Four Steps to the Epiphany*,[4] deals with customer development; another, *The Startup Owners' Manual*,[5] seems to explain itself. In both of these Blank books, anecdote, experience, success, failure, and understanding come together in an overview, both practical and theoretical, of high-tech business needs and practices.

In *The Four Steps*, Blank urges a change of attitude concerning the practices of "customer development." He explains that the innovation has to fill a general customer need beyond just being an intriguing piece of technology. This applies to product development as well as to marketing. Blank advocates the idea of a "lean startup," along with getting the innovators "out of the building" to talk to potential customers. Customer feedback on the idea must be incorporated into the new technology. The entrepreneur needs to talk to customers *before* the gadget is finished. Through his concept of customer development, Blank brings at least some sense of order to the idiosyncratic business of high-tech startups and, not so obviously, to university education. All of this should sound obvious, as good ideas do when they are presented in organized form. But it was not at all obvious on the ground, as the number of startup failures indicates.

Having retired from startups and IPOs, Blank still gives advice in his role as a radio host as well as a professor of entrepreneurship. He now teaches others how to do what he has already done. Even in the constant churn of technological innovation, there is a right way to approach customer development and manage a startup and a coherent way to understand the business.

Steve Blank has explicitly applied some of his ideas to universities. He laid these out to the education committee of the National Governors' Association in 2012. Blank suggested that the university and its faculty need to improve their customer development skills. One of the important customers is the governor of the state. Every governor with a budget problem, and that is all of them, always, needs help in solving fiscal shortfalls. Universities ought to be helpful in this process, from teaching to research, grants, contracts, and technology transfer. Other customers include students and their parents, who, it turns out, sometimes want different things. Students prefer rec centers; parents want the kid to graduate. Soon. Fortunately, both want to feel that the university and its staff care about them. This doesn't always happen. But it is not impossible or even difficult. It begins with an attitude adjustment. Blank argued that the university ought to look outward, facing the world, not inward, facing the quad.[6] Customer development is, in itself, an entrepreneurial activity, no less for a university than for an IPO.

University administrators (and even some faculty) are painfully aware of all this. In the past half century, universities have moved away from "belonging" to the citizens of their state. Administrators used to be local citizens; now they are often high-priced migrant workers of the professional class. Professors who used to be local now come from everywhere. Citizens used to feel that the university was part of their state patrimony; their kids were entitled to attend. Every in-state employer would accept the degree from the state university. Now, only the football team has an overwhelmingly local identity. The rest of the university has moved away from belonging to the state to becoming an international research institution, with its faculty receiving grants running into the tens of millions each year. Borders between the university and the community once were porous, with citizens coming on campus for classes, debates, concerts, and drama. There's less of that now. It's not that the university is actively hostile to the world outside: it is merely indifferent—and a bit supercilious. That kind of attitude does not develop customers; it antagonizes them. Blank was on to something when he suggested improved customer development.

Blank was talking to governors and their educational assistants, people involved with universities but not belonging to universities. He brought them a welcome perspective. He told them that universities ought to be facing outward, developing good customer relations, and not just begging the state for money. For governors, let it be noted, "customers" are actually registered voters. The governors and their educational aides, therefore, ought to encourage universities in their search for funds.

Audience matters. Had Steve Blank been talking to university provosts and presidents, he would not have said any of this. They, and often their deans and faculty, often face outward already, looking for grants and support wherever they can. Universities are, after all, like teenagers: always asking for money, always with plans bigger than pockets. University administrators began to become professional panhandlers as early as the 1950s. That role was confirmed by the expansion of grants and federal fellowships in the wake of Sputnik. Now, fundraising is about all they do; some better than others, of course, but there is no university administrator who does not endeavor to raise as much money as possible. No one in the university has any illusions about the ivory tower. Outside, people seem to think it still exists, but that may be the result of seeing too many college movies. Universities have already, and for a generation, adopted the Steve Blank approach to institutional management.

SCOCs

It is sometimes forgotten that students are actually real people, not just "users" within a vast electronic or campus herd. Individual students with specific problems make the academy run a bit less smoothly than deans and parents would like. MOOCs ignore students altogether, but SCOCs, which charge fees and offer academic credit, cannot. SCOCs, after all, are not just broadcasts that are picked up on Mars. They are narrowcasts: specific courses enrolling clearly identified students, offered by particular universities, granting degree credit, and costing a pretty penny. With SCOCs, the campus comes to you, but it is still the campus.

SCOCs do present unfamiliar problems. Let's look at a few examples.[7] Jane, an engineering student minoring in computer science, studies at a major state university. Registered for a full semester of courses there, she has paid her tuition and fee bill. The university owes her a semester's education. Then comes the accident. The second day of the semester, she is run over by a drunk driver, suffering a broken hip and leg. Her person has become temporarily immobile, but her mind has not. Instead of taking the offered medical leave, Jane drops her five on-campus courses and enrolls in five SCOCs, two from Caltech, another from MIT, and one each from Harvard and the University of Pennsylvania. She assures her dean that these are accredited institutions. The courses are appropriate for her degree program, and four similar courses are offered at her own university. She asks the dean if she can get credit for the SCOCs, and if she can get a refund on her tuition. The dean passes the buck to the chancellor. And what does the chancellor do? Ahhhhhh.

Joe is enrolled at a small liberal arts college, which does not offer a couple of specialized courses that he wants. One is statistics and game theory. The other is in econometrics. He enrolls in two SCOCs offered by Harvard and Stanford. He does exceptionally well in both courses. Can he get credit for these courses at his college? And if he does, whom does he pay? His college, or Harvard and Stanford?

Sam is enrolled at a regional university, majoring in physics. He finds that three of the local courses are undistinguished, to say the least. Sam goes online and takes two MOOCs and a SCOC on theoretical physics offered by MIT and Caltech. Should Sam be allowed to substitute these MOOCs and SCOC for his own university's courses? Again, whom should he pay for the two MOOCs and the SCOC?

Madison attends a small private university. She has taken two semesters of geology, enjoying them immensely. Madison takes three SCOCs: two on paleontology and one on paleogeography, which her school does not offer. She wishes to add these SCOCs to local courses in geology and use that as a minor. Should the provost allow that?

Provosts will also face the problem of superscoring, where students take less challenging MOOCs and SCOCs in order to replace more difficult local courses. Physics is never easy, and Jeremy takes two identical physics MOOCs and a similar physics SCOC during his time at the university. He takes the best grade out of the three and asks if the university will give him credit for it and allow him to avoid the local physics course. Does the dean demand that the scores be averaged? Does he demand that Jeremy take the local course? Or does the dean go along with Jeremy's pretense of having learned some physics online? The dean's office, expert at temporizing, promises an investigation.

These individual student issues, and others too numerous to count and too bizarre to recount, are likely to enliven the lives of deans. They also illustrate this important point: SCOCs separate the college offering the course from the college granting credit. A student can attend a college right here and get credit for a course taken from a college over there. Before online education, the students took courses and gained credit from the college they attended. For on-campus students, nothing may have changed. You attend Yale; you take a Yale course; you get Yale credit. Now, and increasingly, you can attend Yale, take a course from MIT, and get Yale credit. You attend LSU–Eunice, take a course from Yale, and get LSU–Eunice credit. The Internet shifts the emphasis from the university to the student. Things haven't worked like that since before Cardinal Robert.

Both student and university might well benefit from the SCOC-driven emphasis on students. Having a care for the student is good customer relations, and most universities are already working harder on that. Further, the university can easily monetize the SCOCs it offers and those it imports. Further still, administrators can fit student and SCOC into appropriate niches for admissions, enrollment, credit, fees, and discipline. When administrators focus on students, everybody can benefit.

At the institutional level, individual universities have created SCOC degree programs, some of them entirely online. Many others follow what Yale calls a "blended" learning model, combining online classes with in-person work, often in more or less equal amounts. These two SCOC models largely involve graduate work and seem particularly well suited for business, computers, and medicine. Arizona State University has decided that all forms of online coursework are equally acceptable and equivalent to its own bricks-and-mortar classes. It allows its students to substitute MOOCs for Arizona State classes. It also offers an entire general education program composed of its own proprietary online courses. A single university seeks a global freshman class, to say nothing of the income that that might produce. Arizona State University is poised to become America's University.

The fourth and most ambitious SCOC model aims to connect various universities into a consortium. Each university will offer for-credit courses to students within the consortium. This arrangement offers students several advantages. The consortium also benefits. If a school drops out, the consortium can continue anyway. It creates a single large online university, which has immense diversity of SCOCs and even larger (potential) economies of scale. It seems like a good idea in every way, a real benefit to students and potentially profitable to universities. The bugs are still being worked out.

In 2012, the Year of the MOOC, ten major universities, Northwestern, Duke, North Carolina, Washington University of St. Louis, Notre Dame, Brandeis, Rochester, Vanderbilt, and Wake Forest, organized an electronic alliance named Semester Online. This consortium planned to offer collectively about thirty SCOCs to start, beginning in the fall of 2013. Semester Online acquired a technical partner, 2U, which would help with the launch and the students.

The Semester Online consortium would offer credit-bearing courses to students of the ten universities, but students registered elsewhere might possibly also get credit. Students enrolled in the ten universities would get a consortium course for local tuition. Students enrolled elsewhere would pay a fee of $4,000 per course. These non-consortium students would also have to apply to one of the universities involved to take courses and be formally accepted. Unlike MOOCs, the Semester Online SCOCs would not have open enrollment. In addition, the consortium would have a good grasp on how well prepared the students were and would be able to aim the courses accordingly. That was the plan.

Semester Online tried to make its distance-learning experience as much like an actual classroom as possible. The colleges anticipated small classes: stiff fees and admission procedures would ensure that result. The courses promised to be highly interactive and adaptive, with students raising electronic hands at any time. For students, the virtual classroom might have some unattractive features. No one could slip in late, and no one could hide in the back row. There was no back row. From our experience, which goes back to the nineteen-fifties, students find these characteristics of virtual classrooms to be a real drawback. The medium may change, but the audience does not.

None of it worked out. Faculty members at some participating universities opposed the whole thing. Duke and UNC dropped out before the ship set sail. The other universities had a difficult time getting their courses up and running. Student demand was disappointingly low, and some courses, much like those on campus, enrolled single-digit numbers. Semester Online crashed and burned in its first year of operation, 2013–2014.[8] SCOCs are not an automatic success in every venue. Semester Online wound up its affairs in 2014, having struggled on for a single year.

Semester Online has shown that the most important part of going online is anticipating problems. You have to check the SCOC constantly. A university consortium requires serious supervision. It's like cooking. Professors need to make psychological as well as pedagogical and technological adjustments. Administrators really must be elbow-deep in every level of online courses. Problems are constant and permanent. There's a lot of work involved by everyone involved and a lot of money is at stake.

SCOCs differ a bit from courses on campus, but a SCOC consortium differs enormously from ordinary academic life. At Semester Online, nobody saw that. A SCOC consortium is not an academic department, where faculty endlessly discuss everything. A SCOC consortium is a business, requiring marketing, quality control, and customer service. Semester Online did not prepare the professors to become SCOC stars. Where were the marketing experts/academic counselors selling these courses to the students? Students will take anything to get credit to graduate. A consortium needs, and Semester Online did not have, a strong customer service component, ensuring that students whom nobody ever saw were taking the right courses, learning material, and passing the courses they needed to graduate. If a SCOC can be considered a television show, a consortium is a network.[9] Or, in baseball terms, Semester Online began the season without bothering to get a manager, a team, a support staff, or spring training. Failure should have surprised no one.

Semester Online may not have worked out as well as everyone hoped, but other institutions and administrators learned from its mistakes. In January 2014, Georgia Tech began offering a master's degree in computer science online. The university called its program a MOOC, but it turned out to be a program of SCOCs. Georgia Tech admitted about three hundred students for the spring semester, 2014, upped it to 350 for the summer, and expanded that to around 400 for the fall of 2014. By the spring semester of 2016, the Georgia Tech program had risen to over 3,000 students and had issued its first degrees. Originally, the university had hoped to get around *10,000* students, a huge number for a SCOC degree program. The university is not going to reach that number, as even the president of Georgia Tech admits.

The online master's program is not free. But it does cost far less than a student would pay for instruction on campus. The online SCOC series costs $6,600, rather than the $45,000 for being there. The planned discount is around 85 percent, more if you count the costs of commuting and daily expenses.

This online degree program is a partnership between Georgia Tech and Udacity. Georgia Tech provides the course content, the degree requirements, and the professors; Udacity supplies the "course platform" and "course assistants." Udacity is filling a need that Semester Online overlooked. Georgia Tech keeps 60 percent of the anticipated revenue, while Udacity gets the remaining 40 percent. Georgia Tech also acquired a second partner, AT&T, which put up more than $2 million to help with the startup costs. In return, AT&T got the right to put its employees in the online degree program, and to trawl the rest of the students for possible new hires.

Georgia Tech anticipated an immediate profit of $240,000, split by the partners. By the third year, the computer science degree program was projected to cost $14.3 million but make $4.7 million in profits.[10] The online master's degree has not been a bonanza. It did not realize the anticipated profit by 2016. But the program achieved a small positive cash flow.

Georgia Tech has taken care of the essential academic housekeeping. Students in the online degree program take monitored examinations and have access to tutoring and online office hours. Georgia Tech sets admission standards, but students who cannot meet them may gain provisional acceptance, with continuation in the degree program dependent on how well they do in the first couple of courses.[11] The general housekeeping arrangements follow standard academic routine. Georgia Tech has combined the exotic with the ordinary in what it clearly hopes will be a permanent addition to the campus curriculum. Doubtless, the students, prospective as well as current, have the same hopes. Georgia Tech alumni seem far less sanguine. They fear the new program will cut the value of their degrees. It's too early to tell which is the appropriate attitude.

So far, the Georgia Tech program is going pretty well. There are downs as well as ups. The program has attracted fewer students than anticipated. The Georgia Tech SCOC program has cost more than the school had anticipated. Still, the online students are surviving and achieving about the same GPA as students in class. In one first-semester course, 309 of 380 entrants passed, far, far better than the standard MOOC success rate of about 3 to 5 percent. And so the ship sails on.

Georgia Tech's online master's degree program has drawn a lot of interest. Dr. Zvi Galil, the head of the shop, acknowledges that a graduate degree-granting online program is "uncharted territory." He argues that it can be done at an eventual profit to the university and at a low cost to the consumer. The message is certainly clear. Sam Walton showed you could discount just about everything; Georgia Tech says, "Why not graduate education?" Some critics have wondered if the new online venture will cannibalize on-campus instruction, both at Georgia Tech and elsewhere. Dr. Galil admits it's too early to tell. Everyone will find out soon enough. Some faculty at Georgia Tech, and elsewhere, doubt that the online degree will have the same quality as the more expensive classroom version. Now, who knows, but in the fullness of time...

Beyond all that, doubters suspect that large numbers of students won't be able to do the work. They won't be prepared. This limitation is particularly serious for online undergraduate courses. Remember Udacity and San Jose State? They had to suspend their basic math MOOCs. Students couldn't do introductory algebra. Fortunately for Georgia Tech, its master's degree does not involve beginning students. And, even more fortunately, admission to the program requires a bachelor's degree or its equivalent.[12] Georgia Tech will lose some students; that always happens. But the collapse of this program for academic reasons, as opposed to fiscal ones, seems unlikely.

Questions remain about how the Georgia Tech venture will settle out.

Start with turf. Before the degree program began, the chair of Georgia Tech's graduate curriculum committee said that his group had not received any proposal to review, and they had questions about the Udacity partnership. Move on to personnel. Dr. Galil, who runs the Online Master's of Science in Computer Science (OMSCS), hired only a few new instructors. Udacity picks up the slack by hiring mentors, teaching assistants, and graders. Unfortunately, some of the new personnel have drawn adverse comment. They don't seem to be up to par. Technical issues always exist, particularly with course content and production values. One pioneering Georgia Tech MOOC, "Fundamentals of Online Education: Planning and Application," had such thin content and such wretched production values that the university cancelled the thing in a mercy killing after a few weeks. OMSCS does not face these precise problems; computer science is not education. But Dr. Galil's comments about uncharted territory must be taken seriously.

Georgia Tech is not alone in launching a graduate-/professional-level SCOC. Yale has done so as well. Twice, in fact. In 2011, the Yale School of Nursing inaugurated a partially online doctoral program. It has been sufficiently successful over time, so Yale decided to start another one. In March 2015, the Yale School of Medicine announced a partially online program to train Physicians' Assistants (PAs). Both sequences are designed to be as close as possible to the residential program in New Haven. The online courses include video conferencing technology to keep the students in touch with each other as well as with the Yale staff. Both new programs require some hands-on study at a clinic or hospital approved by Yale.

Yale has planned a substantial program. A university spokeswoman announced that the "…on-campus and online programs would be equivalent in admission criteria, student curriculum and assessment, clinical placements, and summative student assessment." The online program will include the 2,000 hours of clinical training. That will be hands-on rather than just eyes-on. Hence the designation of "blended." Yale has also planned for a fairly large program: not the millions of users currently viewing MOOCs, but at least 350 students. On campus, the Yale PA program teaches 40 students. The PA curriculum requires a serious commitment in time. Yale has designed the program to take 28 months. This stint adds up to at least two academic years and three, perhaps four, summers. And, finally, Yale will charge the online students the same tuition and fees paid by those on campus. The cost is (now, more later) $83,000.[13] Given the huge amount of hospital and clinic work, the Yale online PA program cannot be considered a shortcut or a second-rate degree.

The PA and nursing doctorate were not Yale's first efforts in electronic education. As early as 2007, Yale put course lectures online at no charge. In 2011, Yale began online summer school courses for undergraduates, and those courses carry academic credit. Two years later, Yale joined Coursera and began to manufacture MOOCs.

Yale has had enough experience in several varieties of online education to manage the twin problems of costs and credit. It made three decisions that increased its chances for success. The university offered graduate-level SCOCs. True, that cut the pool of possible applicants back a bit, but it also ensured that applications, which are far from free, would be made by serious students. Secondly, Yale chose to offer graduate SCOCs in a popular field, health care, which, along with computer science and business, have an economic future requiring advanced credentials. Finally, Yale enlisted the services of a private company, 2U, an "online enabler," which provides an essential service for the university: an online platform for the new degree program. The enabler companies frequently offer assistance with course design as well as with recruitment (not a big problem for Yale) and customer service (student support, always a problem at every university). They promise universities that they'll get online programs running quickly without incurring large startup costs. The enabler companies cut the university's risks in return for a large slice of university revenue.

Alas for Yale, the online PA program encountered more grumble than applause. Students and alumni claimed that the administration did not consult them sufficiently; more importantly, they feared that the online program would devalue the campus degree. Worse yet, the accreditation review committee rejected Yale's application in 2015, meaning that the program cannot begin until 2017, with the first students matriculating in 2018.[14]

The Yale School of Medicine had to reply to all the official criticism. No way around that. A suspicious domestic community added to a hostile accreditation agency cannot be a good thing. So Dr. Richard Belitsky, Deputy Dean for Education at the Yale School of Medicine, conducted an explanatory educational/charm campaign. Dean Belitsky held several town hall meetings with the current (and on-campus) PA students and added a temporary note to the website:

> Along with the potential benefits and opportunities a Yale PA Online Program might create, we also heard a number of concerns. For example, some of you are worried about the potential negative impact on the reputation of the PA profession, which is admittedly young and still working to achieve a better understanding and broader acceptance by the public. In addition, there are concerns about the challenges of providing high-quality clinical education and ensuring appropriate oversight using sites and practices that are geographically dispersed and distant from New Haven.[15]

Dr. Belitsky was reassuring but left no doubt that Yale was continuing with its plans to establish a large online Physicians' Assistant program. The online PA program would be separate from the on-campus degree. Dr. Belitsky argued that a strong Yale PA program would be valuable for students and society at large. The PA level of medical education is increasingly necessary to "meet the nation's growing healthcare needs, especially in primary care." Yale remains "committed to excellence" with the online program, and Dr. Belitsky promised to keep the residential students in the picture. Still, Yale plans to move ahead in full.[16]

In an era of disinvestment, individuals as well as universities are constantly launching new online courses. Two professors at the University of Texas at Austin, James Pennebaker and Samuel Gosling, have launched an "Introduction to Psychology" course to several hundred students enrolled on campus. They have a "studio audience" of 25 kids or so and a broadcast audience into the thousands. Experience has led them to adopt a TV format of looking into the camera rather than at the students in class. They have divided the course into small segments and have introduced specialized topics such as "What's Cooking in the Lab" and "The Expert's Chair." The course intentionally resembles a late-night TV talk show. They call their creation a Synchronous Massive Online Course (SMOC). In putting together this SMOC for an electronic audience, professors Pennebaker and Gosling have found that lecturers, programmers, online mentors, teaching assistants, and production crew have ballooned past 125 people. Costs, doubtless, mount in equal measure. That's in one course for local students. Georgia Tech, by contrast, wants ten thousand students nationwide and is counting on the economies of scale to allow the degree program to succeed.

A further example of exotic online fauna can be found in a DOCC, a Distributed Open Collaborative Course.[17] In the fall semester of 2013, a DOCC in feminist theory was offered at seventeen colleges for credit, presumably for a fee. Class size was pegged at 15–20 students. The DOCC format required instructors from the various colleges to fit their lectures into a single course framework that offered a "theme of the week." An online panel of discussants would introduce an important topic. Students were invited to comment on the professor's approach to the topic. The DOCC was based on the egalitarian notion that shared experiences and attitudes were preferable to expertise.

The founder of the DOCC program obtained some small grants totaling $17,000 from Brown University, the New School, and Pitzer College and made do with that. The grants covered the costs of video, and that's all the DOCC organizers worried about. The seventeen colleges would presumably cover their own costs. The videos could, in the fullness of time, find a larger audience, but the object was not to make money. It was to empower and enlighten.

The idea behind the DOCC was shared learning. It's not just the professors (online and local) who matter: the students count as well. Their contributions in this course were considered as valuable as anything the professors would bring to the shared learning experience. It is important to remember that who you learn from is just as important as what you learn. The DOCC has no single syllabus. The discussants open with a theme: professors in the 17 colleges develop their courses in the ways that work best for them and their students. The course never "is"; it is always "becoming." The intellectual input is collaborative. It is also un-policed. There are no established standards for anything. The grading is entirely ad hoc. A course in one college may be nothing like a course in another. Content bubbles up from below more than it is imposed from above. The ghosts of Paulo Freire and Wikipedia loom over the enterprise.

Skeptics might suggest that the DOCC is just a touchy feely bull session for college credit. Take it out of the dorm and put it on the Internet. Give it a name (DOCC). Then give it a go. The nature of this highly collaborative course makes external evaluation difficult. The outcome of the DOCC might be individual illumination and social solidarity (AKA consciousness raising). Still, we agree that there are many ways to learn things, and this approach, for some students, doubtless works.

The SMOC in basic psychology and the DOCC in feminist theory illustrate the idiosyncratic, desktop-publishing, do-it-yourself version of SCOC World. Other universities have more of a businesslike approach to their online versions of education. The entrepreneurial Arizona State shows what a major research university can do when it creates SCOCs en masse. Over the past few years, it has made a profit from its stable of SCOCs. The executive vice provost of Arizona State University Online, Dr. Philip Regier, has a clear grasp of online courses for credit and for profit. It's a numbers game. A school may not need millions of students, but it does need several thousand to make an online program work. And competition matters. Dr. Regier worries, "if Georgia Tech attracts five thousand students, I don't want to be doubling down on our computer science master's program. You have to know your market."

Dr. Regier's sense of the market goes beyond sales; it also involves product, which includes course content, production values, and professors. It all boils down to the cost of professors. He explains: "What we're seeing is different price points for different levels of faculty involvement. If you want no-touch, or very limited touch, they'll deliver that for $6,000. If you want a higher-touch program, taught and graded by regular faculty, and a lot of faculty interaction, it's going to be more expensive."[18] You cut costs by cutting faculty. You may well cut educational quality as well. Too bad for the students who have to go online. There's more realism than mercy in Regier's comments. But in an age of public disinvestment in universities, it's hard to ignore the bottom line.

Arizona State has taken a major step in expanding its SCOC footprint. It has announced the opening of an "Online Global Freshman Academy" for the academic year 2016–17. Students entering the Online Global Freshman Academy (OGFA) will face no admission requirements, no test scores, no high school GPA minimums, and no need for letters of recommendation. You just log in and sign up. You can take some MOOCs or some Arizona State courses or both. You can just audit them if you like. Costs nothing. To take an ASU course for credit, you pay a $45 fee to verify your identity and a larger fee, around somewhere between $200 and $543 a credit hour, for academic services. These fees will be assessed for each course, which, over a 30-credit-hour program of ten to 20 courses, will add up to a nice round sum.

Everybody has heard at least one, and probably more than one, advertisement for OGFA on radio and TV. Arizona State kicked off OGFA with an introductory course in astronomy, a precursor to the whole program. It opened the fall semester of 2015. ASU plans to expand its program with at least eight courses a calendar year until it reaches a full general education program. The freshman courses will include the humanities, along with all their difficulties in student assistance and assessment included therein. Dr. Regier, dean of ASU Online's 30,000 students, acknowledges the problems of online humanities. Arizona State will probably introduce English composition as the last of its online courses. Still, tough as this may be, "actual people" will read, edit, and grade the thousands and thousands of student essays that OGFA will generate. In Arizona, at least, teaching assistant is going to be a growth profession.

The ASU Online Global Freshman Academy SCOCs will run for seven and a half weeks, which is half a semester. Presumably, the student will take two SCOCs in any subject to earn three credit hours. At any rate, Arizona State insists that the Freshman Academy provides the same education as is available on campus. Regier reassures everyone that the courses will have the same content and presumably the same assessment as those on campus. Regier hopes for 25,000 students in some courses, but enrollment figures alone will be the main difference between monitor and classroom.

Dr. Regier pitches the Global Freshman Academy as simply another alternative for students wishing to attend ASU. He notes that the kids have four options. Students can enroll on campus or transfer in from a community college. They can attend through the SCOCs offered through ASU Online. And now, or at least soon, they can take the general education courses of their first year through the OGFA. Each alternative increases the university's outreach to students who might (in some cases surely would) be unable to attend college otherwise. Certainly the absence of entrance requirements for OGFA should encourage enrollment. And, through the Freshman Academy, college will cost the student and the state far less than attending in person. Finally, OGFA illustrates how universities have changed. Seventy-five years ago, they advertised junior year abroad; now they advertise freshman year at home.

Arizona State is not alone in the Global Freshman Academy business. ASU partners with edX, the Harvard/MIT manufacturer of MOOCs. Anent Argawal, the CEO of edX, claims that edX will solve, or at least attempt to solve, the two biggest problems in MOOC World: no academic credit for courses and gigantic student wastage. Nothing has yet been said about monetizing the MOOCs, though this issue will certainly arise. EdX and ASU will probably have an effective partnership, bringing together experience and leadership from both sides. It's early days yet, but the ASU Global Freshman Academy SCOCs seem likely to fly.[19] Arizona State may well become "America's University."

Problems and issues still remain with SCOCs, and MOOCs as well. The market monetizes everything, turning education into a commodity. Bacow and Bowen acknowledge this transformation, albeit a bit reluctantly: "Technology and the market have a way of creating commodities out of what were previously value-added services. This is true of some aspects of teaching: certain parts of the bundle that were previously considered part of teaching a course will in the future be provided as commodities."[20] A certain dispassionate chill characterizes this assessment of online courses as a standard system. Clearly, there is nothing inherently student-oriented about MOOCs and SCOCs. Nor will online courses be kind to professors or to learning generally. The market is about profit.

The quality of courses and programs is also a problem. The success of any college course depends in large measure on the personality of the teacher. Teaching is hard enough in class; over the Internet, personality matters even more. Can SCOCs transmit personality, in other words, provide enchantment over distance? That's hard to do. Those working in broadcasting and advertising have long been aware of this sad reality. Does his voice have the right tone and timbre? Does she have the attitude of warmth and caring and intimacy to sell the product? The secret to enchantment over distance remains hidden in the art and mystery of teaching/persuading over the air. Gifted teachers can embrace the student/viewer. In stage, screen, and radio they call it star quality, but that is a name, not an explanation. Still, the magic shines, whether you heard Franklin D. Roosevelt or Mary Margaret McBride over the radio or Ira Glass on a podcast or saw Katharine Hepburn on screen, Bishop Fulton Sheen or Carl Sagan on television, Steve Jobs onstage, or Andrew Solomon on a TED talk. All other problems of MOOCs or SCOCs may be solved by current administrative procedures, by technology, and by understanding that the expense may well outweigh the income. And, as for a great course that everyone will love, critics need only remember that enchantment over distance is a rare personal quality, not a business plan.

And now for the sad news about SCOCs (SMOCs and DOCCs as well). Administrators base their decisions to offer/require online courses on the bottom line. They tend to be indifferent to the quality of electronic education. Great teaching doesn't matter. Poor teaching doesn't matter. The students need the courses to graduate and get a good job, which they need to pay off the student loans. In the end, accountants run online education.

And what do they run, exactly? Online courses that require rote memory work pretty well, even when they're deadly dull. Students can be evaluated by precise measurement. Deficiencies can be spotted early and addressed at once, and, if need be, addressed again and again. So far, just fine. But move to lab sciences. Hands-on differs from eyes-on, and lab work is a hands-on activity, requiring personal supervision. Labs introduce people into the learning equation, and the economics of online education require teaching costs be kept as low as possible. That can only be done by cutting back on the people. And course quality? Profit is the real measure of excellence.

Online courses will proliferate, no matter their deficiencies, because of the incessant demand for additional certification. One student of our acquaintance, already an RN with a BS in education, took her BSN (Bachelor of Science in Nursing) degree online. She slogged through a lot of busywork, along with some assignments apparently designed to test basic literacy. She didn't learn much about nursing that she didn't already know. Still, hoops are hoops. There are tradeoffs in everything.

More yet, an online course lacks a collaborative student learning community. Physical presence itself matters. A classroom of students is a living organism, as anyone who has ever taught will attest. Kids look at each other, whisper among themselves, blurt out relevant or irrelevant personal anecdotes about the topic under consideration, stare blankly, argue with other students' positions, communicate through their body language what they themselves may not even be aware of, exchange sympathetic comments about homework, respond as a group to the teacher's lame jokes and interesting examples, clarify for each other course concepts. Every class has interesting students who alter the dynamic of the class by their mere presence. Online students really do miss a lot; and often, they find it all too easy to retreat from the learning community.

A while back, we had lunch with a recent graduate. She had obtained an excellent job after graduation, making a good living and even working in her field of public relations. She should be a happy camper. We asked her what she thought about her college education. Her reply was realistic rather than nostalgic. She had hated one thing about college: the large classes, 400 students or more packed into an auditorium. It was so impersonal, she said; there was no sense of community because students tended to hunker down into passive mode. Even when a professor would try to encourage interaction with large-class pedagogies like "clicker questions" or polls, the group would not gel. She complained that she hadn't really learned much in those classes, although she had had to memorize quite a bit to pass the tests. Multiply her experience to include the hundreds of thousands, probably millions, isolated in all the SCOCs offered by all the universities in all the land. Online isolation can only be worse than being an invisible part of a large crowd.

SCOCs may lead to a new kind of university, simply by being an efficient delivery system of information. That sort of education (actually, mostly training) seems inevitable, at least to some extent. Electronic distance learning, of the SCOC–ish variety, anyway, will make some money, though nowhere near enough to support research universities, medical schools, law schools, graduate programs, research institutes, et al. But electronic education's most serious weakness is that SCOCS, *de rerum natura*, lead *away* from the mentoring and the intimacy and the mutual support that alone makes good education possible. The Internet does not lead inevitably toward excellence, which gives education its value. For individuals and society, in work and in school, excellence is the necessary goal. These are not the conclusions we hoped for when beginning our essay, but hopes give way to reality. So we recommend an attitude of resigned acceptance of the serious limitations inherent in online education. As Voltaire noted, the future may not be pleasing, but it will certainly be interesting.

Vocational Education Focus

The movie *Failure to Launch* (2006) presented a familiar American nightmare: a college graduate who can't seem to establish himself. And since the crash, kids living at home have become even more of a sad social cliché. They do not become independent, as their parents and grandparents did. They refill empty nests, reluctantly roosting in parental basements or over the garage. Re-nesting happens because the recent graduates cannot find good jobs or perhaps any job at all. Some graduates have taken jobs that did not previously require a college education.[21] Even television commercials deal with moving back home, the returning child often bringing a baby and sometimes a spouse. Difficulties in launching the new generation into (mostly) self-sufficiency fill social media. Re-nesting and underemployment have also caught the attention of politicians trawling for votes. Something has to be wrong here.[22]

In matters of public policy, fixing blame is as important as fixing problems. Americans fix part of the blame on the national economy. Job creation has recently lagged behind population growth. There is no one person to take the rap for the whole economy. But for pieces of the problem, like education costs, frustrated parents and students find a villain. That villain is the university. It is not preparing students for the real world. But maybe that can be fixed? Rework a college education to give it a more practical perspective. Prepare the students for the world of work. Teach the students what the business world needs them to know and do. Social skills are at the top of the list, beginning with respect for the job. Students must learn to follow dress and conduct codes, to hone their work ethic, and to play well with others as well as become familiar with recent technology. Whatever the position sought, the student needs to graduate ready for employment, in attitude no less than training. This sort of college education can to be called "the vo-ed paradigm."

Business leaders as well as politicians have been agitating for the vo-ed paradigm. They are responding to an unsettling social reality. The issues are depressingly familiar. Many recent graduates do not seem prepared for the jobs that exist. More, state budgets have taken a hell of a hit since the fiscal crisis of 2008, and universities are a large budget item. More again, student debt has risen steadily, and parents are registered voters who actually vote. How about making public education more responsive to the public needs? Doesn't that seem like a good idea?

The vo-ed paradigm of university education begins with the idea of thrift, both of time and money. In Texas, the state board of education has suggested that students should get a degree in four years for a total tuition cost of $10,000. The University of Texas should come up with a plan to make that happen. What sort of plan might that be? Well, since you asked, first cut the soft courses, like art, music, literature, philosophy, and any history beyond that of Texas and the United States. Who can afford that stuff? If you think you need it, get it on your own, rather than at public expense. The state can't afford to subsidize it.

Reformers move beyond negative proposals (trimming courses) to positive proposals (getting students ready for work). Universities should teach useful skills and specific courses that business might require. Everybody should take accounting, for example. Those doing the hiring can help here. They know what they need and what current job applicants lack. With that in mind, AT&T recently invested almost $3 million in Georgia Tech's online computer science program, and it will hire the best graduates. That's a good model to follow. The kids get a job; the company gets a useful employee. Other universities should, and likely will, offer what is commercially required.

It takes a lot more than business leaders and politicians making their pitches to change the universities to fit perceived student needs. Professors also have to be convinced, and many, not just in Texas, have tended to be skeptical, sometimes hostile, occasionally apoplectic. They say that the vo-ed paradigm demands a new kind of university—and not a good one. Instead of research, imagination, publication, and good teaching, a university will be judged on how many students are gainfully employed upon graduation.[23] Only one standard will be held over from the old system and that applies to professors in science and technology. They will continue to be judged on how many grants they bring to the university. Grants, after all, help the state pay the freight. Getting a few grants is the least a chemist or biologist can do, in gratitude for the job. Professors ought to be rewarded for doing a job that benefits students and the state directly. And why shouldn't it be that way, politicians and business owners ask.

The vo-ed paradigm raises difficult questions that vo-ed supporters have trouble answering. Even in Texas, many wonder why the vo-ed vision should be applied to the University of Texas at Austin. Turning UT–Austin into a vo-ed undergraduate institution will involve a long, expensive, bitter, and unsuccessful campaign. Although the regents in Texas have broad political powers, they will fail. Appointing top administrators will not do the job. Chancellors and presidents can suggest, urge, and, within limits, reward. But they can rarely command. They must rely on moral authority, and no one suitable to the regents is going to have any of that within the university. Academic freedom, the First Amendment, and tenure contracts give professors the right to criticize and the ability to evade what comes down from the administrative suites. The medieval university of Cardinal Robert may seem far distant from modern Texas, but the position of professors remains pretty much the same from that day to this.

The regents' suggestions regarding UT–Austin are also unnecessary. The vo-ed system is already up and running in Texas. The ideals of community-oriented education, found in the Ivy Tech community college system in Indiana, seems close to the regents' hearts. Just copy that. Surely Texas could organize its community colleges into a system even more comprehensive than Ivy Tech's. This is Texas we're talking about! Copying Ivy Tech is clearly the rational path to take.[24]

The Texas regents are trying to apply a workable ideal to the wrong institution. Why would anyone wish to diminish the economic future of Texas? In the knowledge society of the twenty-first century, a world-class research university is a continuing engine for economic growth. Research universities are among the greatest assets a state can have. North Carolina has its Research Triangle. California benefits enormously from Silicon Valley and Stanford University. Austin is already a high-tech hub, and UT–Austin is part of the reason why. Even suggesting damage to UT–Austin requires a level of ignorance or malice that is hard to imagine. Universities lie at the heart of economic growth.

Finally, the regents appear to assume that the university's sole function is training undergraduates in job skills. Everything else, football excepted, is secondary. When applied to community college, this assumption is narrow but makes some sense. In a research university context, the vo-tech paradigm makes no sense at all. A research university educates the faculty by encouraging imagination and innovation. The vo-ed enthusiasts are calling for the end of the idea factories. How could this help anyone? Idea factories are precisely what good public policy seeks to create and support.

But what about money? MOOCs, SCOCs, and the vo-ed paradigm have all grown like mushrooms after a rain, precisely because they appear to be the broad way to university solvency. Surely a fiscally efficient university is the way to go. Nonetheless, the research university will remain essentially the same, doing in the future what it has done in the past. Moreover, in a knowledge society, those institutions that create knowledge should be supported as lavishly as possible. If they are not, the creation of knowledge will not cease, but it will migrate overseas to other countries, to the Pentagon, to military contractors, to think tanks, and to corporate labs, where information is proprietary. It's probably better all around that collateral damage from public disinvestment in research universities does not include the future.

"Even When They Say It's Not..."

We began with money. In the academy, imagination creates technology, but money will determine how most universities integrate the new electronic distance learning into their campus offerings. Harvard and MIT are not concerned about the money; but other universities will not be quite so insouciant when it comes to the accountant's tale. Certainly Arizona State University is interested in paying its bills. At that level of commitment, money determines the direction and tempo of expansion.

Let's suppose that SCOCs make a modest profit for many universities. Nothing spectacular, mind, but enough to continue the SCOC program. How would the academic world react if this happened? In the first place, the on-campus world of courses, labs, libraries, residence halls, food courts, and classrooms would continue basically unchanged. Established colleges would remain primarily in-person and on-campus institutions.

But electronic distance learning will undoubtedly expand, not just for virtual students but also for on-campus students who take on online or semi-online classes as needed. With similar courses offered in classrooms and online, universities are beginning to offer a dual-track education. The top, of course, is the traditional university experience, going back in some ways to Cardinal Robert and before. The student comes to the campus, learns from dorm life, from other students, and from professors in class. The university experience includes dating and study skills. Lower-tier education is electronic and distant. The student is taught less and must teach herself more. The college experience narrows to the kitchen table. The degree will be the same formally, but inferior intellectually and socially.

Money, both in time spent and direct costs, is the basic reason for a looming division of higher education into a higher on-campus tier and a lower electronic tier. College costs continue to rise. The Internet has opened the discounted way to college. And as Melissa Francis, host of *MONEY* with Melissa Frances on the Fox Business Network, notes, "it's always about the money."

• SEVEN •

For-Profit Universities
The American Dream Redefined

An episode of a recent television show, *The King of Queens,* presents a moment of social reflection. While complaining about his day, the leading character wonders why he hadn't gone to college. That had been a life-changing mistake. The comedy rolls on, and the topic is never broached again. No one has to. The whole show is about the limitations of life for someone who might have gone to college but did not.

Many adults who ask themselves, "Why didn't I go to college?" *do* decide to do something about it. Their choices are limited. Hemmed in by jobs, family, responsibilities, and insecurity, people find it nearly impossible to leave their current lives and enroll at a university. But there is a way to get more education, offering several different options. The way ahead is online distance learning, and the options available include local universities, community colleges, national universities, and for-profit institutions. The four basic options seem to present a prospective student with different paths. He can see his choices: the major universities, such as Maryland and Arizona State, have huge campuses alongside a growing online presence. They award prestigious degrees. *But the courses are probably hard. I might not do so well. The community colleges will have easier courses; but you have to attend most of them in person, and that's a problem for me. The local university is really for kids, and I see them every day in the restaurant. And I may have been a kid once, but I'm not one now. I don't think I'll fit in. The online for-profits look pretty good. I can do that on my computer at home. If I don't do so well, nobody has to know about it. And it probably won't be too hard. Nobody in my family has been to college, and I'm not sure about this, but I don't see any other yellow brick road out of this fast food place. So here goes.*

The paths for that prospective student may be different, but whatever the choice, some things are always the same. The online road is steep, costs time and money, and demands commitment and perseverance, two social virtues always in short supply. There is no guarantee of success and no refund or consolation prize to cushion failure. It's not easy to combine school with life when you're not on campus.

For-Profit Universities

Making money from education is an old idea, but few people have ever been successful at it. Universities went into a fiscal hole the minute they acquired buildings and libraries; they have remained there since. But in post–World War II America, for-profit colleges have been able to buck the long-term fiscal reality. Now, around 13 percent of American undergraduates attend for-profit colleges, whose numbers increased from about 200 in 1990 to almost 1,000 by 2007. The for-profits are often housed in large corporations, such as Apollo, DeVry, American Public Education, Capella, Corinthian. And Laureate, the largest U.S.-based for-profit higher educator, is reported to have 800,000 students worldwide, in the Americas, Europe, the Middle East, Africa, and Asia Pacific.[1]

Several trends in American life have come together to allow for-profit universities to flourish. The G.I. Bill provides government support for veterans' education. Since wars have never ended, the supply of veterans remains strong. Now the Internet allows veterans to choose for-profit schools rather than traditional universities. Secondly, manufacturing began to slow in the 1970s, making a college credential essential for advancing in the workplace. The for-profits offered a convenient way to that degree or a certificate.[2] Thirdly, the federal government's role in education has expanded. After Sputnik (1957), the federal government spread grants across the land. NDEA (National Defense Education Act) grants went to the most qualified students. Pell Grants went to the least qualified. Grants reinforced the effects of the G.I. Bill and job market forces.

For-profit universities have also benefited from the electronic revolution. Increasingly, workers need to know how to manipulate ever-changing technology. And you don't pick up these skills on the playground. The for-profit universities make money from that vo-ed need, which they satisfy cheaper and faster than do liberal arts colleges. These social trends opened a niche, which the electron has brought to a profitable scale. That's the American way.

But opportunity does not come without cost. Federal and state officials worry about what they see as low rates of post-graduation employment by the for-profit students. And there are a lot of those students. The 13 percent of college students attending for-profit institutions involves some two and a half million people. They receive about 25 percent of federally backed loans. But a quarter of these loans are overdue or in default, indicating post-graduation unemployment.[3] It's not a pretty picture. The students owe a lot. Many, even with new jobs, go into default on their loans. Those new jobs aren't much better than the old jobs were. They may not be better at all.[4] The problems interconnect. Students from low socioeconomic origins reach for poor, for-profit education and are then afflicted with large student debt, get a modest post-graduation job, and default. It's a general failure at great expense.

For-profit universities lack both academic prestige and political acceptance. Public authorities have been vigorously moving against the for-profits, more in an effort to kill them off than to fix them up. California has cut state scholarships, the Cal Grants, for students attending 154 schools, almost all for-profit. The reason given was high student debt and higher debt default. The reason not given appears to be that many for-profits are considered bad schools. Neither state nor student is getting value for the money.

Federal officials agree. In 2015, the United States Department of Education implemented a "gainful-employment rule," which will eliminate a lot of student aid to career-oriented for-profit schools. The gainful-employment rule ties student loans and debt to certificate completion in career training programs and subsequent employment success. For-profit institutions are held to a high standard of degrees-to-jobs-to-debt repayment success. Public and private nonprofit institutions are exempt.

Government bureaucracies, once set to the task of creating administrative guidelines, will pursue that effort until every conceivable guideline has been written. On October 30, 2014, the Department of Education took the first step toward enacting the "gainful employment" standard. It issued its 945-page set of regulations concerning the eligibility of colleges and universities to enroll students who had federal loans and grants. These new regulations prohibited students at certain institutions (primarily for-profits) from receiving federal aid unless "the program can show that their graduates' annual loan payments do not exceed 20 percent of discretionary income, or 8 percent of total earnings."[5] Not-for-profit institutions, both public and private, are generally exempt from the requirements, which would hit a large number of community colleges.

Not everyone agrees with the official animus against for-profit institutions.

Critics complain that such discrimination will create some serious collateral damage. After the DOE published its lengthy set of regulations, Steve Gunderson, head of the Association of Private Sector Colleges and Universities, wrote an open letter to Arne Duncan, Secretary of Education. Gunderson claimed that the proposed rule would, if applied fairly, eliminate the law program at George Washington University and the social work program at Virginia Commonwealth University. He argued, "If the vast majority of programs give graduates an earnings gain, then shutting down those programs will deprive those students of that earnings gain." Gunderson added a hard truth:

> Our students are those who are underserved by traditional higher education and we are meeting their needs today in a way that heavily subsidized state universities and private nonprofits are not. Our students are not the highest earners among recipients of credentials, but they are better off than they were prior to pursuing an education. Stripping these students of that opportunity is the wrong thing to do and is, in fact, contrary to the stated goals of this Administration.[6]

No one paid any official attention to these observations, serious though they are. The campaign against for-profit schools has only intensified since then.

Gunderson and the Association of Private Sector Colleges and Universities opposed the regulations with more than an open letter. They filed a lawsuit. It lost in federal district court. Gunderson protested,

> The gainful employment regulation will impact millions of students enrolled in thousands of programs over the next decade. We believe this regulation is arbitrary and capricious and in violation of federal law. The regulation is harmful to students and inconsistent with the intent of the Congress under the Higher Education Act. It needlessly complicates the efforts of new traditional students to achieve a career-focused education that helps them get jobs and we will continue to fight to keep opportunities open for students who are often struggling to juggle family, work, and school.[7]

Although the lawsuit failed upon appeal also, the Association raised serious issues that will reappear, both judicially and politically.

Officials in the Department of Education disdain the for-profits. And they appear to have little empathy for the poor jobs, wretched prospects, often dismal academic preparation, and real needs of many students. These kids and adults are unlikely to attend traditional universities. In the absence of for-profits, a significant segment of the public will lose an educational opportunity. True enough, community colleges can fill some of that gap, and it is government policy to make community college education free and perhaps even compulsory. Still, the very success of the for-profits indicates that community college can't do it all. For-profit universities and technical institutes appear as a kind of domestic Ellis Island for those who wish to migrate from dead-end jobs to the lower rungs on a career ladder.

Students in for-profits genuinely need a good deal of help. Almost a third—31 percent—of African American college graduates and 28 percent of Hispanic college graduates got their degrees in for-profit schools in 2012–2013. For-profit institutions, whatever their weaknesses, continue to play a substantial role in adult education and social mobility. The for-profit schools may be officially regarded as counterfeit universities, not up to appropriate academic standards, and engaged in predatory enrollment just to get federal grants. Maybe so. Maybe not. But the Golden Door they open for working Americans is genuine enough.

The United States Department of Education officials have already put some for-profits out of business. Not everyone is unhappy about that. Holly Petraeus, wife of General David Petraeus, who works at the Consumer Financial Protection Bureau (CFPB), has argued that for-profit universities prey heavily upon military personnel. For-profits have recruited service members to sign up for courses and pay for them with government-secured loans. Those in the enlisted ranks know that they will need more education than they now have, so they make an easy target.

But it's not just those in the military who seek loans. Of those attending for-profit colleges, almost all students, 96 percent, apply for federal student loans. Regardless of their origin, loans are essential to the for-profits; many will fold without them. Observers can reasonably suppose that folding up the for-profits lies at the core of federal policy. Of course, no one will admit that. And, of course, regardless of the for-profits, poor and poorly prepared students will continue to need help with education.

Federal policy, as is so often the case, appears to cut both ways. President Obama set as an administration aim that "by 2020, America will once again have the highest proportion of college graduates in the world."[8] The Secretary of Education endorses college for everyone and opposes for-profits for anyone. But for-profits do educate, to some extent, anyway, a significant percentage of American college graduates. Many of these graduates could not get a degree without the for-profits. So which is it to be—supporting college for working Americans or cutting back on the for-profits? Everyone is familiar with schizophrenic government action, which holds federal policy up with one hand and knocks it down with the other. In any event, federal policy will not reduce the number or the need of working adults who have to have that college degree. The Feds may, however, make it harder to get one.

From the students' perspective, the real problem is their academic preparation. The for-profits often enroll students with abysmal academic records. They can read, but not well or comfortably. For-profits have altered their instructional methods to accommodate poorly prepared students and their work and family schedules. These schools try to meet the students where they live. They offer shorter teaching units: instead of semesters, pods. The teaching pods average 20–24 hours of faculty contact rather than the normal semester standard of 40–45 hours. For-profits offer classes in the evenings, when the students may be exhausted but can at least log on. They also include a good deal of class time in the form of student learning groups, which are given projects to explore and reports to deliver. The educational experience is often a combination of traditional lecture and the trendy "flipped classroom." In this, the for-profits are, unsurprisingly, not different at all from SCOCs, and they have many of the same strengths and weaknesses.

The University of Phoenix uses pods for its standard undergraduate format. Although the pods tend to split about 50/50 between classroom and student projects, Phoenix bases its final exam only on the classroom hours. So the course actually runs only four nights, sixteen hours, which is the classroom component. The difference between pod and semester speaks for itself. Still, the for-profits are generally accredited institutions, approved by the American Commission of Career Schools and Colleges. Oddly, perhaps, the U.S. Department of Education appears to have no problem with that accreditation.[9]

The pod system is based on the idea that the adult students will be able to teach themselves as much as the instructor teaches them. They will complete their homework, whether on their own or in groups. The idea is noble, but the results have been discouraging. Students do not seem to learn as much as they would in a college semester. No surprise here, since the instruction is approximately one-fourth of what a college semester would contain. Teaching under these circumstances can be unrewarding; learning under these circumstances can be both limited and difficult.

People generally suspect that for-profits offer a second-line degree. The credential may be the same, but it means less. There are examples aplenty involving for-profit graduates applying for jobs using colloquial and inappropriate English and writing reports that are ungrammatical and almost unreadable. It's all anecdotal, but the anecdotes reinforce the popular impression. Students may get a credential without learning enough to justify the time, the money, the effort, or the prize. But whatever the quality of the degree, the loans must be repaid.

A further difference between for-profit and the rest involves student recruitment. For-profits often recruit students the way coaches recruit players. The for-profit colleges, so to speak, get in your face. They urge you to sign up. They bombard you with enticements of a better job. They insist that you can, on your own, act to improve your life. They don't wait for you to decide. They get you off the dime and on the march. That is a genuine social service—and also a source of complaint as an improper practice.

Much of the selling of an education is done on television. The University of Phoenix is the most prominent of the for-profit advertisers, if for no reason other than it has bought the naming rights to a Phoenix football stadium. But advertising cannot solve every problem. The University of Phoenix has suffered from the recent recession. In 2010, Phoenix had around 600,000 students, making it the largest college system in the country. By fall 2014, this number diminished to 250,000, still a lot. In 2010, it had over 200 on-site classrooms and offices around the country; by 2014 that had fallen to 112. The success of the for-profits demands scale, and economic growth makes scale possible.

But the University of Phoenix continues to teach its educationally offbeat demographic. The average age of the Phoenix undergrad is 33, and almost all of these students have jobs and families. For graduate students, the age is 36. Two-thirds of their students are women, who are socially vulnerable to the pressures of family and the need for credentials. Around 25 percent of the students are African American and another 15 percent Hispanic. Phoenix continues to graduate more minority students with graduate degrees in business, education, and health care than any other school. The for-profit universities advertise hope and promote a positive social attitude.

With the for-profits, some success coexists with a lot of failure. The overall graduation rate is 16 percent, largely because one of their core constituencies has been students-at-risk most of their lives. Even so, the University of Phoenix graduates a higher percentage than pass most of the MOOCs, where the percentage of student wastage can reach into the mid-90s. Taking it all in all, the University of Phoenix and other for-profits as well are making much of their living out of human reclamation projects. It's the social equivalent of recycling, or, better yet, upcycling. How can anyone oppose that?

Well, Arne Duncan, secretary of the Department of Education, has his doubts. In April 2015, the Department of Education levied a $29.6 million fine on Corinthian's Heald College system for "misrepresentation of job placement possibilities" for its students. Secretary Duncan announced, "This should be a wake-up call for consumers across the country about the abuses that can exist within the for-profit college sector." The term "consumers" is instructive, as is Coursera's habit of calling its MOOC enrollees "users." Both imply a commercial rather than an academic relationship. Secretary Duncan also thundered, "We will continue to hold the career-college industry accountable and demand reform for the good of students and taxpayers."[10] His monitory tone drew a fair amount of public support. Debbie Cochrane, research director at the Institute for College Access and Success, approved both the fine and the press release. She suggested that others who oversee colleges, such as accreditation agencies, should follow the secretary's lead and increase scrutiny of for-profit colleges. Expand the regulatory state. That'll fix things.

It certainly fixed Corinthian. Within a month of the Department's fine, Corinthian had closed its Heald campus system. Closure left a lot of students high, dry, and in debt. Corinthian's Heald students were like homeowners underwater, paying for something that didn't exist. Many simply ceased repaying their student loans altogether, going from compliance or deferred into default. Somehow, the Department of Education failed to anticipate this, which seemed obvious to everyone else. Students began to complain, both as individuals and en masse, and filed lawsuits. After some confused hemming and hawing, Secretary Duncan decided to look into the possibility of assuming student debt for the bereft Heald alums-to-be. The lawsuits continue. The poor suffer the most.

The for-profit universities face a mixed forecast. The economic climate for private sector education remains a bit sour. But for-profits are also seeing a shift in student demographics. They used to admit older, employed students; recently, they have opened their doors to a wider group of applicants who are younger, marginally qualified, and substantially at academic risk. On the other side, the online for-profits face increased competition from traditional universities such as Arizona State or Maryland. And the U.S. Department of Education continues to be aggressively hostile to the for-profits.

But the long-term social trends seem to favor the for-profits. People will continue to need one more credential or degree beyond what they currently have. After all, what employee can drive across town to a college campus, find the necessary courses, and then try to fit a work schedule around that course schedule? Salvation lies with the online for-profits, which offer the necessary convenience that traditional universities do not. For-profit universities, when focused on their comparative advantages, should survive.

But the for-profits must be flexible. The University of Phoenix, after rapid growth, with its original demographic of adults who were employed, continued its growth by opening Axia, an associates degree college. Phoenix now admitted adolescents, many unemployed and most unprepared for college work. The plan paid off temporarily, but by 2010–11, the effects of the fiscal crisis hit Phoenix pretty hard. Enrollment declines and completion declines undercut the original business plan. By 2016, enrollment was 162,000. Phoenix abolished Axia and is replacing it with certification programs, somewhat in the Ivy Tech model. These certificates can be "stacked," so to say, into course credits for a degree. Phoenix has good reason to hope that these changes will revive the brand, increase graduation rates, cut student losses, and produce a better "product." Phoenix is returning to its original demographic constituency of employed adults moving up the career ladder.

Phoenix has added a counseling component. It now begins its program with a three-week online orientation, which all students must take when they seek to enroll. Orientation is free, and the evaluation of student skills is part of it. Those unready will be shunted to remedial courses. Those who barely make the cut are offered increased tutoring and student support. Phoenix hopes that it can exploit the student services opportunity. The institution can maintain continuous contact with its students online, providing support and encouragement that include chat rooms and counseling sessions, along with the usual tutoring and academic help. In the oral cultures that the for-profits serve, constant student contact provides a genuine comparative advantage.

The main obstacle for many for-profits may not be the federal government or the economy but StraighterLine. Burck Smith founded StraighterLine in 2009, a year after the big crash. College costs were a major social issue. StraighterLine would charge only $99 a month as a standard student fee. It would guarantee transfer credit for its courses to both for-profit and not-for-profit colleges. More than 100 institutions currently accept StraighterLine courses, and at least 2,000 others have agreed to consider them. Additionally, StraighterLine provides online counseling along with the usual pep talks.

StraighterLine has taken advantage of the two crucial strengths of online education: it has cut the cost of college, and it provides student counseling. And StraighterLine spares students the embarrassment of a weak online degree by guaranteeing transfer to known, accredited, bricks-and-mortar institutions. With a StraighterLine start, students can obtain a standard respectable degree. StraighterLine has mastered the difficulties of initial admission to college, and that's not nothing.

The whole idea is working out. Over 10,000 students were enrolled in 2014. StraighterLine offered more than 60 college courses. Smith expects more, and he's likely to get them. The U.S. Department of Education is not threatening StraighterLine with extinction, and StraighterLine has avoided all the problems of the "gainful-employment rule." It has bundled cheaper courses, effective administration, and guaranteed college acceptance. It's a winning formula, as community colleges have already shown.

Future success depends on focus. The for-profits can survive if they concentrate on their core constituency of minorities, the working poor, and employed adults who need that next credential. They must improve their student services, from orientation to counseling and tutoring. The other policy that for-profits may follow has been blazed by StraighterLine. The federal employment guidelines apply to graduates. Just slough off that role to the brick-and-mortar non-profits. The for-profits can provide an entrance to the already accredited state and private colleges. For-profits can continue to offer degrees to adults who need another credential and are going to finish the program.

The Community College Solution

State and federal officials think that there should be a way to reduce the footprint of for-profit universities. Well, maybe that can be done. How about sending students to community colleges instead? They award recognized credentials, teach courses in semesters rather than pods, don't cost too much, and reach a lot of working adult students. And community colleges are part of the public sector.

So, let's take an example, an avatar representing some common social characteristics: Joe Smith, the first in his family to go to college, has graduated somewhere in the middle of his class from a typically abysmal urban high school. That is in itself a personal triumph, but it is not enough. Joe knows that he doesn't want to work in fast food all his life. The path ahead is clear. He needs more education, but socioeconomic disadvantage has put him as far behind the eight ball as anyone not a convict can possibly be. Perhaps Joe can find an answer to his problems at a community college. They are relatively cheap, invariably open enrollment, and offer remedial courses. They schedule classes most hours of the working day, and Joe needs at least a part-time job. So he enrolls, embarking on the first step of the community college solution to current social deficit and future social mobility.

Community colleges are designed precisely to deal with the Joe Smiths of this world. But difficulties remain. At least half of newly enrolled community college students find they must take one, usually more than one, remedial course, and these don't count toward a degree. Low-functional literacy, whether with words or numbers, is a standard deficit for community college students. Joe perseveres. He takes three remedial courses, learning what they should have taught him in high school. But it goes slowly. At the end of a full year in community college, Joe has acquired only twelve hours of credit, a fifth of what he needs for an associates degree. His education is going to take a lot of time, and time is the enemy of completion. After all, while Joe's in school he can't earn enough money to live on. Hence, the dropout rate.

A student needs to take fifteen credit hours a semester in order to make serious progress toward a degree. Fifteen hours is a psychological benchmark as well. A student taking those fifteen hours feels like a student, with work done on the side. If he carries less than fifteen hours—six, or nine, perhaps—the student feels like a worker taking courses on the side. The difference in attitude sounds modest, but is in fact profound. Those who think of themselves as students have a lot better chance of finishing. Joe understands that, but he has rent to pay and insurance and all the slew of bills that come with being an adult. After his first year, he needs even more hours working at the restaurant. He won't be able to take a full load next semester. He is falling behind, part of a dismal statistical picture: only about 15 percent of students starting at a community college obtain a bachelor's degree after six years.

In January 2015, President Obama proposed a program to help Joe Smith and his fellow students, almost nine million of them. Speaking in Nashville, Tennessee, he addressed the costs of education. He suggested that community college, defined as the first two years of a bachelor's degree (about 60 hours, depending on the curriculum), should be free for every student. Community colleges can form the "essential pathway to the middle class."[11] The president also added criteria for the free tuition. The community college students must attend school at least part-time, defined as six credit hours a semester. They must maintain a GPA of 2.5. They must make progress toward a degree or a certificate, meaning remediation does not count. The total cost of the Obama community college solution has been estimated at a mere $60 billion (probably more) over a decade, with the federal government picking up at least three quarters of it. The president based his program on a Tennessee model, which provides free community college tuition for in-state students.

The president proposed that free public education be extended from a high school diploma to an associates degree, from 12 to 14 or 15 years. The last few years of education may not be compulsory by law, but they are by social demand. President Obama imagines a better-educated America, something last undertaken, in a big way, by President Franklin D. Roosevelt with the G.I. Bill. The caveats to the Obama proposal, a minimum GPA and a part-time attendance requirement, will doubtless be modified by experience and federal guidelines. But the essential plan is clearly in accord with the demands of a knowledge-credential society.[12]

The basic problem with the Obama community college solution is that it is insufficiently inclusive. Joe Smith may be taking a full load, or close to it, but most of his campus colleagues are not. They are dropping in to pick up a course and dropping out when it is over, or when the car insurance bill comes in higher than anticipated. Some are taking a corporate certificate program. Some are taking a remedial course in reading or math so they can do better in their med-tech courses in a proprietary school. Community college students, like Cleopatra, have infinite variety. The president's idea is now only for those heading toward an associates degree. Only by including everybody, whatever their goals, can the president's initiative really help the educationally disadvantaged.[13] It would be better if it lifted all boats.

The president is adding to the free public education school years, which will change the meaning of the term "dropout." Now, dropout refers to those unfortunate kids who do not finish high school, or maybe middle school. President Obama's plan will change that term to mean those who do not complete their associates degrees. The reverse is also true. There seems little doubt that over time the associates degree, not the high school diploma, will become the minimal educational standard. Nothing remains static in a knowledge/credential society.

Credential Creep

Lod Cook, an American businessman who achieved great success in oil and gas, used to talk to students about a business career that really worked. Put yourself in a position to succeed, he would say. Give yourself a chance. Part of that chance to succeed is to have the right credentials, along with the education they represent. But the level of credentials required to get a good spot on the great social chain of being is rising: slowly, it is true, but also persistently. The American Dream, or upward mobility, as it is often called, has become a moving target. To give yourself a chance, you need more and better credentials than would have sufficed a generation ago. In your grandfather's time, a technical certificate would do; now a master's degree will put you in a position to succeed. The social phenomenon may be called "credential creep." It is tough on today's students, and it may not seem fair, but credential creep is an established fact of modern life.

Examples abound. An RN certificate still defines a nurse. But if you want to go from the ward into management, you also need a bachelor's degree in nursing (BSN). That works for now. Ten years down the road, perhaps 15, you will need a master's degree in nursing (MSN). That will be good enough then. And 20 years or so after that, you will need to be a nurse practitioner, with all the further education that that requires. The same is true in other areas of life. In the 1950s, the Army had a lot of officers who lacked college degrees. Now, the Ph.D. is getting to be standard for a general officer. Credential creep has become an established element in the job market and in personal social planning.

The process of credential creep has been going on a long time. The post–Civil War generation lived through an educational watershed. When they were born, simple literacy was enough. If you got out of the fifth grade, you knew everything that you needed to know. When the ranks of the Civil War veterans began to thin, a high school diploma had become a minimum standard for middle-class employment. It wasn't just the new technology (the Edison inventions, for example). It was also the increasing complexity of business and public life. The process has been inexorable: the tempo of credential creep has increased. Of course, the social drift toward more (and better) education was as uneven then as it is today. In World War I, many small-town semi-literate draftees were taught close-order drill by tying hay to one boot and straw to the other. The cadence was not "left, right," which not everyone knew, but "hayfoot, strawfoot." The improvisation worked well. It was not needed a quarter century later in World War II.

Credential creep involved more than years in school. It also meant a change in the organization of public education. One-room schoolhouses did what they did pretty well, but they didn't include high schools. As the new century wore on, there was more to learn, and it took twelve grades to do it. After World War II, credentials oozed upward again. Almost 15 million young veterans went to college on the G.I. Bill, so a college degree gradually became the standard. The bachelor's degree remained standard until the electronic revolution. Twenty-five years of prosperity, from 1983 to 2008, combined with a torrent of invention, has made the college degree seem merely basic. Young people need a graduate degree of some kind, preferably in STEM, law, or medicine. No social critic in modern America supposes that credential creep will stop. It will only accelerate.

Online students are both victims of credential creep and beneficiaries of the increasing opportunity in American higher education. Near the tail end of the credential chain, the online students plunge in, soon learning that school replaces leisure. And you're taking a big chance at big expense. The often-overstressed students do not usually find online education to be easy. There's more work than you expected. You might not finish. The odds are long, but if you never sign up and take your shot, what sort of future does that leave you? So the students enroll in both "for" and "non" universities. The costs of college will not decline, either in money spent for education or social opportunity lost through its lack.

Everyone knows this, perhaps not in sociological detail or broad historical terms, but certainly as a daily reality. Few Americans have not seen someone with better credentials get the leg up. Even fewer escape the fear that their credentials, now adequate, will one day be found wanting. Will the Cisco certificate *always* be adequate for this IT position? The Hall of Fame pitcher Stanley Coveleski, when asked about his career, replied that baseball is a "worrying game."[14] Pursuing the American Dream can also be a worrying game.

Minerva

There have always been for-profit schools in America. The modern for-profit business model, though, came from John Sperling (1921–2014). In 1979 he founded the University of Phoenix. Sperling often said that he had had one single idea in his life, but that idea had been a good one.[15] He had figured out how to subtract enough from the medieval university model to make a profit from education. Of the three elements of that model, he dropped the creation and the collection of knowledge, keeping only the distribution thereof. The energy crisis and the arrival of the Internet turned his good idea into a huge success. The number of students went from the thousands to the hundreds of thousands, and Phoenix began to make money.

Scale is important in economic terms, but it was not the core of Sperling's business plan. The heart of a good business idea is rarely money; rather, it is about a product, service, or process that will help people alter their lives, at least a bit. The entrepreneur hopes to improve the structure of the world we live in, and that is no small thing.

Sperling imagined a mass for-profit university, but his model is sufficiently flexible to accommodate an elite school. The elite online university has been dreamed up by Ben Nelson, a San Francisco business strategist. Nelson embodies the Silicon Valley style of thinking big and thinking new. You take a chance with the most dramatic and plausible idea available. The Minerva Project proclaims itself as America's newest Ivy League university. Minerva will admit only the top-rated applicants for an undergraduate degree. It has Ivy League admissions standards, Ivy League students, and Ivy League courses. Minerva does not have Ivy League prices, because it does not have Ivy League costs. Minerva has no band, no football, no library, labs, or physical plant of any sort. Tuition is $10,000 a year (2016), far less than the $60,000 or so charged in the Ivies. And it is projected to make money. Minerva opened in the fall semester of 2014, with five online faculty members and around 28 students. This first class of students signed on to the deal with the enticing offer of free tuition for four years. The first paying crop, 113 students, began in fall 2015. Minerva began small, trying to work out the gremlins in the first year. It will move to scale as finances permit, as faculty sign on, and as students apply.

Minerva is a for-profit university, designed to remain permanently in the private sector. At some point, if Minerva is a success, there may well be an IPO. Ben Nelson has already thought about the liquidity moment: he has, after all, already completed a successful corporate sale. "Are we going to go public or stay private? I don't know, but the liquidity event is going to be the trading of our shares. We will not sell to another university—they will not be able to afford us."[16] Minerva University may eventually appear in the primary public markets. The possibility of owning a piece of Minerva raises an interesting question. If you bought some Minerva shares, would that affect the admission of your child to the university? A decision for the future: now it is only a query.

Compare Minerva to the rest of the higher education spectrum, and it appears somewhat like a platypus. It resembles both Phoenix and traditional institutions. All have online components and seek to make money from cuts in costs. But the differences really catch the eye. The University of Phoenix finds a reliable core constituency among the approximately 34 percent of high school graduates who do not go directly to college. Minerva seeks students among the academic elite, who are certainly going to college[17]; the only question is where. In the first Minerva class, 58 percent were women, which is getting to be a standard for the brick-and-mortar colleges.

The same percentage of Minerva students came from outside the United States (largely Asia and Europe), which is far from the campus (or Phoenix) standard. Minerva plans to be a world, not just an American, university.

To teach these brilliant students, Minerva recruits its own faculty. Minerva does not treat them in the manner of traditional universities but more like other online institutions. Minerva does not offer tenure. Nelson has said that Minerva does not expect its professors to be there forever, which suggests that he expects substantial turnover. In return, Nelson promises "freedom" to his faculty. They will be, so to speak, independent contractors. They may keep the profits from their patents and IPOs, as well as the income from their grants. As Nelson would tell a potential faculty member: "So the level of control you have over your life, your IP, where you live, who your colleagues are: that is a level of control no other faculty has."[18] Though Nelson does not say it, Minerva faculty will function essentially as adjuncts do at traditional colleges. Faculty will have freedom, no doubts there: but that's all they'll have. If you teach at Minerva, you better invent something or have a private income.

Ben Nelson views his university, faculty, students, and electronic education as something brand new. Not entirely. His attitude toward students resembles that of Thomas Jefferson and Cardinal Newman. Students come first. The university is built around them. Teaching is the primary faculty duty. Research and publication are secondary. But Nelson's attitude toward faculty does have innovative elements. The faculty is an outside force brought electronically to the students. They rarely, or perhaps never, meet the students personally. The faculty members are interchangeable parts, added or discarded as needed. If the discipline were sufficiently standardized and precise, such as calculus, the instructor might be a robot, perhaps photographically portrayed as R2-D2 or Winnie-the-Pooh.

Basically, Nelson thinks that professors ought to have an intense relationship with their students, while having only the most minimal contact among themselves. They are isolated gurus. They have no collective influence on the university and its policies. Traditional colleges do not function anything like this.[19] They are intensely communal. Departments, degree programs, team-taught courses, and the horrors of faculty meetings: all call upon the collective resources of the faculty. Nelson wants a university with individual professors but with no faculty. Cardinal Robert brought professors together and assumed (correctly) that the students would follow. Ben Nelson has turned this arrangement on its head. He wants to bring students together and have professors drop in occasionally from afar and disappear when class is done. How well does that work?

Minerva's most dramatic innovations lie in the area of pedagogy and curriculum. Nelson believes that his students have been so carefully selected that Minerva does not have to offer the basic freshman/sophomore courses. All other universities, from Yale to Baton Rouge Community College, insist that their freshmen take those basic courses, in writing, mathematics, sciences, and humanities. Minerva's students, Nelson assumes, will already know the basic material. If a Minerva student does have an area of intellectual weakness, she would simply go to a MOOC and learn it there.

Nelson has replaced the discarded basic courses with multidisciplinary modules. One such module is a formal systems course, covering statistics, mathematics, logic, and economics. Minerva also offers a communications course on language, covering linguistics, literature, rhetoric, and composition. The modules, Nelson argues, emphasize skills as well as knowledge. They deal with broad patterns and interpretations rather than with specific detail within academic disciplines. These interdisciplinary modules work better when team taught, with a learning group on both sides of the electronic podium. The interdisciplinary modules are not entirely novel; they resemble the core courses based on the Columbia model.[20]

The Minerva plan does imply an unusual system of student assessment. At Minerva, assessment is based heavily on oral (sometimes typed, sometimes Skyped) student performance in live online seminars. The high grades, insofar as there are grades, go to students who demonstrate critical thinking, speak clearly, are intellectually nimble, and show a firm grasp of the concepts, equations, and formulae involved. The professor grades by examining and re-examining recorded videos of the seminars and posted chat. Examinations, obviously, are obsolete, and Minerva will not use them. Students will still write essays and reports. This system sounds pretty good, for the exceptional students that Minerva admits. The standards reflect English aristocratic practice where social success depends on saying things well.[21]

Nelson's classes resemble nothing so much as an honors college. All classes are seminars, which Minerva monitors to make sure that professors don't talk too much. A timer warns them if they lecture for more than five minutes at a time.[22] Minerva also breaks the seminars down into smaller groups. The breakout groups share "whiteboards" and files, and the professor can electronically visit any group at any time. These arrangements, now and then, anyway, will create the intimacy of a small group, which supports active learning and student participation.

Nelson builds on the active learning by emphasizing Socratic dialogue:

> The worst case scenario is that the student knows the answer, and then the conversation is over. The point is engaging them in analysis, so you want to avoid the right answer. In Minerva, they type their answers. You can pick the most interesting wrong answer first and then engage the students who had the right answer to walk the student with the wrong answer through it.[23]

The pedagogy is designed to reduce the professorial role of providing information, that is, lectures. It emphasizes student discussion, much of it about wrong answers and faulty interpretations, along with connections to related disciplines and information. This teaching process is slow and often infuriating, but it demands critical reading and thinking. Why are some answers wrong? Why do others sound good but won't work? Why are still other propositions just silly? The professors can contribute data and intellectual patterns. They can prod discussion toward the right answer in STEM courses and toward sensible solutions in politics and the humanities. The students do most of the talking. They will come to understand important ideas, usually, sometimes painfully, from thrashing out details and examples. Minerva expects to have only students who can prosper within that system.

Finally, Nelson believes that having the students move from wrong answers/solutions to right ones is something one can do much more easily online than offline. This idea may be the greatest strength of online education. If everyone is in class, the professor, who knows a lot, inevitably leads the discussion among the students, who do not. But online, where faces do not always face other faces, the professor can guide the discussion by silence as well as by speech. Sometimes she rings a gong to interrupt one student's answer and signal to another student to continue the discussion. The social parameters of this online pedagogical strategy are narrow: it succeeds only with small numbers of serious students. But that is what Minerva now has. As Minerva scales up toward the projected 20,000 students, the "wrong answer discussion" may no longer work. But that's the future. Now, as Minerva launches the educational ship (still a skiff, actually), the pedagogical techniques seem reasonable, creative, and likely to succeed.

Ben Nelson also has an imaginative proposal for the Minerva campus. For the first year, the student cohort is housed in a San Francisco hotel. For the last six semesters, they rotate around the world together. The idea is to expand junior year abroad to three full years abroad, in world cities that offer a learning environment in themselves. Nelson has chosen Berlin and Buenos Aires for the second-year students. In the year following, they will visit Bangalore and Seoul; the final year is spent in Istanbul and London.

Minerva combines online courses, contact among the students, and residence in culturally important cities. The Minerva students ought to be ready to compete in the knowledge society. And, Nelson thinks, it can be done at a (comparatively) modest cost in time—four years—and in money—say, $60,000—and with world travel thrown in.

The Minerva idea has been sufficiently enticing to gain outside support. It has received a $25 million initial investment from Benchmark Capital, which is a financial move for them and instant endowment for Minerva. This money will allow Nelson to scale up the Minerva Project from interesting experiment to a profitable company. Basically, the Benchmark investment has bought Minerva time. During these first couple of years, it has gained some sort of professional acceptance. The Western Association of Schools and Colleges (WASC) has granted accreditation to four Minerva programs and is currently looking at a fifth. The speed at which Minerva's programs got accredited has raised eyebrows in the academic world. Minerva was able to skip over the demanding, lengthy, difficult evaluation process by simply becoming a program of the already accredited Keck Graduate Institute.[24] Minerva's official name is Minerva Schools at KGI.

Minerva's current business outlook seems rosy, but the future will pose serious financial challenges. The Minerva system is labor intensive, to a degree that would make administrators in standard universities shudder. When Minerva is scaled up, the number of faculty will go from five to God knows how many. Even if the professors are not paid very much, and it looks like they won't be, there will still be enough of them to cost a bundle. At a student ratio of one to ten, Nelson is going to need 2,000 professors for his high-estimate figure of 20,000 students. That's a lot of faculty. And if some of them are superstars, they will need faculty assistants. Moreover, research, intellectual discovery, and publication are what the best professors generally do.[25] Minerva takes no account of this; so how can Nelson possibly expect to have the top faculty teaching those top students? Good schools need good professors, and this is as true for Ben Nelson as it was for Cardinal Robert.

An additional problem will involve housing. The courses may come from anywhere, but the kids are all supposed to be in one place. First in San Francisco, then Berlin and Buenos Aires, then Bangalore and Seoul, and so on. Where are these kids going to live? It's not a struggle now to find housing for forty students, or even a couple hundred; several thousand or more may well stretch the housing capacity of a good-sized city. You can't put them all in tents in a soccer stadium. Nelson has not mentioned any solution to that issue, probably because there isn't any.

Beyond that, students in science, technology, and engineering require labs, frequently large and expensive, with millions of dollars' worth of equipment. They also need lab partners, mentors, and colleagues, not appearing on screen but being there in person. There is no substitute for hands-on, face-to-face instruction and encouragement in the lab.[26] How are these STEM students going to learn their disciplines, which require an enormous amount of doing rather than watching? Can Minerva borrow, or afford to borrow, the needed lab space, equipment, instructors, computers, for semesters at a time? That's expensive space and expertise. It's like asking for a loan of the Large Hadron Collider. There are reasons why universities own an enormous amount of laboratory space and equipment. And those reasons are learning and research.

The fundamental problem with Nelson's plan does not involve housing or even money. Nelson does not understand what a university is. Nelson assumes that a university is just an instructional delivery system for students. Cardinal Robert knew better. The university is actually a place that creates a learning community; educates the faculty; maintains laboratories, libraries, and museums; and creates knowledge. Each of those activities enhances the others. The town crier is an information delivery system, as is the theatre, radio programs, and the Internet. No one confuses any of these things with a university.

Ben Nelson's dream does not lack nobility, nor is it disconnected from current technology and economics. It is an effort to modernize the university's undergraduate educational delivery system. Nelson does not have anything to say about other essential university functions. In that, alas, he is not alone, but is in the company of thousands of state legislators across the land. He differs from them in one essential way. The politicians just want cheap. Nelson wants excellence plus the next big thing. The politicians deal with the entire educational infrastructure and establishment. Nelson is concerned about a tiny elite. But neither cheap (meaning not excellent) nor elite (meaning not inclusive) will become the future of American universities.

The economist Joseph Schumpeter noted that free market capitalism involves continuing creative destruction.[27] New technologies replace old ones, new companies replace old ones, new ways of doing business put the old ways out of business. Once there were switchboards and telephone operators; now we have cell phones. Once brush salesmen went door to door; now a celebrity sells brushes on television. Is it the same with research universities? Will the personal touch be replaced by machines? Again, the answer is no. Universities are built with people, not technology.

Proportion

The for-profits, mostly online, perform only one of the essential university functions and seem likely to occupy the fringes of American higher education. Minerva searches the world for the most creative kids, but it will skim only the tiniest drop of cream from the annual student cohort. Minerva's class will make no difference in the general student pool. Phoenix et al. do have a target student pool, though it remains a minority of those going to college. Both the "up" and the "down" recruits form an academic niche, large enough to draw a lot of attention but too small to be a model for education. Teaching students only makes the online for-profits an adjunct to a full description of American universities.

In a democracy, mass solutions are required for large public problems, such as the perceived deficiencies of universities.[28] The for-profits do not offer a mass solution. They will continue to change the lives of individual students, but they cannot be universities. Making money is what for-profits are supposed to do.

• EIGHT •

The Limitations of Reform

Western universities have remained much the same since Magna Carta. There have been some changes, naturally, particularly in America. American universities have seen new curricula, with the addition of engineering, agriculture, business, and teaching; with graduate education on the German model; with elective courses and multiple majors, and with a general reform and expansion of professional education. These reforms changed the student experience a lot, and expanded the size of universities. But the medieval structure and functions are still intact. Cardinal Robert's university may have gone on steroids, but it is still his vision expanded to American scale and needs.

Since the 1960s, social expectations for the university have changed. The climate of opinion about universities has swung from approval to complaint. Critics now think universities should be changed from root to branch to twig to bud. They attack the idea that the old ways can still work, even while the old ways are still working. These new critics concentrate on nostrums, not normalcy.[1] In due course they forecast a new kind of university, though exact details remain scarce. Never mind that. Complaints abound anyway. They center on issues of institutional democracy, effective education (that phrase has multiple meanings), and student costs. Many critics denounce the university as elitist, of maintaining itself as a bastion of privilege that restricts opportunity and supports a non-egalitarian society. This alone, so deleterious to a good society, will force universities to change. Beyond that, a slew of critics allege that the university has taught students only a very little. This elitist and inadequate education costs huge sums, driving students, parents, and states into debt. Money and privilege dominate the current conversation about universities, whether critics, students, parents, or politicians are doing the talking.

So what is to be done?[2] Academic costs, on the minus side, and new technology, on the plus side, have convinced administrators to regard online courses as a way to go. Deans and provosts can economize at home and expand university outreach abroad. Perhaps they can even improve instruction. About the importance of the Internet, none can have any "possible probable shadow of doubt, no possible doubt whatever."[3] The absence of doubt, however, is no guarantee of truth.

It is always possible that some of the promised nostrums might work. At least to some extent. Perhaps online courses and curricula will allow colleges to reduce instructional costs, thus easing the fiscal strain. Some students might learn more online than they do in class. A large selection of SCOCs and MOOCs could reinforce the offerings of smaller colleges. Through the Internet, universities could reach students who are now shut out, though no one really knows who or where they are. One thing, at least, is clear. All reform proposals will be tried somewhere, and online courses are now being tried everywhere. Desperation, as much as necessity, is the mother of invention.

Finances and outreach are not the only problems. It is alleged that students who pay a lot do not seem to be learning a lot. A dollop of online courses won't help much. Reformers suggest that students must be tested and the faculty held accountable for the results of those tests. As Donald Rumsfeld noted, only things that are measured will improve.[4] Of course, it's nice to know what is being measured, and with teaching, the variables, many still unknown, vastly outnumber the certainties, mostly still uncertain. Never mind. Testing remains unfailingly attractive, and it can easily be done. Possibly testing and accountability might help.

As proposals proliferate, it's time to inquire if these reform suggestions have any chance of becoming reality. Even if what is to be done, whatever that is, is done, will the American research university change in structurally useful ways? Are the ideas for academic reform much ado about very little? So we ask: will *any* reform ideas help with academic costs, university outreach, student learning, or faculty accountability? Or are they all the "stuff that dreams are made of"?[5]

Academic Reform

Reform, in its nature, is a dodgy business. Reformers project gauzy hopes on the hard face of experience. But pursuit of the golden future contains more than impossible dreams. Reform also means compulsion. Those who do not share the dream must share the consequences. Early in the twentieth century, an Ohio editor, Robert Ryder, observed that "a hardened reformer can never decide which is the most beautiful word in the English language, compulsory or forbidden."[6]

Nor is there any guarantee of success. Even the most desirable change, brimming with righteous intent, will fall short of perfection. Consider a recent example. School administrators contemplating the probable results of mandatory testing under federal legislation (the No Child Left Behind Act) expected some "teaching to the test." More realistic principals thought that there might be a bit of cheating, since the rewards for school and teachers were so high and the risks seemed so low. Most educators expected only the usual small fudging, ignored by all and which, thereby, would lose the name of cheating. Shockingly few reformers anticipated that the number of teachers cheating would be sufficient to create a national scandal, one large enough to embarrass politicians of both parties.[7] The best intentions and loveliest nostrums can go badly awry.

A determined academic reformer is rarely deterred by such experiences. Take student evaluation of professors, which is done everywhere. Evaluations have not noticeably improved teaching, but they frequently, indeed usually, help to improve student grades. But academic administrators do not seem to be discouraged. Sometimes they take evaluations at face value (a mistake), then quantify them (mistake compounded), and then use them as a basis for pedagogical policy (mistake compounded to the nth degree). They continue to measure an art that cannot be measured using evaluations that do not evaluate who excels in a mystery that can scarcely be defined.[8] Increasingly precise accountability of university faculty is one of those ideas that sounds good and works badly. Does that mean it will be abandoned? Quite otherwise. It will be accelerated. It would be odd indeed if anyone expected anything else.

Academic reform is not just the pursuit of laudable goals, often bringing bad results. The techniques of reform also matter. Administrators ought to consult the people involved, but they rarely do. It takes too long and it is too much trouble. Even worse, consulting those about to be reformed has the unfortunate effect of moving the conversation from laudable goals to adverse side effects. No reformer wants that discussion. Better just impose the moral good from on high, whether it is banning smoking on campus, establishing sensitivity training, or adding a new curriculum.[9] There really is no getting away from one of the inherent contradictions of institutional administration: good personnel management (consulting everyone) is the enemy of efficiency and reform.

Process is important. If you want to institute an academic reform, you go with the grain rather than across it. Does the academic culture suggest a new course or program? All that takes is a wee bit of lobbying, combined with the implication that those who oppose it are stodgy, or something worse. Reforms succeed when they fit the system. You gotta go with the flow.[10] But going with the flow makes serious reform almost impossible to achieve. The normal is always the enemy of the radical. Reformers frequently find that their most beautiful ideas are just out of reach.

A final caveat: Reforms, once up and running, work pretty much as does the rest of the institution. Reforms become part of the establishment. The chair of the new department becomes another academic administrator. In almost everything outside of football, the academic dog wags the tail. The university will absorb the new reforms just as it assimilated the addition of science, engineering, and business programs, just as it adjusted to the astounding idea of elective courses, to say nothing of women in college.[11] The past you always bring with you.

Paths Not Taken

Formal education within Western culture goes back at least to Socrates and the Sophists. During the millennia since, someone somewhere has tried everything. From monastic cloisters to military schools to the public square; from pre–K through grade twelve; from the Internet, prisons, apprenticeships, internships, tutoring, and homeschooling to universities, it's been tried and has succeeded. All pedagogical initiatives have proven to have flaws and virtues, along with endless efforts to fix what had gone wrong. Those now proposing university reforms simply cover once again the same educational waterfront.

Begin with two university educational systems that have previously worked well. One involves continuous tutoring to keep the student advancing at a comfortable pace. A second path forward is a rigorous elitism, refusing to allow unqualified students to enroll in universities in the first place. Tutoring was used to good effect in one-room schoolhouses in America. Elitism has succeeded in European universities, particularly before World War II. Neither is going to be tried today on a massive scale in America, not because they don't work but because of fiscal and social costs.

The one-room schoolhouse had a single teacher and perhaps thirty-odd kids, ranging from the first to the eighth grade. One-room education relied on the invaluable virtues of cooperation and mutual support. The older kids tutored the younger, who got a good bit of one-on-one instruction.

In the upper grades, the majority of the remaining students were girls, who often brought care and compassion to the drudgery of routine recitation. The students also heard the teacher present more difficult material along with the basic stuff, and so advanced at their own pace, faster in some subjects than others, faster this year than last. Finally, the one-room schoolhouse usually produced a strong sense of community.[12]

Constant tutoring and student assessment can be brought to the university, without any real change in standard practice. Just make the student learning community more robust. Older students, who have already passed the basic courses, attend them again and then tutor the freshmen, individually and in groups. At LSU, the program is called Supplementary Instruction (SI), and is used in the large introductory courses such as chemistry, biology, history, or psychology. SI complements the large lecture sections, and does so with the usual good results. The kids get some personal instruction, which they need. The juniors and seniors who teach SI *really* learn the basic stuff. The SI instructors have a campus job, which cuts back on college costs and student debt. SI doesn't cost colleges very much, relatively speaking, and the students gain substantial benefits. But good as it is, SI can fill only part of the educational gap. Too many kids are too far behind.

Universities can also add to the faculty. They can hire enough faculty to cut class size from 200 or more down to perhaps 25 or so. Universities can also add academic and social counselors, who help guide a student's professional career and give support for the vicissitudes of life. Instructors and counselors can tutor the freshmen, who always need help and all too rarely get it. The university becomes more supportive generally. It's just a matter of hiring a lot of people and giving a small-college touch to a large research university. Tutoring has been done, for centuries, at every level of learning. It always works. When the small learning units flourish, the whole university does as well. Success seems inevitable. So does expense.

Now let's consider the other kind of reform. Suppose, in a moment of horror, the university must fall back on the elite solution in order to stay open. It restricts university enrollment drastically, to a small number of truly brilliant students and a larger number of rich ones. The brilliant students will go on to graduate school and contribute to the knowledge society. The university will be more efficient. It will enhance the education of both students and faculty. And the elite reform of universities will help solve the problems of costs.

This solution will not be popular, as Simon Newman can attest. Mr. Newman was appointed president of Mount Saint Mary's in Maryland (about 2,200 students, 500 of them in graduate programs) because of his business experience. Mount Saint Mary's had been feeling the fiscal pinch. Perhaps a businesslike approach to a private sector business would improve the university's efficiency and outreach. Mr. Newman does not possess a doctorate, but he is a devout Catholic and an elegant man, well suited to the business of raising money without departing from the university's mission of a serious Catholic education.

But President Newman sent off an indiscreet email. He suggested that the university ought to "drown the bunnies," students who were unlikely to make the grade.[13] No point in wasting instructional time and resources on those who would not be reasonably expected to graduate. The phrase "drown the bunnies" caught the public's attention. Two professors objected publicly to the policy. Mr. Newman, accustomed to business, promptly fired them, even though one was tenured, for "disloyalty to the university." That got the faculty's attention.

Faculty dismissal caught the attention of professors all over the country. Almost 8,000 of them signed a digital petition asking that the two victims of inadequate discretion be reinstated. Organizations followed suit. The American Association of University Professors, the Student Press Law Center, and the Foundation for Individual Rights in Education protested as well. Papers published the news. Taken aback by all the fuss, President Newman reinstated the two professors on the grounds of unmerited grace, since 2016 was a year of Extraordinary Jubilee of Mercy. The Mount Saint Mary faculty asked President Newman to resign, and within a few weeks, he did. Neither town nor gown (faculty and the wider public) was going to forgive his expression of social truth and educational philosophy.

Since America knows what will work to cut costs and/or pay for college, and in the process improve student academic success, politicians can put that knowledge to work. Right? Wrong. The elite solution closes the Golden Door of higher education to most citizens. They will be condemned to limited social and economic life chances. Increased exclusion is undemocratic, a real violation of the implied social contract that the state will make opportunity available to its citizens. The elite solution violates the *norma recte vivendi*. We can't exclude and we won't.

The populist solution might be even worse. The problem is money. The wolf at the university door is a depleted state budget and consequent disinvestment in higher education. Democratic ideals support a robust student learning community, but states cannot afford even the current thin institutional gruel. Oliver Wendell Holmes, Jr., commented in a Supreme Court dissent that "General propositions do not decide concrete cases."[14] A concrete case, one that both authors know as student and faculty, involves

Eight • The Limitations of Reform

Louisiana State University. Its modest entrance requirements admit many freshmen badly in need of help, especially in languages. Language problems run into real money, as well as time, which is also money. To provide that help, LSU, even with SI, needs about one faculty member for every five freshmen. Add a tutor, at the ratio of about one to three, and a counselor, on the basis of one to 20. LSU today has about 30,000 students enrolled, with around 10,000 or so in their first two years. At this level of enrollment, funding for faculty, tutors, and counselors would run up to about $40 million. But on the bright side, that includes offices, parking, health care, insurance, pension contributions, and so on. Of course, that's every year, not just once.

As a society, we will not spend much more money to educate students. Nor will we purge the university of those unready to learn. Not every problem can be solved.

These populist and elite proposals are, as they say in politics and divorce negotiations, off the table. Some other predicted futures for the university appear to be off the wall. One is the frequently suggested demise of most provincial liberal arts colleges and second-line state universities. True enough, colleges do go broke, but the number of institutions newly opened exceeds those that close. Equally true, denominational and private liberal arts colleges are in the greatest peril, with rising tuitions having limits and rising costs and rising student expectations having none. Nonetheless, pastors and teachers direct a continuing stream of students to these colleges, promising parents an education in character and the true faith as well as academic learning and athletic opportunity. Among the newer schools, Liberty University comes to mind; among the older universities, think of Notre Dame. We believe both will survive.

State colleges and universities are almost entirely free from the danger of extinction. They may be undistinguished, but they are vitally important locally. Some are relatively small, others quite substantial, but all anchor local economies. The same applies to junior colleges scattered over thousands of American towns. City colleges, from the City University of New York (CUNY) to much smaller places, enjoy the same political strengths. Politicians defend them to the last ditch and beyond. Having acquired a community college, towns from Eunice, Louisiana, to Miami, Florida, will not give them up. Nothing short of the sun becoming a red giant will close them down. The whole network of universities, colleges, junior and community colleges, denominational institutions, vocational schools, will not only survive the problems of rising costs and rising student debt: they will prevail.

Politics is not the only reason why state governments cannot close a public college. And that is basic economics. The state cannot afford to "save" money by closing a college. Take an example, one among (literally) thousands. LSU–Alexandria was founded as a community college and was later converted into a four-year college. Its budget in 2014–2015 was around $16 million, about $5 million of which came as a state appropriation and $11 million was self-generated by LSUA. Suppose you close LSUA to save the $5 million. The state loses $11 million at a single stroke. It gets worse. All who can retire do so, and the state must pay pensions rather than collecting pension contributions. The other employees go on unemployment, and the state pays again. Closing the college damages the local economy, cutting back on sales tax receipts, adding to unemployment, and reducing property tax values. And worse: You can't abandon the buildings, so the campus police and maintenance staff must be retained, maybe even increased. And worse: You can't leave the buildings vacant; you have to put them to work. So a state agency suggests spending $30 million to convert the vacant campus into regional government offices. The locals love it. The governor needs some votes in the legislature. So the deal goes through. The state lost $11 million to save $5 million, saved nothing because the closing, pension, and maintenance costs ate it all up, and then spent $30 million after losing $11 million and not saving the $5 million. The state is millions in the hole. And the state still needs to put a junior college, at least, in Alexandria. Shutting down government work is no simple thing.

Problems abound beyond economics and politics. Academics also predict doom and destruction for the faculty. Many professors suspect that online instruction will encourage administrators to record their courses and then dispense with them. The new system seems simple and ominous. Hire a professor. Digitize his courses. Keep the poor blighter for a few years of revision. Then lay the bum off forever. The number of professors will drop to a small group of distinguished scholars.[15] The rest will be history.

Maybe so, but more likely, maybe not. The unlikely doomsday scenario for faculty rests upon three assumptions, which seem a bit unlikely: (1) Students will prefer computers at home to the social life on campus. Really? (2) Communities will willingly give up much of their economic base. (3) Studios, IT personnel, directors, and technology will be free. Do these assumptions make any sense to anyone?

Actually, the faculty, as a whole, including SI instructors, will probably increase. Any effective campus learning committee requires instructors, usually quite a few. Some lecturers may come from the Internet, but the instructors on the spot will tailor the seminar sections, create the tests, do the grading, hold the students' hands (when needed, which is always), and do the supplementary tutoring for the course. College, which students prefer to the kitchen table, has to have a faculty.

The mix of professional roles and responsibilities will probably change. Automation of any sort always does that. Colleges have already begun to hire fewer tenure-track professors and more part-time instructors. Tutors hired to support online classes fit into this pattern. Some universities have already gone pretty far down this path. Temporary, part-time, and adjunct faculty makes up the bulk of their hiring. Declining state appropriations, rather than online education, drives this trend. Academic administrators are simply trying to square the circle by simultaneously hiring more faculty and lowering the cost of instruction.

These four futures for American universities are theoretically possible, of course, but they are socially unlikely. Money is the reason why. The future of American universities depends on funding, not on reform proposals. And, in general, the university of the foreseeable future is going to be pretty much like the universities of today.

Brave New World

Your view of nostrums is determined by your view of normalcy. Politicians tend to see universities as another public utility, not unlike roads and water, to be judged by the quality of service they provide. Sometimes that service needs improvement, or even, God forbid, more funding. The road to reform is always open.

On August 22, 2013, President Barack Obama spoke at the University of Buffalo on higher education. He began by saying that the current academic "trajectory is not sustainable." The president recognized that higher education is always going to be expensive. The real problem lies in the results. Students are not graduating on time and in appropriate numbers. And graduates have trouble in the job market. These results are worse, as is always the case, with students from lower socioeconomic backgrounds.

President Obama proposed a revised college rating system. It would replace the one issued by *U.S. News and World Report,* which attempts to measure academic excellence and has become the college rating gold standard. The president suggested a rating system based on how "valuable" an education the colleges offer. The new ratings would be based on the cost of an education compared to the return a student received in the job market.

Obviously, the net value of an education would vary from college to college and major to major, with STEM from Caltech or MIT near the top of both costs and benefits. A humanities degree from a small state college branch campus would be at the low end, again in both costs and benefits.

Once the value of a college education has been computed, the government could then adjust federal support, notably the Pell grants. Colleges that cost less, graduate more, and have recent graduates employed at a good salary will get either a larger Pell grant or a cohort of reduced interest loans, or both. Colleges providing a market-oriented education would benefit through enrollment increases, as students follow the best values. Colleges and universities would be judged on the basis of comparative educational advantage. No matter what area of the economy is considered, it's hard to get away from Adam Smith.

President Obama's speech drew a good deal of attention from academic administrators. Federal student aid runs close to $150 *billion* a year, and states chip in another $70 billion. These totals may not rise much in the next few years, but even small changes in a yearly sum of $220 billion will make a real budget impact on most colleges. So academic administrators have made some hasty calculations about graduation rates, especially among students with state or federal aid. Not every provost or bursar was pleased with the results of these calculations.

The president did not give a follow-up speech. His ideas began to seem more suggestion than proposal. *U.S. News* issued its annual rankings for colleges, universities, and graduate/professional programs based on the usual categories and the usual methodology. Harvard remained at the top of the academic heap, as usual.

But business as usual was interrupted by a report from a nonpartisan foundation, The Education Trust. The Trust noted that around 600,000 students attend colleges that have a dropout rate of over 85 percent, a level comparable to MOOCs. Just as bad, and maybe worse, the students at those institutions have a loan default rate of 25 to 30 percent.

The Education Trust made some recommendations based on President Obama's ideas. Colleges and universities should show a social conscience and have an enrollment of not less than 17 percent poor and Pell grant students, combined with a six-year graduation rate of at least 15 percent of these low-income students. The loan default rate should not exceed 28 percent for low-income students. These standards, high for low-income students and low for general student performance, should be the basis for federal actions concerning university efficiency. The Trust's suggestions did not produce any immediate federal action.

Nonetheless, President Obama did not lose interest in higher education. He added a new proposal to his previous suggestions. Speaking in Nashville, Tennessee, on January 9, 2015, the president suggested making community college free, adding the first two years of college to the previous twelve of public education. This idea, also, has remained just a suggestion. The Department of Education has issued no guidelines concerning free public education through the associates degree. Nonetheless, the Obama proposals point to the academic road ahead.

Educational reform does not depend only on the federal government. States, those "laboratories of democracy," have addressed issues in higher education. They focused on money. State governments cut appropriations for universities but also moved in a positive direction. In 1999, Louisiana started its "TOPS" program, which paid the college tuition for around half of a school's graduating class.[16] Since it began, TOPS has helped over 600,000 students at a cost of $1.8 billion to the state. The Legislature did not address the market value of a college education. Nor did TOPS slow the rise in college tuition, which continued to rise in Louisiana as elsewhere. But TOPS does help directly with student debt.

Tennessee has also moved to lighten the students' debt burden. It anticipated President Obama and began offering free community college tuition in February 2014. By the fall semester of 2015, about 15,000 Tennessee students were taking advantage of the plan. Tennessee also saw an increase in technical college enrollment. That same year, in Chicago, mayor Rahm Emanuel inaugurated a "Star Initiative," providing tuition, books, and transportation for city students in city community colleges. Chicago wants a 3.0 GPA for students to continue. Oregon is watching these programs closely. It expects 10,000 applicants for a tuition program that may begin in 2016. President Obama's idea is catching on, at least in bits and pieces.

The brave new academic world can also occur within the universities. One of the most important recent reforms, for institution and student alike, is dual enrollment. Students take courses in high school and college simultaneously, receiving credit in both places. Dual enrollment is the logical extension of advanced placement, which is entirely confined to the high school. It guarantees nothing with regard to college credit. With dual enrollment, students enroll in college courses while still in high school. You can, in theory, graduate from high school and community college at the same time. Dual enrollment began in the 1980s, and by 2012 almost every state had large-scale dual enrollment.

Colorado has been a leader in pushing dual enrollment, and the showcase has been the Aurora School District. Superintendent John Barry has pushed the idea relentlessly. Of his 40,000 students, around 1,200 were simultaneously enrolled in high school and college. In the 2011–2012 school year, 29 students received high school diplomas and associates degrees in the same week, the associates degree oddly coming earlier. It's just expanded from there.

Success on this level requires close cooperation between high school and college. You can't do something like this alone. Superintendent Barry and Aurora Community College President Linda Bowman committed the time, resources, and energy to make the program work. The cooperation between school and college continues with Dr. Bowman's successor, Dr. Betsy Oudenhoven. Teamwork of this sort is quite rare, and we mention it as the exception rather than the rule.

Recently, colleges and universities around the country have greatly increased their dual enrollment "outreach." They present it to the high schools as a community service. But the impetus is money as well as time, which is also money. As states have disinvested in higher education, universities have sought new students as an additional form of revenue. At Louisiana State University, for example, a high school student (or his parents or school board) will fork over $100 per credit hour for a dual enrollment course. A thousand students a semester can produce more money than SCOCs and at less cost. And the parents are keen to have their high schooler get a leg up on college, the high schools are eager to offer this perk to their students, and school boards must get on the bandwagon lest its schools fall behind the trend.

Ask your college's administrators and they will tell you that offering dual enrollment courses is a no-brainer. SCOCs may or may not pay off, but dual enrollment is a sure thing. The only problem is competition. Various colleges and universities are all scrambling to scoop up high school students into their dual enrollment (DE) programs. The price per class varies dramatically from university to university. Some colleges offer DE courses for as low as $25 a credit hour. It happens that high schools are lured away from one university's DE program to another based on how well it is implemented in the classrooms. Since there is no accreditation board supervising and standardizing learning outcomes in dual enrollment classes, high school teachers and university admissions officials see a lot of astonishing things.

Dual enrollment can pose problems, often related to quality of instruction and course content. It's not common in math classes; a computer program runs instruction at both levels. But in English, a successful pedagogy

Eight • The Limitations of Reform

still depends on people. Can teachers at both levels create a course satisfactory on both levels? Dual enrollment teaching mainly occurs at the high schools, while curricular direction comes mostly from the college. Dual enrollment is a consequential nostrum, making money for the university and changing the first two years of college for the student. It can bring together a high school, college, and computer for those students deemed "ready" for that level of work.[17]

A third certain element of the brave new academic world is the Internet. MOOCs and SCOCs seem to be the universal nostrum. They promise to cut instructional costs and extend the educational outreach to universities that offer them. These impressions (and that's all they are) suggest that online learning is the broad way to the university of the future. The biggest nostrum of them all is the one we log on to.

But how much will the Internet transform universities? Online learning does have all the steam of a fad. It's trendy and it's gaudy.[18] You can attend college via phone; while driving you can answer a quiz at the same time as you run into pedestrians and parked cars. Go to school on the beach, showing up on campus only for the occasional class, labs, and exams. Perhaps this way the students will learn more. Or maybe not. The whole prospect of the campus coexisting with the Internet gives one furiously to think.

Steve Kolowich, technology reporter for *The Chronicle of Higher Education*, examined the process and the fragments of experience in marrying the Internet and the university.[19] Universities have had large and predictable problems in starting online programs. Technology has been hard to master, but marketing has been worse. SCOCs involve more than filming professors teaching courses or putting assignments online or sprinkling quizzes like raisins in bread pudding. Universities have to market their SCOCs, recruit online students, and provide tutoring, counseling, and customer service. All these problems must be solved for the SCOCs to succeed as courses, to say nothing about supporting the university.

Capitalism is a wonderful thing. Universities needed help, and private companies sprang up to provide it: Pearson, 2U, Embanet,[20] Bisk, and others were some of the early entrepreneur-partners. A university would remain responsible for pedagogy, course content, examinations, and course credit. It also would offer the prestige of its name and the skills of its professors.

The company offers some pedagogical technology, and it would take responsibility for licenses and state regulation. The private sector company assumes responsibility, and costs, of marketing the new SCOCs, as well as recruiting students and supporting their efforts to finish the course. The university and the company split the costs, which are never insignificant, and the profits, which always are.

The company takes the greater fiscal risk. If the scheme dies, the company loses a lot of money and may fold, but the university remains to try again. So the company takes, and ought to take, the lion's share of the tuition revenue, usually in the 60 percent to 80 percent range. This sounds like a good deal for the company. But the university, receiving as much as 30 or 40 percent of the revenue, gets a lot of money for very little risk.

How does it all work in practice? Kolowich gives a couple of examples, one from the University of Florida and Bisk, the other between Pearson, Embanet, and the California State University system. Begin on the West Coast. With the help of Pearson and Embanet, the 23 campuses of the California state university system contracted to build Cal State Online, a central online "campus" to be used by students in all 23 of the Cal State institutions. Cal State Online opened in the 2012–2013 academic year. And the results? The SCOC dreams did not come true. Cal State Online and Pearson, the high contracting parties, anticipated 17,000 students in their first year. The actual number was less, 138 full-time students in the two programs up and running on the 23 campuses. Part of the problem lay with the universities, as it always does. The two programs were too few, and the too few were not too good. Part of the problem lay with Pearson. Their marketing and recruiting had been inadequate, to give it the sunniest interpretation possible. Apportion the blame as you will, there was plenty of failure on both sides.

In Florida, Bisk and the university cooperated on a certificate in "executive education." The business plan projected that the first five years of operation would produce $1.6 million in profits for Florida and $6.3 million in profits for Bisk. The program did not live up to expectations. But even if the Bisk/Florida program had met every target, profits for the university could only be described as insignificant. Contracts like this are not going to ease the University of Florida's fiscal problems.

But suppose the university/enabler partnership does work out. If the online enabler companies do become a massive presence on campus, the nature of the university will change. Non-profit universities will become for-profit schools. State universities will take on some of the characteristics of Phoenix. We do not see much academic or political support for that contingency. But turning public universities into semi-private institutions does not seem likely.

As always, size matters. University/corporate enabler contracts are now pretty small beer. By the end of five years, Florida may get $1.6 million, while tenuring a young associate professor, even in the humanities, is (potentially) more than a $2 million business decision. Only if the university and company can scale up to scores of millions (which means every student now enrolled in every college) will the income make any difference in university finances. Advocates for online education find failures of scale the biggest disappointment of them all.

And then there are the students. They continue to come to campus, 20 million or so in 2012–2013. No reason to suppose that will change. True enough, the kids taking a campus degree take online courses. Campus and Internet are not mutually exclusive watertight educational compartments.[21] The University of Florida in the spring semester of 2015 told over 3,000 students who had already been admitted that they could only take online courses. The students did not apply for anything like that, but they were stuck with it if they planned to "attend." Florida had to take extraordinary steps to help Pearson fill its quota so that the online programs could work. The administration regarded these kids as customers (though suckers might be a better term) who go to college by staying home. Hard to find many happy campers here. Will the Florida expedient become standard in the brave new academic world? Arizona State University offers the same sort of program; California's legislature recently discussed a bill to make all state colleges' first-year courses completely online. But compulsion, not persuasion, will be needed to make these programs work.

Finally, Kolowich confirms that the United States Department of Education has no objection to the online-enabler companies, even though they are private sector and seek a profit. Federal approval, or at least neutrality, regarding the online enabler companies may be the crucial factor in allowing lots of non-profit universities to mount a serious online effort. Most universities could use the help, as Semester Online showed. And, can the online-enabler companies develop a system-wide program to recruit and retain millions of students? Now, no. But in the future?

The brave new world of the academy includes one change that is not directly about money. That change involves accountability. Online professors will be held accountable by profits in the market. For professors who teach in person, the assessment/accountability program will be intrusive, bureaucratic, and burdensome. The faculty will create portfolios, endure interviews, and complain a lot.[22] But, after all the sludge of evaluation, it will come down to retention. If the students pass the course and come back to college next semester the faculty who taught them have done their job. Still, a CLA of some sort will be part of the future. Universities must at least pretend to hold faculty accountable.

Important parts of the brave new world come from the larger society beyond the university walls. The social need for more credentials is sufficiently strong for colleges and universities to grow in size and number, no matter what the cost to students. Credential creep is also pushed by politics. The war on dropouts is as old as the war on drugs and has been much more successful. Dropout once meant high school; it is coming to mean failure to complete an associates degree in a community college. This rise in the standard credential is presented as increasing equality and opportunity, and these are magic words in a democratic society. Surely, no one can oppose these values.

Finally, there is always money. Disinvestment has removed money from the university budgets, but universities raise money through tuition, fees, grants, and gifts. Research and innovation are a main contribution that universities make to the larger society. Costs of medical and technological innovation always rise. The tension between the costs and benefits of university research may be regarded as permanent.

The combination of internal stability and external pressure tilts that brave new academic world toward continuity more than change. Because continuity in the university dominates, current trends are the place to look for future trends. Colleges and universities will continue to expand, though more slowly than they did in the postwar decades. Reforms in academic practice, such as using the Internet, will reinforce the old ways within the university, which are hierarchical, labor-intensive, and costly. Reformers will face the hard irony that the university absorbs reforms, not the other way around.[23] Now and then the black swan swims by, but not this time.[24]

And So It Goes

The idea certainly sounds simple. Create a university *ab initio*. Perhaps the Minerva Project might be an attractive model. Minerva is electronically sophisticated. It seems to solve the problems of a ruinously expensive campus. It deals with those pesky professors with their high salaries and tenure by reducing them to part-time piecework knowledge workers. But Ben Nelson has left the student problems untouched. At their current numbers, it's easy to put them all up in a San Francisco hotel, not the St. Francis, of course, but still somewhere. Even a student body of 500, a really small college indeed, is a hotel problem in a lot of cities. Numbers large enough to matter, whether students, faculty, or administrators, seem to lead inexorably toward the brick-and-mortar universities we now have. But Minerva is an effort to get away from the standard university with its campus, not a scheme to replicate it.

So the Minerva Project may not be the best option to begin an American university anew. How about the Phoenix system? John Sperling had virtual students, virtual faculty, and a virtual campus. At least in theory, there is no limit on the size of the University of Phoenix, and that's no small virtue in a country with scores of millions of students needing an education. It turns out, though, that with Phoenix, size has been the enemy of the virtual, as students need help face-to-face, though not through the ether. As Phoenix bulked up, it had to add in-person student services. Nothing unexpected, as the bell curve and experience with MOOCs and SCOCs indicate. But offices for student tutoring and counseling, though absolutely necessary for many students to succeed, are the thin wedge leading to a brick-and-mortar campus—and the costs that come with it.

Then we come to the problem of excellence. The law of large numbers and the bell curve indicate how difficult it will be to create an excellent mass university online. But excellence, by students as well as faculty, is essential in a modern knowledge society. Perhaps Phoenix also has inherent drawbacks; as Minerva cannot grow, Phoenix cannot excel. Efforts toward excellence also seem likely to lead to the brick-and-mortar universities. It's not so easy to invent a new university.

Perhaps we can bypass academic visions and discuss privilege and money. American higher education has become too expensive for public fisc or private purse. Could online courses alone, like the cavalry, ride to the financial rescue? Moreover, the very structure of the university often seems unsuited for modern, democratic mass education. The faculty, with their privileges and autonomy, seem to stand athwart egalitarian reforms. But with money and privilege, critics may find much to criticize but few solutions and no new university model. Complaint alone is not reform.

The distress is also simple enough: all the ills aforementioned are permanent. Some have lasted for centuries; others are more recent. Previous reform efforts, such as new curricula or academic freedom, have just reinforced the old ways. Universities have absorbed ideas considered radical and turned them into normalcy. Still the university remains a place that supports faculty, educates students, and collects knowledge. Academic reformers hope a new university will differ from the old in every way, and it will, with the single exception of being the same in every way. If you want a university, with all three of its interconnecting functions, then what you have is what you're going to get. Like the wheel, the university has already been invented. And like the wheel, it works pretty well. Even if you think the university works badly, like the wheel, you can fix the trim but the basic design remains the same always.

V. "Much Ado..."

The Sloane Foundation ran a survey in 2011 about electronic distance learning. Sloane found that some six million students had taken, or were taking, at least one online course. The promise of an online bonanza is the Next Big Thing in Higher Education.[25] But the real question is less what the next big thing is and more what the next big thing will do. Will the entire university be changed merely by a change in the delivery of instruction?

Probably not. College life will remain about the same. Students will continue to prefer attending college on campus, with electronic courses forming an auxiliary based on need or convenience. Life on campus is more fun than life at the kitchen table, and students on campus are more likely to graduate. It's better to be there. And then there is the money already spent building the campus and the stadium. The investments made on campus, along with town planning and infrastructure, are too substantial to be abandoned. More, dual enrollment blurs the difference between high school and college, but students will attend in person. Online courses may democratize a university education, but attracting lots of new students also means that few graduate. More yet, political opinion will demand more accountability for faculty as well as students; that works best on campus. Yet more again, the gap in excellence and scholarship between the best, both schools and people, and the rest will not diminish. Even if the wine is new, the bottles are not.

New technology may replace the old, but it can also reinforce the old ways. Driverless cars will spur campaigns to improve the roads. The same process operates with universities. Though online instruction may replace some lectures in some schools, it will add tutors and teaching assistants and increase the need for a college degree. The old ways and attitudes never quite disappear. Hopes invested in university reform always encounter reality.

F. Scott Fitzgerald recognized the juxtaposition of hope and reality in American society: "Gatsby believed in the green light, the orgiastic future that year by year recedes before us. It eluded us then, but that's no matter—tomorrow we will run faster, stretch out our arms farther—and one fine morning—"[26] The fine morning never comes. The green light beckons

Eight • The Limitations of Reform

but does not fulfill. Everyone knows the bittersweet taste of hoped-for change, change that did not really change the way things were. "So we beat on, boats against the current, borne back ceaselessly into the past."[27] American universities will follow the path of American law. What will be comes from what we are.[28] The university will be changed, not into something new but into what it has always been.

Bibliographical Essay

This bibliographical essay comments on the social, economic, and technological context within which universities now exist. Universities now stand far less apart from society than they did a century ago, when their special relationship to society was still recognized by current practice as well as long tradition. That was then. With World War II and increasingly thereafter, universities have become an integral part of the wider society beyond their gates. Colleges and universities educate more than 20 million students a year, and the number is rising. Academic research in medicine, genetics, agriculture, physics, geology, et al., undergird the modern Western economy. The university affects the world beyond the walls in ways it did not when Abraham Lincoln took office.

The outside world also leans over the academy's walls in ways it did not when Teddy Roosevelt rode up San Juan Hill. Universities are now heavily regulated by government, from federal to local, and compliance bureaucrats will some day certainly outnumber faculty. Money from outside the university, mostly public but private as well, underwrites the academy. In the absence of outside money, the place shuts down. If outside funds run a bit short, excellence within the academy is the first casualty. In a democratic society, the university participates in the general contract and cannot be understood apart from the broader world.

The books discussed herein illuminate the social role research universities play. American research universities remain the best in the world, an essential prerequisite for a prosperous national future in a globalized knowledge society. No serious observer of the modern world thinks that the knowledge society will disappear or that globalization will diminish. Universities will function within a globalized knowledge culture. A topic this broad lies beyond the scope of our essay. So the bibliographical note hints at that wider context and acts as a reminder that universities do not function in a social vacuum.

The book with the widest social and historical focus is Niall Ferguson's *Civilization: The West and the Rest* (New York: Penguin, 2011).[1] Professor Ferguson describes the rise of Western scientific and industrial culture from the Renaissance to the twenty-first-century world of CAD/CAM, iPhones, and a modern university education. How did it all happen and why only in the West and its colonies? And what does it mean that the rest wants what we have and does not want to become what we are? He asserts that research universities have played a significant role in creating that scientific, secular, and technological culture and will play a similar role in sustaining it.

Professor Ferguson explores the development of a Western culture that embraced the ideas of competition and progress. This society had its beginning in the Renaissance, a crucial period of intellectual growth and technological change in Western Europe. Bits and pieces of the Western Renaissance did appear elsewhere in the sixteenth century, as with Turkish cannons and ship design, but imported Western technology did nothing to change the tribal and traditional Turkish society. Only in the West did the entire culture change, and it continued to change in the centuries following Cosimo de' Medici and Henry V. In the Renaissance and Baroque periods, roughly 1400–1750, the West (often grudgingly) accepted the fundamental ideas of science, which would lead directly into the secular and increasingly democratic attitudes of the Enlightenment (circa 1680–1820). In the Renaissance, the West and its universities began the painful journey toward modernity. Like it or not, and they will not like it, the rest may well have to follow.

Ferguson argues that permanent progress involves six distinct factors, which he calls, using electronic merchandising patter, "killer apps." The six killer apps exist collectively in the West but appear only individually, if at all, among the rest. Ferguson's killer apps are partially social/cultural and partially intellectual/cultural. Those mainly social are the habit of competition; the practice of consumerism of goods, gadgets, and ideas; and the work ethic, which honors diligence rather than leisure. The primarily intellectual apps are science, modern medicine, and the rule of law. The killer apps are all part of a university education, for faculty and students alike. Social apps are necessary tools of learning. In the modern research university, a curriculum of science and technology has replaced theology, and the university has updated the medieval intellectual apps of law and medicine. The role of research universities in teaching and expanding the six killer apps may be a bit fuzzy to Americans, but it is blindingly obvious to the foreign students who come here to study. They know, as all ought, that killer apps require killer universities.

Ferguson argues that international politics forms largely around the cultural gap between the West and the rest. The essence of the gap is imbalance: power, affluence, and opportunity in the West and rage, envy, and resentment for the rest. Within this environment, it is a life-changing event for a student from the rest to enroll in a Western university. What Western universities teach, from STEM to history and art, is, one and all, subversive of some aspect of traditional societies and cultures. Teaching as well as learning is a political act and, sometimes, a revolutionary one as well.[2] Niall Ferguson implies that the research universities, both as a Golden Door and a locus of scientific, legal, and medical research, will only grow through the twenty-first century and beyond.[3] Who can doubt that he is correct?

The cultural health of the West depends on progress in goods, gadgets, ideas, and technology, every bit as much as the continuation of traditional cultures depends upon their absence. The Western world of work and consumption rests upon constant and accelerating intellectual growth. How can that happen without universities?

An examination of the killer apps and American universities can deal with deficiencies as well as strengths. Current conditions in America and competition from abroad form the basic theme of a book by Thomas Friedman, *The New York Times* Pulitzer Prize-winning columnist, and Michael Mandelbaum, the Christian Herter professor at The Johns Hopkins University. They have analyzed the current world in *That Used to Be Us: How America Fell Behind in the World It Invented and How We Can Come Back* (New York: Farrar, Straus and Giroux, 2011). Friedman and Mandelbaum identify four challenges to modern America. These are basically economic and technological, and their solution will require changes in public attitudes and policy. The most difficult challenge involves the American adjustment to globalization. After the twentieth-century war, which began in 1914, finally ended in 1989, American policies of free markets and economic cooperation were expanded to include the entire world.[4] The global economic system has meant outsourced American jobs to low-wage countries, international technological competition, capital flight to overseas investment opportunities, and systematic theft of American intellectual property.[5] Thomas Friedman had explained the often-disruptive impacts of globalization in *The Lexus and the Olive Tree*,[6] noting how the phenomenon of globalization posed a real threat to organized labor and the environment through a worldwide race to the bottom of production costs. A decade later, he and Mandelbaum see the West, especially America, as seriously damaged by that competition. Comparative advantage does not always favor the West, especially in low labor costs and modest governmental regulation.

Friedman and Mandelbaum see a second challenge in the technology of communication, from computers to smartphones to cyber insecurity, all becoming constantly more sophisticated. Already, most electronic gear is manufactured overseas, usually in Asia, and both the jobs and intellectual property are lost to America. Only innovation is still primarily domestic. In a knowledge society, imagination is our most important product. The jobs that imagination creates are the foundation of our future.

Friedman and Mandelbaum recognize that the challenges of global competition and information technology also involve American university research and education. Two of the first three parts of *That Used to Be Us* are entitled "The Educational Challenge" and "The War on Math and Physics."[7] "The Educational Challenge" treats the perceived decline in the quality of American university education and the concomitant decline in the number of students in the STEM disciplines. Educational decline can be repaired by a change in popular attitudes. It cannot change without it. More money, probably an awful lot of money, would help. Education must again become fashionable. It has all been done before, after Sputnik in 1957, and the solution lies now, as it did then, in national leadership. Almost no one expects money to flow, or attitudes to change in the absence of strong political leadership. And, alas, saying something is not enough. After all, "if the trumpet makes an uncertain sound, who will heed the call to battle?"[8] The president must issue the fabled clarion call. President Kennedy set the nation on course to the moon and all the technology associated with that endeavor.[9]

Friedman and Mandelbaum's third and fourth challenges concern the technology of energy and our massive public fiscal deficits. The authors quote the Italian saying that "arithmetic is not an opinion" and suggest that good public policy extends to fixing the fisc. Good public policy also extends to the fourth challenge, the production and consumption of energy. Friedman and Mandelbaum claim that America uses too much energy based on hydrocarbons. Importing oil adversely affects our international current accounts, and its use warms the globe.[10] Academic expertise can help frame fiscal policy, but research, innovation, and universities will play an even more important role in developing green energy. Friedman and Mandelbaum have chosen challenges that link America's future to research universities. The general aim of their commentary is to regain (or maintain) American preeminence in imagination, innovation, and technology. Research universities are certainly part of that policy.

A third book deals directly with education. Charles A. Murray, in *Real Education: Four Simple Truths for Bringing American Schools Back to Reality*

(New York: Crown Forum, 2008) presents American education from the various perspectives of its clients, customers, acolytes, beneficiaries, inmates, sufferers, and dropouts. These terms all describe the students, from preschool to graduate school. Murray thinks the schools, at all levels, are failing the students, though for quite different reasons in different situations. From the slow learners too much is asked. Learning to read is hard, and so is learning the symbolic language of mathematics. Many in schools can manage only the barest literacy and numeracy. No real point in asking more. The average student is taught the wrong stuff. Their curriculum is excessively academic and not sufficiently commercial. The gifted are not pushed hard enough and so learn too little. The schools fail everyone, which is certainly democratic, though it can hardly be called desirable. Murray explains that diversity in failure has made skeptics of everyone.

Educational reform has become extremely difficult and intensely controversial. It's easy to see why. Murray warns that a change that benefits the vast middle of the bell curve will quite likely damage those that lag behind or those that need to push ahead. Equally, an emphasis on improving either end of the bell curve will take attention and resources away from the other. Doing just about anything is a standing assault on political correctness and social equality.

No overriding solution to educational problems exists. Those who suppose that there is a comprehensive solution suffer from "educational romanticism," according to Murray. Educational romantics are not merely wrong, which is obvious; they also retard beneficial educational change everywhere.

In *Real Education*, Murray deals primarily with the small group of really smart kids, known as the "academically gifted." He accepts the unpleasant social reality that ability varies and that half of students are below average.[11] Not every kid will prosper in college. Murray suggests limiting college enrollment, even though it has the undemocratic result of limiting opportunity. Murray here enters the never-to-be-solved controversy about the benefits of a university education. Is it worth the cost in time and money, for the university as well as the student, to admit the less-than-gifted? True enough, every student will benefit from college to some extent. But the equation includes more than university or student cost/benefit ratios. The social good also matters. Murray argues that the future of the American economy depends on how well universities educate the academically gifted, which is somewhere between 10 and 20 percent of a student cohort.[12] By supporting the best, America will ensure the welfare of all.

In place of college for 21 million or so students (2011), Murray proposes a group of professional and occupational entrance/competence exams. This system already exists in graduate education, medicine, law, and many crafts. Murray would like to see this form of credential greatly expanded so it could replace, to some degree, a college degree. Educational romanticism is the problem here. Romantics believe that every student can succeed in college with the right kind of support. This is obviously untrue. Murray draws from this reality his position that higher education must be offered to those who can use it best. That is Murray's basic premise. Tough social realism is Murray's basic attitude.

In another book, Charles Murray explores the social results of inadequate education and the relentless movement of western economies toward knowledge-based technology. Murray's *Coming Apart: The State of White America, 1960–2010* (New York: Crown Forum, 2012) examines the gradual emergence of an upper class increasingly separated from a lower class. The differences are cultural as well as economic and residential. They involve language and marriage as well as profession and income. Moreover, in a society as litigious as America, formal academic credentials have become the benchmark of social status and economic opportunity. If you have a degree, you are more likely to be in than out.

As Murray notes, this increasing social separation has been a long time coming. Over the course of two working generations, equality of opportunity has increasingly come to depend upon academic credentials. They are needed to get a foot in the door, as well as to climb the ladder. Murray argues that the social middle has been stretched to the point where the top and bottom that have drifted too far apart for the general good. A less structural analysis can also be made. The critic may concentrate on practical social virtues, such as marriage, legitimate children, a general absence of addictive behavior, and the avoidance of violence. These social strengths are unequally distributed, less common in the lower than the upper groups, in spite of the fact that money enables indulgence. Whether one emphasizes education, class structure, or social virtue, many critics find an American society where class divisions have grown too great. Social classes should tend to merge rather than separate.

Murray confines his analysis of a half century of social history to white America, but the same thing can be seen among African Americans. Eugene Robinson, in *Disintegration: The Splintering of Black America* (New York: Anchor, 2011) found the same social separation that Murray had seen in the majority community. The bottom 40 percent or so of African Americans, most of whom live in urban ghettos, endure a social culture that is not promising. Most are undereducated and come from dysfunctional homes and neighborhoods. Surrounded by drugs and violence, they are massively unemployed or in the system (prison, parole, mental health). Within that urban culture, impulse control is often preached but rarely practiced. Success in the larger society is difficult for these kids. In addition to the usual tasks of mastering educational and social skills, they must also become adept at a different culture and a different language. Little wonder that Robinson called the bottom group the "abandoned," though the abandonment has been as much by self as by society.

The gap between the upper and lower levels of African American society is audible. Language in the urban neighborhoods tends heavily toward dialect rather than the Queen's English. Or it can be visible. Drive north though Washington from Anacostia to the Maryland suburbs in Montgomery County. The social ladder becomes visible, along with the tragic distance between top and bottom.

However large the gap between the affluent and the abandoned, the main road from bottom to top remains education. At the primary and secondary levels, this means Kidd Academies, parochial schools, vouchers, and the like, all in an effort to counteract dysfunctional neighborhood values. But it's no longer 1950, Murray reminds us. The information and technological society demands more education and greater facility with languages, symbolic and linguistic. However one views modern American social history, the way to ameliorate class separation has always been through education. Experts know that. Students and their parents know it also. The Pew Research Center found that over 90 percent of the parents interviewed said that their kids were going to college. The university is still the Golden Door, and the glitter of promise reaches almost every abode.

The social and educational gap between the classes is expanding at a time of rapid and profound technological change. Erik Brynjolfsson and Andrew McAfee describe these changes in *The Second Machine Age: Work, Progress, and Prosperity in a Time of Brilliant Technology* (New York: W.W. Norton, 2014). The authors make four assertions: first, that the pace of technological change is increasing; second, that new technology is changing the job mix from people to machines, rather than merely from muscle to precision; as a result, technology is creating unemployment whereas previously it had added jobs; finally, they claim that social adjustment lags far behind technological progress.

The process of technological progress and unemployment has three major characteristics. The first involves tempo. In the digital age, Moore's Law speeds up and includes more and more categories of jobs and machines.[13]

The second deals with Big Data, which is constantly becoming bigger. Since there is more information to work with, more data applications are technically possible, and these new applications come online more rapidly. The third element of technological change concerns the process of innovation. Much, perhaps most, current technological change involves combining and recombining existing technology and existing applications in new ways. There is recombinant DNA and recombinant electronic technology. The technological mix changes faster than society can adjust and in ways that cannot be anticipated. Everyone and every institution and every piece of technology is always behind the innovation curve.

Technological unemployment is the most ominous aspect of new technology and its applications. Technology has always changed the job mix, going back to James Watt and beyond, but the new industrial technology had always created more jobs than it erased. Now, maybe not. Digital technology is creating employment obsolescence further and further up the educational and skill chains. People with college and more than college, like CPAs or corporate middle management or those working with routine information in government, insurance, or transportation, will inexorably be replaced by computers. Distributive computer networks can turn repetitive information into a digital superorganism, which can process the information more efficiently than the clerks and managers who are being replaced. Previously, the new jobs have outnumbered the old. As the general economy grew, the numbers of jobs grew with it. That has been the pattern for two centuries. Brynjolfsson and McAfee doubt that the old economic patterns will continue into the digital age.

The worst is yet to come. The larger the GDP gets, the larger the pool of individual economic casualties becomes. Rewards will be concentrated at the top, and the median income will stagnate. That's the current (2016) American economic pattern. Only those jobs requiring personal service (like nursing) or inter-personal relationships, or those that demand extraordinary imagination or innovative skills, will increase. The direction of economic efficiency is clear, say, Brynjolfsson and McAfee. People are expensive and computers are cheap. And the time may come when having a job is a privilege.

In such an economy, a college degree, or even two, will provide imperfect protection, but it is the place to start. Students attending a university can both prepare themselves for a career and defend themselves against technological unemployment. Finally, an academic tip, both from us and Brynjolfsson and McAfee: while at college, attend class, study, read, learn as much as possible, and perfect your language skills. The degree may get the graduate in the door, but knowledge, understanding, diligence, and imagination make the career. The student is responsible for what is learned. The university is the Golden Door only if you walk through.

A final book that illuminates the current political world is Moises Naim's, *The End of Power: From Boardrooms to Battlefields to States, Why Being in Charge Is Not What It Used to Be* (New York: Basic Books, 2013). Moises Naim, once Venezuela's trade and industry minister, has written a treatise on the sociology of governance. He argues that running the show is harder than once it was and likely to become harder yet. He gives three reasons for that. The first is "more": an increase of persons and things, of technology, enterprises, information, and activities that have collectively caused a lot of pain for administrators. The second is "mobility." The movement of people, information, ideas, and money has become so rapid and so massive that governments and corporations cannot keep up. The third is "mentality," which consists of an increase in skepticism, in lack of trust in institutions, in a rising disinclination to follow established leaders, in a growing absence of loyalty to anything but self and family and a willingness to try new political directions. Mentality includes the vast increase of easily available information, along with an enhanced view of self. It is democratic ideals internalized and expanded to their logical conclusions. Mentality may be summed up in the phenomenon of personal publicity exemplified by Facebook.

Naim's three postulates explain the fragility of bosses and institutions. The trend toward electronic communication has real consequences. When popular trust in power declines, then social upheavals, from family to state, increase.

Within universities, "more" and "mobility" hardly matter. Universities can also absorb the distrust involved in "mentality." Faculties are always skeptical and usually cynical. A tenured professor generally teaches what he or she wants, does research of choice, publishes at will, goes to meetings he or she chooses, accepts or refuses graduate students, grades as he or she thinks fit, and all those things comprise the *norma recte vivendi* of academic life. The story of a professor in Chicago who moved his office to a bar, taught a graduate seminar there, had his mail picked up, and did not come to the department for a decade illustrates the extreme—but not by much.

As for the students, they are even more detached. They know they are at the university for a short time, and their goal is to leave as soon as may be with degree in hand. In institutional terms, students are concerned with hoops, barriers, and requirements, all of which they wish to see diminished. These attitudes are certainly reasonable. After all, the student pays to be at a university and profits by rapid completion. There is nothing to be gained by staying a day longer than one must.

The decline of effective public and private power described by Moises Naim only marginally affects university governance. The university designed by Cardinal Robert resembles a confederation or the Holy Roman Empire more than a modern corporation or state. Tenured professors who publish still resemble the medieval knights on whom they were originally modeled. We have said this before, but don't stop us. It needs to be said again. Professors rarely have power, but they do have autonomy. To the extent that Naim is correct, university governance, instead of being obsolete, may be a model of future institutional administration.

We have examined books that show a conservative bent (Murray) and a liberal perspective (Robinson, Friedman, and Mandelbaum). A couple of books (Naim and Brynjolfsson and McAfee) are basically technical in their analysis. We have sought a broad cultural and historical context (Fergusson) and looked for diversity in commentary.

All of these books, with their diverse approaches to the modern world, agree on globalization, in economic, social, fiscal, and intellectual terms. The different civilizations pointed out by Samuel P. Huntington in 1993 have different attitudes toward modernity; (much of Islam is notoriously hostile) but globalization is relentless.[14]

The several authors also agree on the technological future. Instant communication through watch, pad, phone, and laptop connects individuals with markets, labs, libraries, or the office. And technology is a one-way road; things cannot be un-invented. Technology is the carrier of globalization. Universities must live in this world, and they seem to be doing well. Governments must recognize that globalized universities will cost enormous sums, and there is no future without them. Reformers must adapt their often outré schemes of university change to a globalized knowledge society. The "killer apps" of Niall Ferguson are the way of the future.

Finally, each author implies that universities should be better rather than changed. Excellence is a challenge far greater than reform and goes to the teaching, innovation, and imagination that are the heart of the university. These virtues are always in short supply. So the issues today are what they have always been. It is not how the university must change. It is how the university, both masters and scholars, can become better.

Chapter Notes

Preface

1. Peter Brooks of *The New York Times* is one of the few modern observers who agrees with us:

> To me, the university is a precious and fragile institution, one that lives with crisis—since education, like psychoanalysis, is an "impossible profession"—but at its best thrives on it. It has endured through many transformations of ideology and purpose, but at its best remained faithful to a vision of disinterested pursuit and transmission of knowledge. Research and teaching have always cohabited: anyone who teaches a subject well wants to know more about it, and when she knows more, to impart that knowledge. Universities when true to themselves have always been places that harbor recondite subjects of little immediate utility—places where you can study hieroglyphics and Coptic as well as string theory and the habits of lemmings—places half in and half out of the world. No country needs that more than the U.S., where the pragmatic has always dominated.

Peter Brooks, "Our Universities: How Bad? How Good?" *New York Review of Books*, March 24, 2011.

Chapter 1

1. The rules of 1215 for the University of Paris may be found in English translation by D. C. Munro in *University of Pennsylvania Translations and Reprints*, vol. 2, no. 3 (Philadelphia: University of Pennsylvania Press, 1895). The Latin comes from the *Chartularium Universitatis Parisiensis*, vol. 1, 78–79.

The basic treatise on medieval universities remains Hastings Rashdall, *The Universities of Europe in the Middle Ages*, 2 vols. (Cambridge: Cambridge University Press, 2010).

2. See Michael Oakeshott, *The Voice of Liberal Learning: Michael Oakeshott on Education*, ed. Timothy Fuller (New Haven: Yale University Press, 1989). Oakeshott's study is an essential part of understanding what a university is as well as what a university does, especially in light of the proliferation of MOOCs and online higher education.

3. See chapter 7, which discusses the Minerva Project of Ben Nelson. Nelson houses his students in downtown hotels, an unconscious (perhaps) re-creation of the medieval student experience.

4. Every university student, in most places outside of Italy, was a "clerk," that is, either a priest, a brother, or in minor orders. Minor orders, that is, clerks who were not ordained, were permitted to marry. The minor orders were sub-deacon, lector, sacristan, exorcist, ostler, and sexton. These were professions, with salaries and benefits, which could include room and board. One of the advantages was "benefit of clergy," which exempted the fortunate possessor from some secular tribunals and the most brutal secular punishments. We can find those in minor orders in literature, notably the two lascivious males of Chaucer's "Miller's Tale." Both Nicholas and Absolom fit the medieval view of those in minor orders as lewd, lazy, and inclined to take every advantage. They were not, of course, as vile as millers or as violent as weavers, but they were reputed to be a close second in both regards. Being in minor orders was an excellent position for a second son of a craftsman, a small merchant, or a minor landowner.

5. From the early Middle Ages, there were two kinds of clergy. Regular clergy swore obedience to a rule, *regula*; hence the name. Secular clergy had an apostolate in the world, *saecula*; hence the name. The secular clergy were, in descending order, pope, bishops, priests, deacons. Regular clergy were monastic brothers, usually

of the Benedictine rule or some variant. In the thirteenth century, a new form of rule emerged. Friars, Franciscan, Dominican, Augustinian, Carmelite, Sulpician, swore obedience to a rule but also lived in the world. These distinctions mattered greatly at the time, as various institutions in the Church fought for turf.

6. This system lasted quite a while. When Oliver Wendell Holmes, Jr., enrolled in Harvard Law School after the war, all it took to enter was a college degree and fifty dollars. The medieval informality in admissions does not really end in American universities until the twentieth century.

7. Notably missing from the medieval university is the entire superstructure of the modern admissions process. Scholars simply appeared, recommended by family and friends, able to pay fees, welcomed by those already at the university, accepted by the abbot of a local monastery, or just arriving. The scholars attended lectures. Soon enough, they were among those who were already there. It was all casual and personal.

8. In 1174, the student guild first appears in the historical record. In 1202, the town recognized the student guild, and in 1245 the town and the student guild came to terms. From the viewpoint of the town, the students *were* the university.

9. See Gordon Leff, *Paris and Oxford Universities in the Thirteenth and Fourteenth Centuries* (New York: John Wiley, 1968); the Rashdall, of course, always applies.

10. It's like that today, not just in churches or government or business but in universities. We all are more comfortable with those we know, especially when they will come to occupy important positions. This may be called "better the devil we know" theory, even if only one person on the hiring committee knows the devil.

11. A modern story seems to add a bit of light to the Cardinal's promotion. In the days of John Paul II, papal finances were in some disarray. Father Paul Marcinkus came from Chicago to help out. The pope liked him and put him in charge of the Vatican Bank in 1971. Nobody would speak to him. Pope John Paul made him a monsignor. A few people talked, but not enough. The pope made him a bishop. Things got better, but not good. The pope made him an archbishop. Finally, he had enough rank to do the job. We suspect that the same solution occurred to Innocent III.

12. The dissension between the arts college, where learning was secular, and the masters of theology was legendary long before Cardinal Robert.

13. Problems with students were not new. Indeed, they went back to classical times.

14. The cardinal was managing a problem that had existed for at least a millennium. St. Augustine complained bitterly of his unregulated students in Carthage, c. AD 400:

The licence of the students is foul and uncontrolled. They impudently break in and with almost mad behavior disrupt the order which each teacher has established for his pupils' benefit. They commit many acts of vandalism with an astonishing mindlessness, which would be punished under law were it not that custom protects them.... When I was a student I refused to have anything to do with these customs; as a professor I was forced to tolerate them in outsiders who were not my own pupils. So I decided to go where all informed people declared that such troubles did not occur.

Augustine set his sights on Rome. There, he had been told, "the young men went quietly about their studies and were kept in order by a stricter imposition of discipline. They did not rush all at once and in a mob into the class of a teacher with whom they were not enrolled, nor were pupils admitted at all unless the teacher gave them leave." *Confessions*, trans. Henry Chadwick (Oxford: Oxford University Press, 1998), 80–81. Augustine went so far as to lie to his devoted mother and slip away. But he was punished for his deception, or his dreams: "I quickly discovered that at Rome students behaved in a way which I would never have had to endure in Africa. Acts of vandalism, it was true, by young hooligans did not occur at Rome; that was made clear to me. But, people told me, to avoid paying the teacher his fee, numbers of young men would suddenly club together and transfer themselves to another tutor, breaking their word, and out of love of money, treating fairness as something to be flouted. I cordially detested them, but not 'with a perfect hatred' (Psalm 138: 22); for I probably felt more resentment for what I personally was to suffer from them than for the wrong they were doing to anyone and everyone.... They loved the passing transient amusements and the filthy lucre, which dirties the hand when it is touched" (*Confessions*, 87). So he went on again to Milan.

15. The "trivium" consisted of grammar, rhetoric, and logic. The "quadrivium" was arithmetic, geometry, music, and astronomy. All are still taught in modern universities.

16. The cardinal's effort is being repeated today with MOOCs, which, without admitting it, present the one, the best, the superstar teacher's version of geology, literature, circuits, quantum mechanics, etc.

17. Rules of 1215.

18. The progress of a Parisian scholar of theology in the thirteenth and fourteenth centuries in Paris was as follows: *auditor*, for six

years; *Biblicus*, for three more; *ordinarius*, for three years; *sententorius*, for however long it took; *baccalarius formatus*. The entire progress took most of two decades, or longer, and included determinations and disputations along the way. It was not easy to become a "regent master," one who was officially recognized as being a part of the university.

19. Leff, *Paris and Oxford Universities*, 6.
20. Rashdall, *The Universities of Europe*, vol. 2, 693.
21. The cardinal's rules find a modern equivalent in the Civil Code, both in France and in Louisiana. Here also, a compilation of rules, injunctions, and prohibitions stand the test of time only through constant adjustment and interpretation. Both systems of rules are broad enough to permit flexibility and adjustment. In each system, the details of specific situations can be fit into the general code, which strengthens the rules while giving justice to individuals.
22. Pope Gregory IX, Papal Bull, *Parens scientiarum*, April 15, 1231.
23. Today's version of Gregory's papal bull is the handbook of student conduct, often supplemented by a faculty handbook. Both are written by lawyers, for lawyers, so they are incomprehensible to their respective audiences. But take heart. Comport yourself so as to stay out of the hands of lawyers, and all will be well. And a second rule: courtesy, particularly in public, disarms almost every complaint by making the plaintiff look like the aggressor. On these two rules hang all the law and doctrine of campus life.
24. These regulations have carried over into the modern world. You can't be an engineer without a PE. You can't be a lawyer without passing the bar. You can't be a doctor without passing your medical board exams. Exclusion via determining the rules of inclusion has, since Gregory, been a hallmark of higher education.
25. The modern climate of political correctness, as well as the McCarthy-era censorship, comes to mind.
26. In the modern university, Ward Churchill comes to mind.
27. An academic calendar for the "Street of Straw," where the arts college lectures were given, survives for the late thirteenth century. The schedule is precise, the holidays numerous, and academic life had become as organized as the schedule for city markets. Markets commoditize everything, and learning was becoming simply another commodity.
28. For a delightful book on the human propensity to sin necessarily and incessantly, see Alan Jacobs, *Original Sin* (New York: Harper, 2009). The notion of Original Sin, that is, sin as our being, rather than just what we do, is, as G. K. Chesterton notes, the one Christian doctrine that can be empirically proved by example and which requires no investment in faith. It is also unpopular, so much so that the name has been changed to the more secular and less emotionally charged term: human nature. The problem is the word "sin." It is too strong and judgmental for effete modern tastes. After all, does anyone really sin any more? Isn't almost anyone merely the hapless victim of an unjust and wicked society? Are not most people underprivileged? Is not everything society's fault? Well, actually...

In spite of the modern affect, which began with Jean-Jacques Rousseau, to shift the location of sin and the responsibility for sin from individuals to society and the state, within the university both masters and scholars (students) continue to behave as they did in the days of Pope Gregory. One can only suppose, as student malcontents always do, that universities are uniquely bad places. We doubt that and point back to Original Sin, which, by Occam's razor, is the preferred explanation for the laziness of students, the looniness of masters, and the inability of administrators to do anything right.

29. The exception, as in so much else concerning universities, was at Bologna, where the student guild ran the whole show and practically eliminated student failure.
30. Today, one of the most common and contentious areas of student complaint involves sexual assault. These cases, of course, vary in legal merit, from quite strong to essentially imaginary. The problem itself, however, is not new. The ghosts of Abelard and Heloise, speaking from the twelfth century, can give testimony to that effect.
31. Gary Gutting observes that

> The raison d'être of a college is to nourish a world of intellectual culture; that is, a world of ideas, dedicated to what we can know scientifically, understand humanistically, or express artistically. In our society, this world is mainly populated by members of college faculties: scientists, humanists, social scientists (who straddle the humanities and the sciences properly speaking), and those who study the fine arts. Law, medicine, and engineering are included to the extent that they are still understood as "learned professions," deploying practical skills that are nonetheless deeply rooted in scientific knowledge or humanistic understanding.
>
> When, as is often the case in business education and teacher training, practical skills far outweigh theoretical understanding, we are moving beyond the intellectual culture that defines higher education.

Gary Gutting, "What Is College For?" *The New York Times*, December 14, 2011.

32. Faculty education is entirely different from "faculty development." Schools are filled with faculty development days, seminars, and workshops. What one learns in these workshops is a new way to teach, assuming one learns anything. Generally speaking, faculty development benefits most first- and second-year teachers. Faculty education, on the other hand, means learning more chemistry, physics, literature, architecture, and so on. The purpose of faculty education is to enhance publication, innovation, and imagination.

33. A modern example of such an institution is the newly minted Minerva University in San Francisco, an accredited and greatly heralded creation. It lacks all support for faculty research, learning, community, and publication. Is this system going to work? It's only just getting started: the jury is still out.

34. Oakeshott, *The Voice of Liberal Learning*, 24.

35. Steve Kolowich, "Can Universities Use Data to Fix What Ails the Lecture?" *The Chronicle of Higher Education*, August 11, 2014.

36. The last few generations of students have grown up watching television, which is mostly passively watching other people talk. They are used to lectures, sometimes in the guise of comedy shows, news shows, reality shows, and so forth, but always with the same relationship of passive viewer to active presenter. We suspect that there is no general demand from either faculty or student to get rid of lectures. We suspect further, that if a secret ballot were taken, everyone but university critics would support the lectures.

37. Aristotle believed in learning by doing, noting in the *Nicomachean Ethics*, book 2, "For what we learn, we learn by doing." Aristotle has modern disciples. The motto of Texas Woman's University (once TSCW) was, and may still be, "Learn by doing." Some have suggested that this is a strange motto for a woman's university.

38. William Faulkner, *Requiem for a Nun* (New York: Vintage International, 1950).

Chapter 2

1. On the Puritan sensibilities of early New England, see Perry Miller, *The New England Mind: From Colony to Province* (Cambridge: Harvard University Press, 1998). Also of interest is Miller's *The New England Mind: The Seventeenth Century* (Cambridge: Harvard University Press, 1982).

2. This assertion originates with the Duc de la Rochefoucauld, *Maximes* (1665 and on). Upon seeing the apparent reconciliation of Cardinal Mazarin with a bitter political enemy, the Duc muttered in disgusted admiration, "Tout arrive en France": "everything happens in France."

3. *Dartmouth College v. Woodward*, 17 U.S. 4 Wheat. 518 (1819).

4. Fewer than 5 percent of Americans, excluding slaves from the calculation, went to college. It was not just a matter of money; it was also a matter of the wise use of time. Lawyers read law and established practices. Doctors apprenticed themselves to the local practitioners. Engineers went to West Point. In the South, sons of planters were most likely to attend university, while northern states sent the sons of clergy and merchants.

5. Exclusivity refers to one's position in the entire small college. Within the fraternity, it is like middle school all over again. There are the cool kids, the rich kids, the jocks, and a sprinkling of geeks and nerds who are accepted to keep the GPA up.

6. A surviving example of the original design can be seen at New College, Oxford (1379), where two academic cloisters were the heart of the basic college design. The cloister migrated across the pond. Harvard built its Harvard Yard, and Yale enclosed its first two buildings with a large quadrangle. In the twentieth century, Louisiana State University built its new campus (1922–1940) as a quadrangle, with the library and campanile at one end and a small engineering quad at the other.

7. The fixed curriculum had intellectual origins in Greek philosophy and medieval practice. It was then thought possible for someone to know everything. Aristotle did, and so did Archimedes and Cicero. Thomas Aquinas did as well; he imitated Aristotle by writing it all down. Since the corpus of knowledge was limited, the number and variety of courses could be limited as well. Graduates did not know all that Aristotle, Archimedes, or Aquinas knew, but they did know something, a smidgen at least, about every branch of moral and natural philosophy. The general education requirements now in vogue also reflect this medieval reality. Modern students, however much they like different majors, hate having to take courses in every discipline. Engineers taking history, poets taking mathematics: the pain is prodigious, and the complaint endless.

8. Schools as part of political organization can be seen most clearly in New York. See D. T. Valentine's *Manual*, issued until 1864, which gave an organizational overview of New York government. Schools occupied a large amount of space. In 1864, the newest school was New Lots. The principal was Mrs. McGillicuddy. She was, naturally, a political appointee of the Irish-dominated Tammany Hall machine.

9. See Hastings Rashdall, *The Universities of Europe in the Middle Ages*, vol. 1 (Oxford: The Clarendon Press, 1895).

10. George Ticknor, *Life, Letters, and Journals*, vol. 2 (Boston, 1877), 485; quoted in Morton Keller, *Affairs of State: Public Life in Late Nineteenth-Century America* (Cambridge: Harvard University Press, 1977), 2.

11. While faculty and overseers were defeated, they were not abashed; opposition to electives lingered on. Modern critics to the contrary, universities are fundamentally conservative.

12. The market for subtraction via community colleges has become part of the political as well as the economic marketplace. In the 2016 presidential campaign, both Democratic candidates supported a national program for free tuition at community colleges. No Republican candidate opposed the idea.

13. Systems can become too large and complex, so they no longer have a tendency to self-organize. Then the process becomes an end in itself, and both customers and workers are subject to the tyranny of inefficiency.

14. We have used two examples from Louisiana because that's where we live. Had we been at a school in Florida, Tennessee, or Michigan, we would be telling similar stories about community colleges there. The details vary, but the phenomena of political pressure and local economic development remain constant always.

15. The most prominent institutions in this process were the companies that would ultimately form I. G. Farben (*Interessen-Gemeinschaft Farbenindustrie AktienGesellschaft*). These included six companies, among them Bayer, BASF, and Hoechst. One of their most important inventions was aspirin, which was Bayer's name for the drug and which became part of the post–Versailles patent controversies. I. G. was formally dissolved after World War II, but the companies all remained alive and well and prosperous, cooperating much as they always have. University graduates continued to call into these corporate ranks.

16. Jon Gernter, *The Idea Factory: Bell Labs and the Great Age of American Innovation* (New York: Penguin Press, 2012). Gertner describes the history, structure, and achievements of Bell Labs, including the stuff they missed (fiber optics), the stuff they got wrong (picture phone), and the stuff they got right.

17. The whole process of empire building can be found in C. Northcote Parkinson, *Parkinson's Law* (Buccaneer Books, 1996). The law is as follows: work expands to fill the time available, regardless of the work to be done, if any. Parkinson's Law accounts for the truism that if you want something done, give it to your busiest worker. In modern society, as all know, the busiest person is invariably a woman.

18. Originally, many towns provided no schools for girls or African-Americans. In the 1830s, most American men believed that a girl's place was in the home and that African-American children, including those who were free, should be at work. Those attitudes would change, but only conditionally. Some towns established separate schools for girls and boys (Atlanta, Georgia); others, separate schools for separate races (Boston and Brooklyn).

19. Being a teacher often provided more than a job. Teaching in the late nineteenth-century one-room schools often led to marriage. Montana, with public schools sprinkled in small settlements across the prairie, wanted only single women to teach the kids. There was a shortage of women on the Montana frontier, and virtually no teacher went a year without acquiring a husband. Montana received a steady stream of young teachers from Midwestern normal schools, who started as teachers and became ranch, farm, or small-town wives. Montana was not alone in having to renew its teacher core annually, particularly in the trans-Mississippi West. Public school teaching played a substantial part in building families and communities.

20. On the growth of federal support and regulation in the area of scientific research, see Michael Hiltzik, *Big Science: Ernest Lawrence and the Invention that Launched the Military-Industrial Complex* (New York: Simon & Schuster, 2015); and Charlotte DeCroes Jacobs, *Jonas Salk: A Life* (Oxford: Oxford University Press, 2015). Hiltzik deals with big physics, centered in part on the life and work of Nobel laureate Ernest Lawrence. Jacobs deals with big biology, a discovery made at a university (Pittsburgh) that inoculates against a disease. In both, the relationship of government to the research university is a basic, though not a keynote, theme.

21. Politicians run for office (and sometimes win) by promising to make government more efficient and less burdensome. These promises are *"merde a la troisieme puissance."* They cannot be kept. The reason is size: the global figure of federal aid to students, professors, and universities runs to scores of billions of dollars, but the money is actually spent a few thousand or a few hundred dollars at a time. The same is true of protocols and reports. The number is too large and the subject too diverse for effective policing of grants and contracts. Both in size and cost, the federal ongoing investment in universities has become too great to be avoided.

But those grants and contracts are not too numerous to be selectively investigated in a search for scandal. Since the rules are both vague and numerous, scandal is always found. Universities are in the uncomfortable position of depending on funds they will inevitably, in some way, misuse.

22. Oakeshott argues that the "pause" is not a sort of time-out from life. It is instead an "interval" in which the loyalties of youth can be examined in light of the wisdom available in an academy. The pause, therefore, is not so much in the race but more in how the student understands that race. Oakeshott writes:

> The characteristic gift of a university is the gift of an interval. Here is an opportunity to put aside the hot allegiances of youth without the necessity of at once acquiring new loyalties to take their place. Here is a break in the tyrannical course of irreparable events; a period in which to look round upon the world and upon oneself without the sense of an enemy at one's back or the insistent pressure to make up one's mind; a moment in which to taste the mystery without the necessity of at once seeking a solution. And all this, not in an intellectual vacuum, but surrounded by all the inherited learning and literature and experience of our civilization; not alone, but in the company of kindred spirits; not as a sole occupation, but combined with the discipline of studying a recognized branch of learning ... it is itself the privilege of being a "student," the enjoyment of *schole*—leisure [113–114].

23. Oakeshott, 24.
24. See Angus Kennedy, "The University: Still Dead," May 25, 2012, http://www.spiked-online.com/review_of_books/article/12484#.WKxdn9BN1Hg.
25. Today, the Catholic University has become the University College of Dublin, having received certification in 1908. There are two universities in Dublin, and they are quite different. Trinity College, Dublin, an Anglican foundation, designed to serve the Ascendancy, is easily distinguished from University College, designed to serve the propertied Roman Catholic majority.
26. Cardinal Newman's *The Idea of a University* (published 1852 and 1871) was a product of both anticipation and experience. He began with the ideal before he took over and concluded with some reference to realities after he had left the school (1872). In this, his treatise is similar to the Rules of Cardinal Robert de Courçon, who was chancellor before he was asked to organize the university.
27. In the nineteenth century, establishing universities in Europe was essentially a government monopoly. In postrevolutionary France, all universities were part of a single system, the University of France, which was instituted by Napoleon. In Great Britain, as new universities were founded, notably the "red bricks," a royal charter signified state approval and support. Strictly private universities went unrecognized by public authorities, both in Britain and on the continent. Their degrees did not officially exist; their "graduates" had not graduated, or even attended. Unlike the American practice, European governments regarded higher education as a state responsibility and a state function. Recently, there has been movement in this direction in America, particularly in the Obama administration's proposals for free tuition and additional oversight in public colleges. In the modern world, generally speaking, the state has replaced the Church as the sponsor and the overseer of universities.
28. Aniline dye was first exhibited there. Some thought it might be a cure for malaria. It may have helped, though an unfortunate side effect was the patient's death. Other uses for aniline dye soon appeared, and these did not involve killing the users.
29. It may be superogation, but we will say it anyway: Newman's sense of the natural and the social world fit the Platonic/Augustinian/scholastic model of a unified natural truth and therefore a unified intellectual system. See Plato's dialogues, the *Theatetus* and the *Republic*, along with Question One of the *Prima Pars* of Thomas Aquinas's *Summa Theologia*. On the personal level, the obvious place to go is Augustine's *Confessions*.
30. Had he written in the twenty-first century, Cardinal Newman might have noted that eight centuries were inadequate. We suspect that there are not enough centuries between now and final entropy to inform legislators about the nature and purpose of a university.
31. John Henry Newman, *The Idea of a University* (New Haven: Yale University Press, 1996).
32. Charles Mackay, *Popular Delusions and the Madness of Crowds*, 1841.
33. Newman, *The Idea of a University*, "Preface."
34. Ibid., Discourse 5.
35. Ibid., Discourse 7.
36. As we hope this essay will show, that is pretty much the main problem with MOOCs, and a lot of SCOCs, too, come to that.
37. Clark Kerr, *The Uses of the University* (Cambridge: Harvard University Press, 1963).

Chapter 3

1. It does depend on how you count. Community college students count, of course, but

how about students in proprietorial schools, such as DeVry or Phoenix and vo-tech schools, that teach things like cosmetology and welding? Do these count? They are post–high school, but not traditionally collegiate. The figure of around 20 million does not include these students.

2. Wikipedia provides an excellent explanation of the Law of Large Numbers. (It includes the law itself, a couple of simple examples of its working, the mathematics of its two forms (strong and weak), and the mathematics of proof. The article is accessible to lay persons as well as mathematicians, and it is clear and easy to follow, even for a couple of humanists.

3. Richard J. Herrnstein and Charles Murray, *The Bell Curve: Intelligence and Class Structure in American Life* (New York: The Free Press, 1994).

4. This idea appears in Thomas Gray, "Elegy in a Country Churchyard," which presents the current liberal view of vast social oppression of intelligence, though with a great deal more grace than is usually now found. A little more social fairness, and huge amounts of talent and intelligence, would rise from obscurity.

5. See the comments by James J. Heckman, especially "Cracked Bell," *Reason* (March 1995). This is a serious article by an important authority who is competent to read the book and has done so.

6. "Character is destiny in mankind" is a fragment from Heraclitus. See Milton Charles Nahm, *Selections from Early Greek Philosophy* (New York: Crofts, 1935).

7. This refers to the famous comment by Justice Potter Stewart that he could not define pornography, but he knew it when he saw it. That has remained the real standard of judgment for both teaching and pornography ever since.

8. One of the authors learned all of this in the United States Army. The Army education course was short, intense, and serious. Grading was pass/fail. The author in question failed.

9. For example, Marc Bousquet's *How the University Works: Higher Education and the Low-Wage Nation* (New York: New York University Press, 2008); Jennifer Washburn's *University, Inc.: The Corporate Corruption of Higher Education* (New York: Basic Books, 2005); and Christopher Newfield's *Unmaking the Public University: The Forty-Year Assault on the Middle Class* (Cambridge: Harvard University Press, 2008).

10. Jeffrey J. Williams, "Deconstructing Academe: The Birth of Critical University Studies," *The Chronicle of Higher Education*, February 19, 2012.

11. Back in 1992, he fired one of the opening salvos in the CUS challenge. Gerald Graff, *Beyond the Culture Wars: How Teaching the Conflicts Can Revitalize American Education* (New York: W. W. Norton & Co., 1992), 214.

12. Paolo Freire, *Pedagogy of the Oppressed*, 30th anniversary ed. (New York: Bloomsbury Academic, 2000). Modern secular ideologies are not psychologically different from older transcendental religions. Modern ideologies have sacred texts and patron saints. Both types of religion, transcendental and immanent, also have disciples who venerate the saints, read the sacred texts, and engage in doctrinal exegesis. We confess here, and do not wish to hide, that this is basically how we view most post-Freire critical university studies and critical pedagogies.

13. Freire was born into, and was writing within, a Roman Catholic society, in which a good deal of education was religious. In Roman Catholic pastoral theology, things socially acceptable are the *norma recte vivendi*, the norms of right living. Their source is the pastoral *officium* of the pope, and they form a core of pastoral education given to Catholic youth. In Brazil, one could easily be a Marxist, and many were, but a Catholic pastoral background was pervasive. It is not too much to say that a good deal of Brazilian Marxism was a reaction against a socially conservative Roman Catholicism.

14. Jean-Jacques Rousseau, in *Emile*, had the same difficulty in describing how students learn without being taught. In general, earnest social reformers were not much given to a sense either of humor or irony.

15. The Shining Path still exists. It is now an important drug cartel in the foothills of the Andes, where it runs maceration pits, turning coca leaves (imported from Bolivia) into raw cocaine.

16. The line of inheritance for critical university studies runs backward through the progressive education ideas of John Dewey through Karl Marx and Georg W. F. Hegel, all the way to Jean-Jacques Rousseau and others in the first generation of the Romantic era. Romantic authors were much concerned with the beneficent influence of nature upon education, particularly of the child. Around the turn of the nineteenth century, Johann Pestalozzi had the idea of combining nature and education in the kindergarten, and he published two books, *How Gertrude Teaches Her Children* and *Education of Man*. More influential was Jean-Jacques Rousseau, who published *Emile, or On Education*, which was burnt by the public hangman as subversive and sacrilegious in 1762. In *Emile*, the most important part of education was moral, and nature would bring out the inherent goodness in humanity, which society

was in the permanent business of crushing. See Jean-Jacques Rousseau's *The Social Contract* on this as well.

A further enduring educational/literary treatise of the period was *Paul et Virginie* by Jacques-Henri Bernadin de Saint-Pierre, first published in 1787. It described two orphan children growing up in nature on a Pacific island. Things came to a bad end, of course; that is required for a sentimental novel. *Paul et Virginie* was several times turned into an opera in the nineteenth century. But the children were happy together, and they lived a moral life in accord with nature. The modern American version is not an opera; America is not a society that loves opera. In America, it is a movie: *The Blue Lagoon*.

The importance of Romantic educational commentary for critical university studies lies in two areas. The first is that people are inherently good, and desirable reforms can bring that goodness out. Universities have now organized oppressed students (see Rousseau's *Social Contract*). But a reformed university will ennoble and enhance them. Secondly, there is a right and natural law of education, which can be found and implemented, if only we discard the tyranny of tradition. Both of these Romantic ideas have resurfaced in critical university studies.

17. The vocabulary of liberation can be used in any circumstance to advocate the liberation of just about anyone. Multimillionaire ballplayers went on strike in 1994, complaining that they were being oppressed. Their salaries were too low. Ten million a year was not enough. Players as a group were getting too small a percentage of gross baseball revenues. The same sort of complaint, on a much more limited scale, of course, can occur in universities. We have no doubt that Freire himself would have been disappointed, but not surprised, at the multiple uses the word "liberation" can embrace.

18. Polybius, *Histories*, trans. Robin Waterfield (Oxford University Press, 2010), I.1.

19. Much of the general information about paper mills comes from David Tomar's *The Shadow Scholar* (2012). By his own admission, Mr. Tomar, a Rutgers graduate, is a thoroughly unpleasant person, much given to whine, self-pity, and a lively sense of victimhood. But he tells a compelling story of years of professional paper-writing for students impaired in energy, intelligence, interest, or language.

20. This exam is hard enough so that a flourishing scheme of substitute test takers was recently uncovered, and the case is now before a United States attorney.

21. Passage rates run from 85 percent for chemical engineers down to 65 percent for industrial engineers. Obtaining the professional license is by no means guaranteed.

22. Those critics are not entirely correct. Students learn things that are taught outside of the classroom. We relate an anecdote: Once upon a time and many years ago, during lunch, a recruiter sat down with one of the authors. It was the only vacant seat in the cafeteria. The recruiter remarked that he was looking for engineers. The author suggested that he was in the wrong place. Why not go to MIT, Cornell, or RPI? They were really good engineering schools, and this university was not. The recruiter smiled indulgently at an inexperienced young professor. Everyone, he said, cannot run the lab or head the research project. There need to be lots of engineers in support roles. The university he was visiting supplied those. And one other thing, he added: support staff engineers need to work well in a group. He looked for kids that had been in fraternities.

23. Richard Arum and Josipa Roska, *Academically Adrift: Limited Learning on College Campuses* (Chicago: University of Chicago Press, 2011).

24. Some years ago, the list of what they knew would have included Oprah Winfrey, the fundamental source of social values for fifteen years of college students. Looking back on it, the kids could have done a lot worse.

25. Although the CLA has not found customers everywhere, it has had astonishing growth in the past decade. In 2004, the University of Texas began using College Learning Assessment at the insistence of the state regents. Other universities soon signed on with the CLA, as the desire for its kind of teaching and learning assessment has spread across the country. Two other major assessment systems, Collegiate Assessment of Academic Proficiency and the Proficiency Profile, were created to satisfy the ever-increasing need for evaluation. By 2012, more than five hundred public colleges had pledged to give one of these assessments to their students.

26. Doug Lederman, editor of *Inside Higher Ed*, observes that "It's hard to think of a study in the last decade that has had a bigger impact on public discourse about higher education and the internal workings of colleges and universities alike than has *Academically Adrift*." Doug Lederman, *Inside Higher Ed*, "Less Academically Adrift?" May 20, 2013.

27. See Steven D. Levitt and Stephen J. Dubner, *Freakonomics: A Rogue Economist Explores the Hidden Side of Everything* (New York: Harper Collins, 2005, 2006), chapter 1. The problems of faculty cheating in Chicago emerged within a couple of years of establishing the student tests. What a surprise.

28. Or, alternatively, a test can be carefully

constructed, as with PhD oral exams, which really are designed to fail the candidate.

29. In these State Department hypotheticals, a serious analysis and a reasonable policy recommendation will result in failing the test. In all Third World "states," the situation is always hopeless but never serious. Nothing can be done to change the state and alter its geopolitical relationship with America and other powers. Well-coached candidates know going in that this analysis, though true, is the wrong answer. Candidates for the CLA corporate memo will, after a couple of years, have the same advantage.

30. "College Graduation: Weighing the Cost ... and the Payoff," *Pew Research Center Publications* (May 12, 2012): 2.

31. See Samuel Lubell, *The Future of American Politics* (Westport, CT: Greenwood, 1984).

32. The word "myth" is used here in its formal definition: a myth is a narrative exposition of truth in which everything is true but the story itself. In the American experience, the details of attaining a college education are so varied that no single story covers them all. The constant truth concerns the value of a college education, which fit all circumstances of travail and success.

33. The number of veterans going to college was so large that Hollywood made a movie about it. *Apartment for Peggy* appeared in 1948.

34. See "Trends in College Enrollment: Completion, Cost, and Debt," *Pew Research Center* (May 15, 2011).

35. Hanna Rosen, "The End of Men," *The Atlantic* (July/August 2010).

36. Generally speaking, private college loans have a default rate of around 3 percent, while federal college loans have a default rate of around 13 percent. The reason for this difference is clear. Private lending institutions are concerned with the ability to repay the loan. Public lenders concentrate on performing a service.

37. The total amount of student debt, and the projected rise in both global and individual amounts, brings to mind the reforms of Solon in 594 BC. These reforms included eliminating debt slavery as part of the "shaking off of burdens" (*seisachtheia*).

38. Pew Research Center, "College Graduates Weighing the Costs," 3.

39. "College Graduation: Weighing the Cost ... and the Payoff," *Pew Research Center Publications* (May 17, 2012).

Chapter 4

1. Leonard J. Hochberg, "Nature of Legitimate Knowledge in Institutions of Higher Education," unpublished manuscript; Professor Hochberg has extensively discussed this article with the authors. We are quite taken with his ideas, which are recognizable in reality without being cynical or disagreeable.

2. Hochberg, "Nature," 1, along with many conversations.

3. Disdain for teachers at research universities is the stuff of anecdotes, not measurement. If an analyst inquires too closely, everyone will deny everything. Of course, the university loves students. Of course, universities love professors who love teaching. Of course, teaching is a primary mission at this university, maybe not so much at others, but certainly here. Why, at our school, we have twenty, perhaps thirty, teaching awards for every award for research. These observations come from experience as well as gossip.

4. See Cardinal Robert de Courçon's rules of 1215 and Pope Gregory's rules of 1231, which are covered in chapter 1. Hierarchy is often implicit in these rules, but is the unquestionable result of living by these rules. The tree may be old, but the apples have not fallen far from it.

5. Hochberg, "Nature," 1ff.

6. See, as an example of differences among those who live close together, Vladimir Jabitinsky, *The Iron Wall* (1923). Jabitinsky describes the utterly different cultures of Palestinian Arabs and Western-educated Jews living in Israel. He anticipates no general conversion of one culture to the other. The iron wall symbolizes cultural differences built into social and educational structures that are essentially unchanging. Research university faculty and student attitudes should be thought of in terms of a symbolic iron wall.

7. Hochberg, "Nature," 1.

8. Ibid., 2.

9. See, for example, Thomas at Millsaps College.

10. The idea that humanity, both persons and society, is essentially mechanical became popular during the Enlightenment. See Julien Offray de La Mettrie, *L'Homme Machine* (1748). Subsequently, society has seemed less mechanical, at least by some and certainly by us. For a more antic view of modern university life, see Hazard Adams, *The Academic Tribes* (Champaign: University of Illinois Press, 1987). See also Jose Ortega y Gasset, *Mission of the University* (New York: Transaction, 2002).

11. See the work of Professor Michael Hochberg, of the University of Delaware and Singapore National University.

12. Stanley Engerman and Robert Fogel, *Time on the Cross* (1974; repr., New York: Norton, 2013).

13. See Ron Soodalter, *Hanging Captain Gordon* (New York: Atria, 2006).

14. See *Plessy v. Ferguson*, 163 U.S. 537

(1896). This case legalized racial separation on public transportation, and this practice was extended to public accommodations and to schools. See also *Gong Lum v. Rice*, 275 U.S. 78 (1927), which accepted racial segregation in public schools.

15. On the Jewish experience, see Moses Rischin, ed., *Grandma Never Lived in America: The New Journalism of Abraham Cahan* (Bloomington: Indiana University Press, 1985) and Moses Rischin, *The Promised City: New York's Jews, 1870–1914* (Cambridge: Harvard University Press, 1962).

16. Discrimination may be summed up in a single case. The state of Illinois denied Myra Bradwell a license to practice law because she was a woman. See *Bradwell v. The State*, 83 U.S. 16 Wall. 130 (1872).

17. George Kubler, *The Shape of Time* (New Haven: Yale University Press, 2008). The salient example used by Kubler was Gothic art and architecture, which fell victim to Renaissance aesthetic judgment.

18. *Huffington Post*, February 11, 2016.

19. *Washington Post*, August 22, 2014.

20. Much has been written lately about the whole adjunct phenomenon. A good overview is provided by Laura McKenna in "The Cost of an Adjunct," *The Atlantic* (May 26, 2015).

21. Truth in advertising compels us to disclose that both authors have had personal experience in the LSU Honors College, as a student and as part of the faculty.

22. Cardozo's great treatise is *The Nature of the Judicial Process* (New Haven: Yale University Press, 1921). It should be required reading for every undergraduate in every discipline in every college; otherwise, they will not know how the courts work. See also Karl Popper, *The Open Society and Its Enemies* (London: Routledge Press, 1945); also note George Orwell's 1945 parable *Animal Farm* (repr., New York: Signet Classics, 1996). These three books collectively provide an effective overview of modern political thought, minus an awful lot of the rant.

23. Nancy West, "What's the Point of an Honors College, Anyway?" *The Chronicle of Higher Education*, January 27, 2014.

24. The full quote goes something like this: "The best LSU students were as good as any at Yale, but as for the rest, oh my God." At the time, LSU was an open-enrollment university: preparation for college was obviously a problem.

25. Long was elected governor in 1928 and served until 1932, even though he had also been elected senator in 1930. He did not trust his lieutenant governor, so he simply stayed in the state until his term was up. Only then did he go to Washington. See T. Harry Williams, *Huey Long* (New York: Knopf, 1969).

26. Louisiana adopted twelve grades for high school only in 1950. Before that, Louisiana high schools only went until the eleventh grade. Governor Long, who believed in "every man a king," also believed that every kid deserved a chance.

27. The law of large numbers did not (and does not) yield to the populist belief that the hinterlands are littered with multitudes of diamonds in the rough who will shine superbly upon application of a university polish. In Great Britain, there is an entire college, Birkbeck, socialist in its political orientation, that is devoted to finding bright working-class kids and providing them with a college education.

28. The Sternbergs owned Goudchaux's, the town's premier local department store (way ahead of Sears in every respect), and an insurance company. See Hans J. Sternberg, *We Were Merchants* (Baton Rouge: Louisiana State University Press, 2009).

29. These are the concluding words from the Catalan oath of allegiance to the kings of Aragon. See Ralph Giesey, *If Not, Not: The Oath of the Aragonese and the Legendary Laws of Sobrarbe* (Princeton: Princeton University Press, 1968). In the opinion of one author, the phrase has entered the language. In the opinion of the other author, it has not. The other author is probably right. Hence the note. Although there are variants, the oath goes much like this: "We, who are no less than you, swear to you who are no better than we, that we will be your faithful subjects as long as you adhere to our laws and customs, but if not, not."

30. Economically though not institutionally, Louisiana was a member of OPEC. The Iranian oil crisis of 1979–80 boosted the price of oil, both spot and contract, and Louisiana benefited enormously. Things were so good that the dean had a little extra money. Two years later, 1984, there wasn't a spare nickel on campus, and the dean would never have been able to support honors.

31. Some lessons can be learned here as we consider how Dean Seay navigated through the bureaucratic labyrinth. There are some things you can do, and they take time. Always go see the other guy in person. Appear to be slightly conspiratorial. But include a lot of people in the loop. Reassure constantly. Always allay suspicion. Suspicion is a major coin of the academic realm. The deeply ingrained suspicions within the academy are one reason for committees. They are a waste of time but not of reassurance.

32. The American Constitution, an Enlightenment document, reflected the eighteenth-century view that rights inhered in persons, not groups. The amendments to the Constitution reinforced this sense of defense

of personality by protecting individuals from the overweening power of the state. Constitutional jurisprudence concerning rights has followed the Enlightenment pattern. The defense of individual rights and civil liberties really began with Oliver Wendell Holmes's dissent in *Abrams v. United States*, 250 U.S. 616 (1919). Subsequent jurisprudence has reinforced the idea that rights belong to persons.

Group rights have their origins in various European philosophers of fascism, notably Marx, Gobineau, and Pareto.

33. See *Regents of Univ. of California v. Bakke*, 438 U.S. 265 (1978). The effort at balance concerning the role of race and ethnicity established by Justice Powell in Bakke has been under continuous judicial review.

34. An analogy can be found in prayer in public schools. See *School Dist. of Abington Tp. v. Schempp*, 374 U.S. 203 (1963). The court held, 8–1, that Bible reading and the Lord's Prayer required daily in school by Pennsylvania law violated the Establishment clause of the First Amendment. For decades, schools went right on holding prayers.

35. After the 1900 election, Mr. Dooley (Finley Peter Dunne) noted that the Supreme Court, in supporting imperialism, had followed the election returns. If the Supreme Court can attend to politics, may not research universities do the same?

36. One need only consider the endless discussion about Professor Jonathan Gruber, the MIT economist who helped write the Romney Plan in Massachusetts and the Affordable Care Act.

37. Alan Charles Kors and Harry Silvergate, *The Shadow University* (New York: Free Press, 1998).

38. See Mark Edmundston, "Dwelling in Possibilities," *The Chronicle of Higher Education*, March 14, 2008. Edmundston points out that it is the student's aim to always be everywhere simultaneously. Students are not interested in being in a single place, doing a serious thing seriously.

39. Oliver Wendell Holmes, Jr., *The Common Law* (Boston: Little, Brown, 1881), 1, Lecture I.

40. See Benjamin Nathan Cardozo, *The Nature of the Judicial Process* (New York: Yale University Press, 1921), 53.

Chapter 5

1. *MONEY with Melissa Francis* on Fox Business Network (2012–2016).

2. Some of the stories about lost opportunities are truly legendary. LSU, a place both authors have some familiarity with, lost the opportunity to be a major center of geopolitical and geostrategic study. The university had a grant-funded Center for Geopolitical Study. But for reasons no one can explain, LSU was unable to integrate the Center's work into the curriculum, fit the Center's personnel into a department, or pick up the necessary institutional expenses. So the Center closed. It reopened in Austin, Texas, as Stratfor, an internationally recognized private intelligence and analysis think tank. The benefits went to the University of Texas. No opportunity like this will come again to LSU.

The most famous of the lost horizons came in 1945 at the University of Pennsylvania. Two faculty members in the Morse School of Electrical Engineering, Harold Mauckley and J. Presper Eckert, worked on an electronic calculator that could figure artillery firing tables. The mathematics were straightforward, but the number of calculations was enormous. Perhaps a machine could speed things up. Mauckley and Eckert came up with a machine called ENIAC, Electronic Numerator and Integrated Arithmetic Calculator. But there were two problems. World War II was over, and the need for firing tables had diminished. Moreover, the administration at the University of Pennsylvania could not arrive at an arrangement with Mauckley and Eckert concerning what to do with ENIAC. So the two left the university and took their computer with them. Mauckley and Eckert did not do well in the computer business, but their ideas and patents were bought by IBM. IBM could do something with computers, and it did. Now we have iPhones, iPads, PCs, servers, supercomputers, microcomputers, and more and more. The University of Pennsylvania, where all that started, had an opportunity to have part of the action. In the administration of the academy, imagination really matters. So does its absence.

3. The origin of this is disputed between Roger Brinner, George Stigler and Frank Kotsonis.

4. These days are different indeed. In March 2015, Sweet Briar College, a women's school founded in 1901 in rural Virginia, announced that it would close at the end of the academic year. The Amherst County Attorney Ellen Bowyer sued to prevent the closure. The case has been appealed to the Virginia Supreme Court. In the meantime, whatever the decision, the closure announcement itself has done enormous damage to the community, the college, and the students.

Sweet Briar has been a Southern equivalent of the Seven Sisters, with considerable prestige and an endowment. But the fiscal problems seemed to be too much. Enrollment was declining; the "discount rate" (the difference between formal tuition costs and what the students actually pay) was growing. At a certain point, the college administrators no longer felt that they could sustain its operations. Sweet Briar is not alone. Two other Virginia colleges, St. Paul and Virginia Intermont, have already closed. Randolph-Macon Woman's College staved off extinction by changing its name and adding male students. For small liberal arts colleges, particularly those in very small towns, the future can seem dim. Disinvestment for private colleges can take the form of students going elsewhere, which is as serious for them as declining state appropriations are for public institutions. See Scott Jaschik, "Shocking Decision at Sweet Briar," *Inside Higher Ed*, March 4, 2015.

"Those were the days" comes from a song by that name. The lyrics were written by Mary Hopkin in 1968, and that version topped the popular music charts. The song is actually older. The music was composed by Boris Fomin, and the Russian lyrics by Konstantin Podrevkskii during the period of the Great War. Its initial recording was in 1925. It was written as a song of youth and love lost, but with the Hopkin lyrics it works equally well as a lament for lost time.

5. *Cumming v. Richmond County Board of Education*, 175 U.S. 528 (1899). The decision was written by John Marshall Harlan, who had dissented three years earlier in *Plessy v. Ferguson*, 163 U.S. 537 (1896). The relationship between income and expense has been described by C. Northcote Parkinson. He suavely explained the relationship between income and expense in *Parkinson's Law: The Pursuit of Progress* (London: John Murray, 1958). Parkinson's Law is as follows: No matter what your income, your expenses rise to exceed it. This Law applies to the state as well as its people.

6. Universities are not alone in the huge rise in costs since the Nixon era. Health care, houses, and automobiles have experienced the same.

7. The numbers for LSU are on the university website under "Budget and Planning." The same is certainly true for other state universities in other states. Tracking the fiscal horror story, state by state, university by university, is beyond the scope of this essay. We have used the local example because it appears to lie within the parameters of the standard model. The university has been damaged but not destroyed, and the primary victims of disinvestment have been the students.

8. Everett Dirkson, a Republican senator from Illinois, was Senate minority leader in the 1960s. A charming, cheerful, and chatty man, he appeared on television a lot because he was good copy. On one memorable occasion, he observed, "A billion here, a billion there, and pretty soon it becomes real money." That remark was made in the days when a billion really was real money, and the total federal budget was *under* $100 billion.

9. See, for example, the silent film *Poppy* (1925), starring W. C. Fields and Carol Dempster. The administration of the Great War, to say nothing of Prohibition, did not leave all Americans breathless with admiration.

10. As of now, 2016, the impact of the Affordable Healthcare Act on public funding cannot be estimated with anything approaching precision. All that can be said is that there will be costs.

11. "Virtual community" sounds like an oxymoron, and grammatically it is, but the effect is clear and observable. Remember the wink that Liberace gave to the camera at the end of his television show. Market research found that plenty of viewers thought Liberace was winking at them. It sounds impossible or at least weird. The success of Liberace on television indicates it was neither. Professors are not Liberace, and students seldom take the wink personally, but there can be a sense of one-on-one communication via electron. Facebook is the living billion-dollar proof on that.

12. Connection between student and professor also occurs in the classroom, at least for those who are not too timid around other people. A personal relationship developed face-to-face is pretty standard. The miracle of the Internet is that this can occur without anyone ever meeting anyone else.

13. Daphne Koller, one of the founders of Coursera, discusses the problems of student cheating in online courses in "Weekend Confidential: Alexandra Wolfe," *The Wall Street Journal*, June 6–7, 2015.

14. We refer back to earlier comments on human nature and Alan Jacobs' *Original Sin* and G. K. Chesterton's comment that original sin is the only Christian doctrine that can be proven empirically.

15. This myth, in all its pathetic strengths, has been staged by Emlyn Williams, *The Corn is Green* (1938). It was made into a movie in 1979.

16. In Great Britain there is an entire college, Birkbeck, that searches for and enrolls working-class students who would not otherwise go to a university. A combination of left-wing zeal, social resentment, and the desire to help animate the faculty at Birkbeck. They know that they are doing God's work, always assuming there is a God. See Caspar Melville, "Saving Our Universities? New Humanist Interviews A. C. Grayling," *New Humanist* 127, no. 5 (September/October 2012). A. C. Grayling, a "man of the left," has founded a new humanities college in London, charging £18,000

a year tuition, which is what the education costs. Grayling is worried that the humanities are being slighted in most universities. A not-surprising side effect of this venture is that his old friends will no longer speak to him. The hard left is quite similar to a gathered church, with its rigid doctrine and strong sense of virtue.

17. As an example, Harvard in the 1930s strongly supported the college entrance examinations on the high moral ground that there might be someone in North Dakota, or even Mississippi, who could benefit from a Harvard education, which should be made available even to bumpkins.

18. See, for example, the outstanding book by Jerome Karabel, *The Chosen: The Hidden History of Admission and Exclusion at Harvard, Yale, and Princeton* (New York: Mariner Books, 2006).

19. See, for example, The New School in New York City.

20. Augustine's works were discussed in Cardinal Robert's university, not least by the patron saint of professors, Thomas Aquinas. The Patristic authority most often cited in the *Summa Theologiae* is Augustine.

21. Actually, the term "MOOC" was not coined until 2008, by Dave Cormier of the University of Prince Edward Island in response to a course called Connectivism and Connective Knowledge.

22. For O'Donnell's own description of the experiment, you might look at "Teaching on the Infobahn," *Religious Studies News* 9, no. 3 (1994): 4. Professor O'Donnell also announced his invention to a broader audience in "The Future Is Now and Always Has Been," *The Chronicle of Higher Education*, September 3, 2012: "I call it the best idea I ever had in the shower. About to teach a standard course, introducing the life and thought of St. Augustine, I wanted to do better. What about, I thought in midshampoo, inviting the rest of the world into the classroom? The Internet, after all...."

23. Organisation for Economic Co-operation and Development, http://www.oecd.org/edu/ceri/36224377.pdf.

24. After all, artificial intelligence is not intelligence, even student intelligence. It is primarily formulae and techniques of problem solving. What AI measures is stuff so basic that it doesn't figure in intelligence tests, which deal with skills in utilizing language, both symbolic and linguistic.

25. *The New York Times*, March 20, 2012.

26. Cardinal Robert also recognized the need to charge fees. In his day, students paid the fee in person to the institution. These days, they pay a fee electronically to a faceless corporation. We are not convinced that the modern system is an improvement.

27. By the end of 2013, Thrun himself was complaining that Udacity provided "a lousy product." He began concentrating on a business model that offered vocational training and the moneymaking "Nanodegrees."

28. *The New York Times* declared 2012 the "Year of the MOOC."

29. This venture was developed because MIT was concerned about the commercialization of online learning. In 2012 MIT created the not-for-profit MITx. Woody Brown reports, "The inaugural course, 6.002x, launched in March 2012. Harvard joined the group, renamed edX, that spring, and University of California, Berkeley joined in the summer. The initiative then added the University of Texas System, Wellesley College, and Georgetown University."

30. College education always does. Humanities and social sciences illustrate, but do not exhaust, the differences between training and education.

31. Some of these courses are typical academic fare, as in Ancient Greek Heroes and Health in Numbers: Quantitative Methods in Clinical & Public Health Research.

32. In order to teach what is essentially a middle-sized nation, Coursera adheres to four basic pedagogical principles: (1) the effectiveness of online learning; (2) "mastery" learning (constant student evaluation); (3) peer assessment (students grading each other); (4) "blended" learning, combining in-class with online. It is not exactly clear how these principles address the problem of scale.

33. Dhawal Shah, "How Does Coursera Make Money?" *EdSurge News*, October 15, 2014, www.edsurge.com/news/2014-10-15-how-does-coursera-make-money.

34. Lawrence S. Bacow, William G. Bowen, Kevin M. Guthrie, Kelly A. Lack, and Matthew P. Long, "Barriers to Adoption of Online Learning Systems in U.S. Higher Education," *Ithaka S+R* (May 1, 2012): 30, appendix, p. 1, https://doi.org/10.18665/sr.22432. This is an important and comprehensive early look at technology-based distance education. Bacow et al. support the establishment and expansion of technology-based instruction. They approve of its cost savings, its educational outreach, and its effectiveness as a learning model. Being university administrators, they take an institutional rather than a scholarly or pedagogical view of online education. They do not avoid the barriers to establishing a coherent regime of online courses and degrees. The Bacow essay is a cautious but optimistic preliminary examination of the opportunities involved in adopting MOOCs and SCOCs as a standard part of the university education.

William G. Bowen has expanded the report

and added to it significantly in a recent book entitled *Higher Education in the Digital Age* (Princeton: Princeton University Press, 2013). Former Princeton president Bowen tends to think that the digital delivery of undergraduate courses will change the entire character of the university. We are more conservative. We suspect, as virtually every page of this essay indicates, that the digital delivery of student courses will change the courses somewhat and will change the university much, much less.

35. Bacow et al., "Barriers," 2, 3.
36. Ibid., 25.
37. In an effort to save money, these tutors and graders will be purchased in bulk. They will be paid as close to the minimum as possible. Training will be superficial. Supervision will be even worse. One professor will have fifty tutors and graders to look after. Everyone will be encouraged to grade rapidly. Many of the new tutors will be moonlighting high school teachers and coaches. When costs outweigh every other consideration, sweatshops are what you get.
38. Daniel A. Bonevac, "MOOCs: The Director's Cut," *Academic Questions* 29, no. 1 (Spring 2016): 64.
39. Bonevac asserts, "MOOCs function largely as continuing education for those who already have college degrees." Bonevac, "MOOCs: The Director's Cut," 61.
40. A recent study in the *Harvard Business Review* reports that "[c]areer benefits are the more common reason for taking a MOOC. Fifty-two percent of the people surveyed report a primary goal of improving their current job or finding a new job—they are 'career builders.'" Chen Zhenghao, Brandon Alcorn, Gayle Christensen, Nicholas Eriksson, Daphne Koller, Ezekiel J. Emanuel, "Who's Benefiting from MOOCs, and Why," *Harvard Business Review*, September 22, 2015.
41. Woody Brown, "More or Less (A Seminar on the Massive Open Online Course (In Seven Easy Lessons) blog, *The Massachuesetta Review.*
42. Carl Sagan had the pedagogical fire within. Like all good teachers, he knew an awful lot of stuff. Sagan was good at using examples to illustrate his point, drawing these examples from the anthropology and psychology of everyday life, as well as from relativity and particle physics. He was entertaining and charismatic. Admittedly, there were those who liked him better on television than in person, but that is inevitable and irrelevant to his role in mass education.
43. See Brian Greene, *The Elegant Universe* (New York: Norton, 2010). One of the authors, who is interested in physics, started to read it but got only into chapter 2 before breaking down completely. This book is not for novices.

44. Carl Straumshein, "MOOCs for (a Year's) Credit," *Inside Higher Ed*, April 23, 2015.
45. Lindsay Gellman, "Wharton's New Online Courses Include Incentives," *The Wall Street Journal*, March 4, 2015.

Chapter 6

1. In those Paleozoic days, E.T. meant educational television. Television critics thought television shows were generally terrible; television reached everybody in the country; television was a "hot medium" (Marshall McLuhan, *Understanding Media: The Extensions of Man*, Critical Edition [Berkeley: Gingko Press, 2013]), and good public policy required that television be uplifting and educational. Reformers proposed educational television, which would be free, appearing on the standard networks as well as on a separate network. Skeptics, and that included everyone who was not an E.T. zealot, doubted that E.T. was either probable or could be successful; certainly not on a mass scale. The skeptics were not entirely right, which is unusual in itself. Reformers gained the half-hour evening news and PBS.
2. See Q. Horatius Flaccus, *Espistola ad Pisonas de arte poetica (Ars Poetica)*. The important purposes of good poetry are to both instruct and delight, to be at the same time *utile et dulce*.
3. Alexandra Wolfe, "Daphne Koller on the Future of Online Education," *The Wall Street Journal*, June 5, 2015.
4. Steve Blank, *The Four Steps to the Epiphany* (Menlo Park: K&S Ranch and Open Library, 2013).
5. Steve Blank, *The Startup Owner's Manual* (Menlo Park: K&S Ranch and Open Library, 2012).
6. Andy H. Palmer, "Steve Blank on Demystifying the Start-up Culture," *Koa Labs* (blog), July 16, 2012.
7. In nature, anything that can happen will happen, and it will happen more than once. See Nassim Nicholas Taleb, *The Black Swan: The Impact of the Highly Improbable* (New York: Random House, 2010).
8. Carl Straumsheim, "2U Ends Semester Online," *Insider Higher Ed*, April 3, 2014.
9. See Bacow et al., "Barriers," 25–27, for an examination of professorial concerns and for the authors' paranoia. A problem with this section is that the authors do not distinguish between MOOCs and SCOCs and professional worries about each. Complaint about online instruction and worries that it will render professors obsolete can be on every academic message board in the country. Many professors have a reasonably accurate view of their instructional charisma, and most of the rest think

they teach an awful lot better than they really do. Even while thinking that they do a good job, these same professors are clearly worried. It's quite likely that many of them should be. Even if MOOCs and SCOCs do not change the general educational framework a whole lot, they can, and likely will, have serious adverse consequences in a lot of individual cases.

10. Tamar Lewin, "Master's Degree is New Frontier of Study Online," *New York Times*, August 17, 2013.

11. It may be possible that a number of those students who gain provisional acceptance will be AT&T employees. That is entirely appropriate. It will provide additional training for AT&T people, and it will fit into the promise of increased educational outreach, which is one of the "better angels" of online education. It is worth noting that Georgia Tech has retained the brand.

12. The August 2014 report by Harvard and MIT indicates that most of those students completing a MOOC already have a college degree and already know at least something about the material of the course. A. D. Ho, I. Chuang, J. Reich, C. Coleman, J. Whitehill, C. Northcutt, J. J. Williams, J. Hansen, G. Lopez, and R. Petersen, "HarvardX and MITx: Two Years of Open Online Courses" (working paper No. 10, HarvardX and the Office of Digital Learning at MIT, 2015), doi:10.2139/ssrn.2586847. So much for educational outreach.

13. See Tamar Lewin, "Yale Medical School's Request to Expand Campus Program Online is Denied." *New York Times*, April 14, 2015.

14. *Inside Higher Ed* reported that the Accreditation Review Commission on Education for the Physician Assistant decided Yale could not treat the hybrid program as an expansion of the face-to-face version. Students and alumni have argued that offering the program online will hurt the reputation of the highly selective face-to-face program. Carl Straumsheim, "Yale Proceeds With Online Physician Assistant Program," *Inside Higher Ed,* September 16, 2015. See also Emma Platoff and Amaka Uchegbu, "Online PA Program Comes Under Harsh Scrutiny," *Yale Daily News*, April 2, 2015: "Currently, roughly 36 students are admitted to Yale's PA program on a rolling basis each year. According to Chandra Goff MED '14, an alumna in the PA program, the University intends to grow that number nearly tenfold to 350 students, answering calls from the medical community to increase the number of primary care clinicians."

15. From the Yale School of Medicine website, September 28, 2015.

16. Steve Kolowich, "Yale Announces 'Blended' Master's Degree" *The Chronicle of Higher Education*, March 10, 2015.

17. Scott Jaschik, "Feminist Anti-MOOC," *Inside Higher Ed*, August 19, 2013.

18. Tamar Lewin, "Master's Degree is New Frontier of Study Online," *New York Times*, August 17, 2013.

19. Carl Straumsheim, "Arizona State, edX Team to Offer Freshman Year Online through MOOCs," *Insider Higher Ed*, April 23, 2015. See also Carl Straumsheim, "Arizona State U 'MOOC for Credit' Program Faces Unanswered Accreditation Questions," *Inside Higher Ed*, April 24, 2015.

20. Bacow et al., "Barriers," 28.

21. This falls into the category of "Social Notes from All Over." During the Great Depression, Macy's department store would hire only young women with college degrees to work behind the store counters. Two things to note here: the stuff learned in college was not needed for the job, but the social graces and personal self-discipline acquired in college were real job assets. Secondly, in times of substantial unemployment, the educational requirements for every job tend to rise. During this current recession, the unemployment rate for those with only high school education has hovered at nearly twice the national average.

22. A bit of economic history may help. In the first half of the twentieth century, multigenerational homes were common. Most clerical, factory, retail, and service jobs then, from 1900–1950, did not pay enough to lead to home ownership. The "Victory Dividend" from World War II produced a sixty-year prosperity (1946–2007), with only one bad decade (1973–1980). Wages rose, veterans got benefits, small businesses prospered, and there were so many new jobs that even minorities were hired. In that economy, home ownership expanded and became the social norm. At least for the time being, that period is over, and things are now more like 1910 than they have been at any time since the Great Depression. For a great many service and clerical jobs, the compensation is no longer sufficient to pay for a house and a car and a family. The multigenerational family home may again become the social norm.

23. These standards are always being measured and released to the public. On June 2, 2013, the Gannett staff published an article on which universities give students the best job value for the money they invest in their education. Not surprisingly, technical and engineering schools ranked near the top. The methodology for rankings was "the earnings differential divided by the weighted cost for a 2012 graduate, annualized to represent the percent of expected ROI received each year after graduation" (www.payscale.com/data-packages/college-roi-2013/methodology). The compensation received is a percentage of educational

costs. Vo-ed is more than a proposal; it is already a statistic. For example, according to AdvisorOne, an online financial news site that supports *Investment Advisor* and *Research* magazines, tiny Louisiana Tech "ranks among the top 25 in nation for best return on investments" (Dave Guerin, "Louisiana Tech ranks among the Top 25 in the nation for best ROI," May 31, 2013).

24. Plenty of people support, and ought to support, the vo-ed idea. In Texas, it is popular in conservative circles, where universities are viewed critically. Universities are seen, more or less accurately, as bastions of liberalism, and cities with large research universities usually vote Democratic. This includes Baton Rouge, Louisiana, and Austin, Texas. Vo-ed proposals, therefore, for UT–Austin may well be based in political animosity. If so, that animosity, though well-placed ideologically and emotionally, is off the mark politically and educationally. UT–Austin is one of the world's great research universities; it is not a soft target. From football to medicine, UT has a strong hold on Texans' affections. The University also has a lot of its own money coming from oil. Texas conservatives would be better advised to build their own vo-ed system out of community colleges. That would certainly be easier, and quicker, and it might even work.

Chapter 7

1. Former President Bill Clinton has served as honorary chancellor for Laureate. He was paid $16 million for his services.

2. See the impressive variety of certificates offered in business, health care, education, technology, humanities, etc., by the University of Phoenix on its website.

3. "For-Profit College Students Less Likely to Be Employed After Graduation and Have Lower Earnings, New Study Finds," *Journal of Economic Perspectives* (Winter 2012).

4. We have been unable to find any hard unemployment statistics that apply only to graduates of for-profit institutions. Both the Department of Education and Senate committees complain that for-profit graduates have higher unemployment rates, but they don't say how high they are. Nor do they appear to recognize that students enrolling in for-profits already had high unemployment rates, perhaps because they come from a significantly lower socioeconomic group; 61 percent come from below 150 percent of the federal poverty line, as contrasted with 38 percent of those in traditional nonprofit institutions. David A. Bergeron, "Examining Gainful Employment in Career Education," *Center for American Progress*, October 31, 2014, www.americanprogress.org/issues/education/news/2014/10/31/100048/examining-gainful-employment-in-career-education/. To sum it all up, meager statistics and plentiful anecdotes indicate that things are pretty bad for poor students entering poor for-profit institutions, which may or may not make things better for them.

5. Steve Gunderson, "Making 'Profit' a Dirty Word in Higher Education," *Wall Street Journal*, November 13, 2014.

6. Association of Private Sector Colleges and Universities, www.career.org/news-and-media/sector-news/open-letter-to-sec-duncan.cfm.

7. On July 2, 2015, the Association of Private Sector Colleges and Universities (APSCU) filed a notice of its intent to appeal the District Court ruling in *APSCU v. Duncan*.

8. President Barack Obama, in his 2009 State of the Union address, called upon every American to obtain at least a year of college or career training.

9. Accreditation is a controversial issue. The Accrediting Commission of Career Schools and Colleges (ACCSC) is a national accrediting body, but regional accrediting bodies, such as the Southern Association of Colleges and Schools (SACS), attest to the worthiness of most not-for-profit institutions. The regional accrediting agencies claim that ACCSC is appropriate for vocational schools but not academic ones. The ACCSC claims that regional accrediting agencies disdain the national accreditation on essentially frivolous and prejudicial grounds. The United States Department of Education takes no official position on this disagreement but has begun to lean more heavily on schools with only national accreditation. However, schools accredited by both national and regional agencies can incur federal displeasure. The Corinthian system is the primary instance thereof.

10. Andy Thomason and Goldie Blumenstyk, "$30-Million Fine for Corinthian May Portend Tougher Scrutiny of For-Profits," *The Chronicle of Higher Education*, April 15, 2015.

11. Trymaine Lee, "Obama Unveils Free Community College 'Game Changer,'" *MSNBC*, January 9, 2015, www.msnbc.com/msnbc/obama-unveils-free-community-college-proposal.

12. Of course, no one can doubt that as the credential completion level rises, the credentials needed will rise even faster. This is a social application of Parkinson's Second Law.

13. Janell Ross, "Where Obama's Community-College Plan Falls Short," *The Atlantic*, January 12, 2015.

14. Lawrence S. Ritter, *The Glory of Their Times* (New York: William Morrow, 1966).

15. On ideas, both quantity and quality, see Isaiah Berlin, *The Hedgehog and the Fox* (Princeton: Princeton University Press, 1953). The title quotes a fragment from the Greek poet Archilochus: "The fox knows many things, but the hedgehog knows one big thing."

16. Wade Roush, "Minerva's Plan to Disrupt Universities: A Talk with CEO Ben Nelson," *Xconomy*, April 18, 2014, www.xconomy.com/national/2014/04/18/minervas-plan-to-disrupt-universities-a-talk-with-ceo-ben-nelson/?single page=true.

17. See Mitchell Stevens, *Creating a Class: College Admissions and the Education of Elites* (Cambridge: Harvard University Press, 2009). Professor Stevens teaches at Stanford and is familiar with the maldistribution of applications, admissions, and attendance at the nearly 5,000 colleges and universities. At the top, among the Ivies, is a huge surplus of applications, and the Ivies, including Amherst, Williams, Chicago, Stanford, et al., admit a tiny percentage of the total pool of applicants. At the bottom end, where there is open enrollment, are vacant seats. Among the secondary school students applying is a strong bias toward admission to a college with the best national reputation; the curriculum is at the top edge of the students' preparation and capacity. The students' admission strategy is usually a few top-rank schools and a couple of safety valves, which are state universities and occasionally compass colleges. Students assume, not entirely unreasonably, that a brand-name degree is essential for a brand-name career. Minerva, unlike Phoenix, seeks to exploit that student preference.

18. Roush, "Minerva's Plan." Nelson has expanded on this view. See the most recent boilerplate from Minerva's website:

> Minerva is assembling an exceptional team, dedicated to reinventing every aspect of the university experience to provide students with the best education possible.
>
> Employees will have the opportunity to work in a dynamic, collaborative, creative environment with other smart, talented people from around the world. Minerva is the right place for those who enjoy challenging assumptions, forging new paths and accomplishing things that have not been done before.
>
> Every individual in our organization is driven to positively impact our collective future by ensuring the most exceptional students in the world fulfill their extraordinary potential.

19. Cardinal Newman wanted the faculty to interact among themselves as their own learning community. Thomas Jefferson thought faculty should live within the academical village.

20. The team-teaching preference comes from long years of attending and teaching in an honors program, where multidisciplinary courses, in the communication module, were taught by historians, philosophers, and literary scholars. It worked quite well. Students got several interpretative approaches, along with differing pedagogical techniques. All to the good. But the basic strength of team teaching is this: no faculty member in a single discipline knows enough about the other disciplines to teach the whole communications show. If Minerva succeeds, Nelson may discover this reality for himself.

21. The system goes back to the Tudors, where success in court was dependent in part on speaking well and writing good poetry. It has been preserved in the public schools and universities there.

22. Nanette Asimov, "San Francisco's Minerva: 'Perfect University' or Student Gamble?" *San Francisco Chronicle*, August 25, 2015.

23. Roush, "Minerva's Plan." It seems that Ben Nelson has gotten to know a few professors pretty well, and they have agreed on this system. It's a lot more work to start with the wrong answer and work up to the right one. Furthermore, students are interested in the right answer, much more than they are interested in how to get there. Still, with really super-bright students, as Minerva promises to have, the whole process of Socratic interrogation and analysis can be interesting in itself, regardless of the answer. Minerva's classes could be the equivalent of music and ballet "master classes," where choreographers like Balanchine work through a ballet with dancers as superb as Robert Helpman or Moira Sheerar. What it will take is the very best on all sides of the discussion. It doesn't seem likely that this will happen very often, promises to the contrary notwithstanding.

24. It may not have hurt Minerva to have hired one of the high-level executives on the accreditation board the day after she left her position.

25. At major research universities, STEM departments often employ professional grant writers. The family experience of one of the authors indicates that grant writing can absorb the entire working day and year. Once you leave the lab, you are professionally dead. Grant writers are an essential academic function.

26. Nelson, the son of a lab scientist, disagrees: "Lab class is a waste." He suggests that students wanting lab experience go get an internship somewhere.

27. Joseph Schumpeter, *Capitalism, Socialism, and Democracy*, 3rd ed. (New York: Harper, 2008).

28. On the nature of a mass society, see Jose

Ortega y Gasset, *The Revolt of the Masses* (1930), particularly the first chapter. Ortega argues that in a mass society, numbers set the tone in everything. He describes the impact of the masses in two primary areas, the "height of life" and plenitude, both of which involve consumption and the democratization of taste.

Chapter 8

1. The phrase "not nostrums, but normalcy," was uttered by Warren Harding in a speech at the Boston Home Market Club on May 20, 1920. That speech played an important role in getting him the Republican nomination.
2. That phrase is the title of a novel by the civic critic Nikolay Chernyshevsky (1863). Dostoeyvsky mocked the book in *Notes from the Underground* (1864); Leo Tolstoy used the title in 1886; and Nikolai Lenin also picked up the title for a 1902 pamphlet. Lenin was so impressed by this turgid novel that scholars have claimed that it, rather than Marx's *Das Kapital*, provided the emotional foundation for the Bolshevik Revolution.
3. William S. Gilbert, "The Grand Inquisitor's Song" from *The Gondoliers*.
4. Donald Rumsfeld, *Rumsfeld's Rules: Leadership Lessons in Business, Politics, War, and Life* (New York: Broadside Books, 2013).
5. This line, from *The Tempest*, is also the last line of the movie *The Maltese Falcon* (1941).
6. Quoted by James Thurber in *The Thurber Album: The Wit, Wisdom, and Surprising Life of James Thurber* (New York: Simon & Schuster, 1971).
7. See Leavitt and Dubner, *Freakonomics* (New York: William Morrow, 2005). Leavitt and Dubner investigated the actual, though oft-ignored, incentive structure of everyday life, from dealing drugs to teaching school. These are remarkably similar economic activities, with almost identical vertical administrative structures and rewards systems. The authors are properly surprised that anyone would be surprised about school cheating.
8. We stand by our earlier definition of good teaching, which occurs when somebody learns something. Really good teaching is when somebody other than the teacher learns something.
9. The first efforts along sensitivity lines involve speech codes. These have become problematic. The Supreme Court decided against them, unanimously, in *R. A. V. v. St. Paul*, 505 U.S. 377 (1992).
10. See again the books on academic caste and tribalism: Hazard Adams, *Academic Tribes*; Lord C. P. Snow, *The Masters* (London: Macmillan, 1951); M. E. Cornford, *Microcosmographia Academica* (Cambridge: Bowes and Bowes,

1964). The reformer's distaste for the past does not diminish its influence, but it does diminish the clarity of the reformer's vision.
11. In the bad old days, this was called "co-education," and the women were called "coeds."
12. In the decades after World War I, the one-room schools were slowly but inexorably abandoned and consolidated into district schools. The consolidation movement seemed up to date and was very popular. Bright, shiny new buses took students on paved state roads to new schools that had electricity and plumbing. The consolidated system required more teachers, bus drivers, maintenance workers, and administrators. Home schooling, particularly when a couple or three families are involved, attempts to regain the genuine virtues of one-room schools.
13. Michael Bayer, "Why So Many Are Alarmed by the Ongoing Controversy at Mount Saint Mary's," *The Washington Post*, February 17, 2016.
14. *Lochner v. New York*, 198 U.S. 45 (1905), Holmes dissent.
15. This exists already, for schools as well as colleges. Online, there are short, engaging lectures—seven, ten, 15 minutes in length—about such topics as Vietnam, chemistry, the Civil War, algebra, and the French Revolution. The Internet is the place for enthusiasts, whether amateurs or professionals, and they are able to transmit their love of the discipline to their electronic students. A ten-minute vignette is not an academic course. It does provide a useful addition to the school or college classroom. It also illustrates the difference between good teaching and merely being in front of the class. See *Crash Course* on YouTube by the Green Brothers.
16. TOPS is the abbreviation for Taylor Opportunity Program for Students. New Orleans oilman Patrick Taylor came up with the idea; a high school student needs a 2.5 GPA in the academic curriculum and to score the state average of 20 on the ACT in order to qualify. Once in college, if you fall below a 2.0, you lose the benefit.
17. See Philip Lapsley, *Exploding the Phone: The Untold Story of the Teenagers and Outlaws Who Hacked Ma Bell* (New York: Grove Press, 2013). For us, the interesting part of the book lies in Ma Bell's continuing automation and technological improvement. In 1940, Ma Bell had 100,000 operators. Then, most people had no phones, and many who did had party lines. Ma Bell looked forward to a future, 20–30 years down the road, when they would have one million operators. Something had to be done. Something was done. Western Electric invented the automatic switching operators based on tones of the scale. Ma Bell went from human operators to electronics, based partially

on tone and partially on light. This extraordinary technological shift is exceptional for modern America only in terms of scale, not at all in terms of direction.

18. All Americans know and respect the power of trends. Barbie and Elvis have lasted for generations. It is hard to imagine America without them. Online learning may follow the Elvis/Barbie pattern and become an established part of the American cultural landscape. Just because something, product or procedure, becomes established does not mean that it escapes criticism. Barbie is routinely excoriated for giving little girls a distorted body image, to their psychological disadvantage. Nonetheless, Barbie and her slutty younger sisters, the Bratz dolls, sell, even while the critics carp. Faculty everywhere, such as the philosophy department at San Jose State University, are already saying that online courses will diminish the quality of education at their institution. Maybe so. Maybe not. Nonetheless, online education continues to expand. There are times when critics are right, at least in part. But it doesn't matter. The established patterns are stronger than the objections.

19. Steve Kolowich, "What You Need to Know About Companies That Run Online Programs for Colleges," *The Chronicle of Higher Education*, September 30, 2014.

20. See the informative article in *The Atlantic*, Derek Newton, "How Companies Profit Off of Education at Nonprofit Schools," June 7, 2016.

21. To give an example among many: at LSU, in January 2014, Jose Antonio Bowen (dean of Goucher College, formerly dean of the Meadows School of the Arts and professor of music at Southern Methodist University) lectured on "Teaching Naked." He discussed college instruction, which is partially in the classroom and which students supplement, voluntarily and independently, by resorting to online videos and crash courses and MOOCs. Bowen argued that these supplementary online sources are the competition for classroom teachers, who need to learn to put them to use. He did not say, and did not need to say, that classroom teachers are going to have to do a hell of a lot better job in order to survive in the new semi-online, semi-personally taught college classroom.

22. This means professors must improve their student recruiting techniques. A new practice is a flashy video preview of the course, put online so the students can be introduced to the material taught and the professor's style. The course and the professor become a "brand."

23. We paraphrase here Oliver Wendell Holmes, Jr., writing for the court in *Baltimore and Ohio R. Co. v. Goodman*, 275 U.S. 66 (1927). Holmes's comment that "you stop for the train; the train does not stop for you" is the classic example for situations best described as a dichotomy. The modern update, of course, is Yoda.

24. Nassim Nicholas Talib, *The Black Swan: The Impact of the Highly Improbable* (New York: Random House, 2007).

25. We offer a local example. In March 2013, Louisiana State University inaugurated a new unit called "LSU Online," a program comprising three master's degrees: in business administration, construction management, and human resource development. Two more SCOCs master's degrees in higher education administration began in May 2013. The degrees in business and construction would cost students a mere $27,000, while the Master of Science in Human Resource and Leadership Development is an incredible bargain at a paltry $15,012.

26. F. Scott Fitzgerald, *The Great Gatsby* (New York: Charles Scribner's Sons, 1925), penultimate paragraph.

27. Fitzgerald, *The Great Gatsby*, last line.

28. See Benjamin Nathan Cardozo, *The Nature of the Judicial Process* (New Haven: Yale University Press, 1921), 53.

Bibliographical Essay

1. We could have used Ian Morris, *Why The West Rules for Now: The Patterns of History, and What They Reveal About the Future* (New York: Farrar, Straus and Giroux, 2010). Professor Morris posits the doctrine of "social development" to distinguish one civilization from another. The elements of social development include the technology of energy, administrative organization as illustrated in urbanization, the capacity to make war, the capacity to store and retrieve information—that is to say, literacy and technology in general. Notice, the list does not include art, music, or literature. Excellence in aesthetics may be found in comparatively undeveloped societies.

We have not used Morris because he goes too far afield. The book really begins with Cro-Magnon man and begins its main argument with Gobekli Tepe, a cultic center that flourished from 10,000 to 9000 BC. He presents the doctrine that culture arose from cult, not the other way around; he is undoubtedly correct. But the book is too general and covers too much to be specifically relevant in any significant measure to the topic of this essay. So we have selected Ferguson instead. Nonetheless, we wish to acknowledge this superb book by Ian Morris and note that the entire sweep of Western culture is relevant to the life of a research university.

2. George Orwell understood that reality, which forms the basis of *1984*. George Orwell, *1984* (New York: Harcourt, Brace, 1949) states this idea in slogan form: "Who controls the present controls the past. Who controls the

past controls the future." This was applied to propaganda, which could be controlled, rather than technological innovation, which cannot. The influence of a specific view of the past on how one sees the future is less deterministic and more an impression than Orwell indicates.

3. The increasing importance of research universities, and the increased funding needed, does not apply to any specific state and its university. It is entirely possible, and likely to happen, that state governments here and there will decide that there are spending priorities more important than the future of the citizens. The future is, after all, both distant and uncertain, and politicians are not guaranteed continuous re-election. There is real political pressure to satisfy the constituents now, rather than act in the best interest of their children.

4. Historians increasingly are coming to see the wars of the twentieth century as a single conflict, beginning with the Great War (1914–1921), through appeasement (1931–1939), World War II (1939–945), and the Cold War (1945–1989) as a single continuous conflict. For most of its duration, it was a war between liberal democracy and various forms of fascism. In dealing with this extended conflict, historians now see more continuity than division.

5. Much the same thing happened to Great Britain, beginning as early as the 1790s. British technology, from steam engines to textile technology to railroads, began to flow overseas, much of it to the United States. Eventually, by the 1870s, Britain fell behind permanently to Germany and the United States, both of which had established science and engineering as part of the university curriculum.

6. Thomas Friedman, *The Lexus and the Olive Tree* (New York: Farrar, Strauss & Giroux, 1999).

7. The chapter on physics begins with a commentary on the 1979 movie *The China Syndrome*. The movie presents the populist prejudice against complex technology, notably that it is dangerous and will blow up the world. *The China Syndrome* combines this prejudice with a traditional liberal view that private enterprise, which seeks profit, is inherently unfair and contrary to the public weal. In the West, the market economy is inextricably tied to the university. In a chapter dealing with education, the example seems odd.

8. 1 Corinthians 14:8.

9. The call for academic excellence, however, is an anti-egalitarian proposal for a society driven by the ideal of equality. But even the most cherished ideals cannot always be realized, no matter how fervently they are believed. The hierarchical research university is in the business of separating sheep from goats at every level of learning. This is a socially necessary but ideologically obnoxious task. Nonetheless, regardless of resentment, universities will continue to participate in the process of social sorting out on the basis of learning and intellect.

10. Friedman and Mandelbaum wrote before the fracking boom, which has improved the American current accounts and reduced emissions through the increased use of natural gas. The authors would probably suggest that these developments, though largely positive, are just details and the general challenge remains. They are, of course, absolutely right.

11. The second postulate violates a cherished American hope, that all kids will be above average. The most popular expression of this ideal appears in Garrison Keillor's *Prairie Home Companion* radio program.

Murray's first two rules passed without comment in this book, though when they appeared in *The Bell Curve* the American left collectively foamed at the mouth and descended into paroxysms of rage. Murray was called a racist and a whole lot of other bad names, which did not prevent the critics from having to admit, at least implicitly, that he and Herrnstein were right.

12. Charles Murray returned to education and its social consequences in 2012 with *Coming Apart* (New York: Crown Forum, 2012). The subtitle indicates that Murray is dealing only with the white community, but the same educationally based social divisions can be seen in San Antonio, Texas, among Hispanics. In the African-American community, one need only compare Anacostia, D.C., to Montgomery County, Maryland. See also Gene Robinson, *Disintegration: The Splintering of Black America* (New York: Anchor, 2011). Mr. Robinson, a journalist, has dealt with the educational, income, and living divisions among African-Americans. His observations are similar to those of Charles Murray. His conclusions, of course, are not.

Murray and Robinson were not the first to notice that life chances and neighborhoods were distinguished by education. In 1958, the popular sociologist Vance Packard, in *The Status Seekers*, divided America into two general classes: the opportunity class, who had a college education and often more and worked in government and the professions; and the limited opportunity class, consisting of those who lacked the socially needed credentials.

13. Gordon Moore, founder and head of Intel, explains that every 18 months computers double in power and halve in price. Both ends of the law matter. Since computers are cheaper and cheaper, more and more people use them. Since they are more and more powerful, it takes greater skill to utilize the bulk of their capacity.

14. Samuel P. Huntington, "The Clash of Civilizations," *Foreign Affairs* 72, no. 3 (Summer 1993): 22–49.

Index

Abelard, Peter 9, 15, 187
academical village 25–27, 61–62, 71, 79, 109, 179
Academically Adrift 61–62
Advanced Placement 65, 165
Alexander, Lamar 94
Allen, George 107
AllLearn 99
American Association of University Professors 160
American Commission of Career Schools and Colleges 139
American Public Education 135
Andreeson Horowitz 107
Apollo 135
Aquinas, Thomas 10, 29, 81
Argawal, Anent 127
Aristotle 12, 20, 22, 33, 71, 81, 91, 112, 118
Arum, Richard 61–62
Association of Private Sector Colleges and Universities 137
AT&T 32
Axia 142

Bacow, Lawrence S. 104, 127
Banking theory of education 54–55
Barrett College, Arizona State University 85
Barriers to Adaptation of Online Learning Systems in U.S. Higher Education 104
Barry, John 166
Baton Rouge Community College 30, 150
Belitsky, Richard 124
bell curve 48–50, 52, 65, 108, 171
Bell Labs 24, 32
Benchmark Capital 152
The Bill and Melinda Gates Foundation 106
Bisk 167
Blank, Steve 114
Bonaventure 10
Bonevac, Daniel 105
Bowen, William G. 104, 127
Bowman, Linda 166
Brandeis University 118
Brookings Institute 24

Brooks, Cleanth 82
Brown, Edmund G. "Pat" 44
Brown University 124
Brynjolfsson, Eric 181–182, 184
Butler, Nicholas Murray 83

Cahan, Abraham 74
California Board of Regents 44
California Institute of Technology 35, 114, 116, 117, 164
Capella 135
Carlyle, Thomas 1
Catholic University, Dublin 38
Chicago school system 63
Churchill, Ward 62, 89
Civil Rights movement 73
Civilization: The West and the Rest 176
Cold War 36, 43, 72, 75
college fraternities 25
College Learning Assessment 60, 62–65, 96, 102, 127, 150, 159
Collegiate Assessment of Academic Proficiency 64
Columbia University 76, 83–85, 99, 114, 130
Coming Apart: The State of White America, 1960–2010 180
Community College of Aurora 166
Corinthian 135, 140–141
Cornell University 35, 76, 107
Corpus Juris Civilis 10
Cosmos 107
Courçon, Robert de 7, 10–20, 38
Coursera 102–107, 123, 141
Crick, Francis 8
Critical University Studies 53–54, 56
Cumming v. Richmond County Board of Education 91–93

Dartmouth 24
DeVry 135
Disintegration: The Splintering of Black America 180
Duesenberg, August, and Frederick 69
Duncan, Arne 137, 140–141

205

The Education Trust 164
edX 101–102, 105–106, 108, 127
Eliot, Charles William 28, 35, 42
Embanet 167–168
The End of Power: From Boardrooms to Battlefields to States, Why Being in Charge Is Not What It Used to Be 183
EPF 103

Fabricius of Acquapendente 45
Fathom 99
Faulkner, William 22
Ferguson, Niall 176–177, 184
fiscal crisis of 2008 1, 36
The Four Steps to the Epiphany 114
Fox, Edward Whiting 76–77
Freire, Paulo Reglus Neves 54–56, 125
Friedman, Thomas 177–178, 184

gainful employment standard 136
Galil, Zvi 121–122
Galileo 45
George Washington University 137
German research universities 28
GI Bill 67, 97
Gilded Age 28–29, 35, 42
Global Freshman Academy 102, 108, 112, 126, 127
Google Alphabet 107
Gosling, Samuel 124
Graff, Gerald 54
Gregory IX, Pope 15–16
Gresham's Law 89
Groves, General Leslie 43
Gunderson, Steve 137

Harvard 23, 27–28, 45, 76, 87, 101–102, 105, 116–117, 127, 133, 164
Harvard Law School 27
Hayes, S. J. H. 76
Heald 140–141
The Heritage Foundation 33
Herrnstein, Richard 49
Hochberg, Leonard 71
Hoover Institute 24, 32
Houston school system 63
Huntington, Samuel P. 184

The Idea of a University 38
Illinois State University at Normal 34
Innocent III, Pope 10
Irnerius 9, 20
Ivy Tech Community College 30–31, 35, 76, 101, 109, 132, 142

The Jazz Singer 74
Jefferson, Thomas 25–27, 39, 41–43, 47, 71, 75, 80, 149
Jewish Daily Forward 74
Johns Hopkins Data Science Specialization 103

Johns Hopkins University 28–29, 53, 103, 177
Jolson, Al 74

Keck Graduate Institute 152
Kerr, Clark 43–45
Khan Academy 106
killer apps 176–177, 184
Kleiner Perkins Caulfield & Byers 107
Koller, Daphne 102
Kolowich, Steve 167

Langer, William 76
Laureate 135
Law of Large Numbers 48, 50, 171
The Lexus and the Olive Tree 177
Liberation theology 55
Litchfield law program 27
Long, Earl 31
Long, Huey P. 83
Louisiana State University at Alexandria 31–32, 162
Louisiana State University at Eunice 32, 117, 161
Louisiana State University Baton Rouge 45, 64, 79–80, 82–85, 92–93, 159, 161
Luther, Martin 14

The MacArthur Foundation 106
Mandelbaum, Michael 177
Manhattan Project 33, 36, 43
Marxism 55–56
Massachusetts Institute of Technology 35
McAfee, Andrew 181–182, 184
McCullough, David 76
McGuffey's Readers 27
Miami Dade Community College System 30
Minerva 147–154, 170–171
Montpellier medical college 27
Morrill Act of 1862 28, 35
Mount Holyoke 24
Mount Saint Mary's 159
multiversity 44
Murray, Charles A. 49, 178–181, 184

Naim, Moises 183
The Name of the Rose 20
National Defense Education Act 44, 135
The National Science Foundation 106
Nelson, Ben 148–153, 170
The New School 124
Newman, John Henry Cardinal 38–43, 47, 57, 80, 85, 149
Newman, Simon 159–160
Ng, Andrew 103
No Child Left Behind Act 60, 65, 157
Northwestern University 118
Notre Dame University 118
Nova Southeastern University 97

Oakeshott, Michael 19, 37
Obama, President Barack 30, 138, 144–145, 163–165

O'Donnell, James 98
Ogden Honors College 79, 85
Oldenburg, Ray 81
Oudenhoven, Betsy 166

paper mills 58
Pearson 107, 167–169
Pedagogy of the Oppressed 54
Pennebaker, James 124
Petraeus, Holly 138
Philip Augustus 11
Pitzer College 124
Pius IX, Pope 38
PLATO 97
Polybius 57
Priscian 20

Real Education: Four Simple Truths for Bringing American Schools Back to Reality 179
Reeve, Tapping 27
Regier, Phil 108
Rensselaer Polytechnic Institute 35
Rhodes College 83
Rice University 45, 71, 103
Robinson, Eugene 180
Roosevelt, Franklin D. 67
Roska, Josipa 61–64
Rumsfeld, Donald 65, 156

Sagan, Carl 107, 128
St. Augustine 65, 98
St. John's College 71
Salerno medical school 27
San Jose State University 101
Seay, William 84–85
The Second Machine Age: Work, Progress, and Prosperity in a Time of Brilliant Technology 182
Semester Online 118–120
Sendero Luminoso 55
Smith, Burck 142
Sperling, John 147–148, 171
Stalin, Joseph 47
Star Initiative 165
Sternberg family 83
StraighterLine 142–143
Sunrise Semester 111

Talmud 41
TED talks 19
That Used to Be Us: How America Fell Behind in the World It Invented and How We Can Come Back 177
Think tanks 34
Thrun, Sebastian 99–101
Ticknor, George 27
Tocqueville, Alexis de 27
Trinity College 23

2U 118
Tyson, Neil deGrasse 52

Udacity 100
University of California at Berkeley 17, 44, 61, 70, 114
University of California, Davis 44
University of California, Irvine 44
University of California, Los Angeles 44
University of California, San Diego 44
University of California, Santa Cruz 44
University of California Extension System 168
University of Edinburgh 103
University of Florida 168–169
University of Illinois at Urbana-Champaign 97
University of Michigan 46, 97, 99
University of Padua 14, 45
University of Paris 1–18, 23–24, 27–29, 38, 46, 77, 80, 85
University of Pennsylvania 34–35, 98, 103, 109, 116
University of Phoenix 32, 98, 139–142, 147–149, 154, 168, 171
University of Rochester 118
University of Salamanca 14
University of Southern California 45
University of Texas at Austin 70, 105, 124, 131–132
University of Toronto 103
University of Toulouse 14
University of Trento 55
University of Virginia 25, 103, 137
The Uses of the University 43
Utah State University for Open and Sustainable Learning 98

Valencia Community College 30
Vanderbilt University 118
Vassar 24
Virginia Commonwealth University 137
Wake Forest University 118
Washington University of St. Louis 118

Watson, James 8
Webster, Daniel 24
West Point 35
Western Association of Schools and Colleges 152
Wharton School of Business 34
Wiley, David 98
World War I 32, 43, 146
World War II 3, 25, 32, 35, 42, 44, 47, 82, 97, 135, 146, 158, 175

Yale 25–26, 35, 71, 82, 99, 117–118, 122–124, 150
Yale School of Medicine 122
Yale School of Nursing 122

www.ingramcontent.com/pod-product-compliance
Ingram Content Group UK Ltd.
Pitfield, Milton Keynes, MK11 3LW, UK
UKHW042002140426
5217IPUK00015B/930